LABOR IN A NEW LAND

Labor in a New Land

ECONOMY AND SOCIETY
IN SEVENTEENTH-CENTURY
SPRINGFIELD

Stephen Innes

Princeton University Press
Princeton, New Jersey

Published by Princeton University Press, 41 William Street,
Princeton, New Jersey 08540
In the United Kingdom: Princeton University Press, Guildford, Surrey

This book has been composed in Linotron Baskerville

Printed in the United States of America by Princeton University Press
Princeton, New Jersey

Library of Congress Cataloging in Publication Data

Innes, Stephen.
Labor in a new land.

Includes index.
1. Springfield (Mass.)—Economic conditions.   2. Springfield (Mass.)—
Social conditions.   3. Springfield (Mass.)—History—17th century.   I. Title.
HC108.S83I56   1983   330.9744'26   82–61369
ISBN 0–691–04698–0
ISBN 0–691–00595–8 (pbk.)

282398

In Memory of Roberta
and
for Julie

Contents

Acknowledgments

MANY generous friends have helped me to write this book. T. H. Breen supervised it in dissertation form and was throughout a model advisor. Stanley N. Katz and Josef Barton provided guidance and support at a number of critical stages of the enterprise. Robert A. Gross, Thomas Slaughter, John M. Murrin, Edward Ayers, W. W. Abbot, Erik Midelfort, Robert Stanley, James Schmotter, Christine Leigh Heyrman, John J. McCusker, and Jean Lee all offered discriminating (and repeated) readings of the manuscript, often at considerable personal sacrifice. Professors Gross and Slaughter, in particular, were tireless in helping me formulate and sharpen my argument, a role also ably played by the two readers for Princeton University Press, Russell Menard and Douglas Greenberg. James A. Henretta penetratingly critiqued the chapter on land while it was at an early stage of gestation, as did Michael McGiffert. Juliette Tomlinson, as Director of the splendid Connecticut Valley Historical Museum, helped me enter the thicket of the Pynchon account books with as little harm as possible. Ruth A. McIntyre's transcription of volume three was equally helpful. Lottie McCauley and Kathleen Miller typed an exceedingly difficult manuscript more times than they would like to recall—both on a typewriter and a word processor. It's impossible to imagine more competent, or more forebearing, typists and proofreaders. Alice Calaprice showed unerring judgment as a copyeditor and was a pleasure to work with besides.

I must reserve special thanks for four people. Gail Filion, Social Sciences Editor at Princeton University Press, saw the virtues of a manuscript still in very rough form and helped immeasurably in bringing it to fruition. Olivier Zunz, while trying to complete his own book, guided mine through the countless arcane procedures needed to computerize the text for printing. My debt to him is immense. Fred V. Carstensen, both in his several readings of the text and in our many conversations about it, was instrumental in clarifying my theoretical assertions, especially in the epilogue. Finally, William M. Daly, as a scholar and a teacher, showed me some years ago that the historian's craft could be an ennobling one. Without his example, this book would never have been written.

Quotations from manuscripts appear as originally written, except that abbreviations have been expanded, certain archaic usages modernized, and punctuation added when necessary. All dates in the text are rendered in New Style (with the year beginning on January 1 rather than March 25, as it did prior to 1752). Readers of the paperback edition are advised to consult the clothbound edition for the Dependency Tables and Wage Tables that form much of the documentary basis for chapters three and four.

Abbreviations

Account Books	John Pynchon's Account Books, 1652–1702, 6 vols. Connecticut Valley Historical Museum, Springfield
CVHM	Connecticut Valley Historical Museum, Springfield
HCPC Rec.	Hampshire County Probate Court Records, Hampden County Courthouse, Springfield
Mass. Archives	Massachusetts Archives, Boston State House
Mass. Recs.	*Records of the Governor and Company of the Massachusetts Bay in New England, 1628–1686*, ed. Nathaniel B. Shurtleff. 5 vols. in 6. Boston, 1853–1854
Pynchon Court Rec.	*Colonial Justice in Western Massachusetts (1639–1702): The Pynchon Court Record . . .*, ed. Joseph H. Smith. Cambridge, Mass., 1961
William Pynchon Account Book	William Pynchon's Record of Accounts with Early Settlers and Indians, 1645–1650. Forbes Library, Northampton, Mass.
Springfield Town Recs.	*The First Century of the History of Springfield: The Official Records from 1636–1736*, ed. Henry M. Burt. 2 vols. Springfield, 1898–1899
WMQ	*William and Mary Quarterly*, 3rd Series
Winthrop's Journal	John Winthrop, *The History of New England from 1630 to 1649*, ed. James Savage. 2 vols. Boston, 1853
Winthrop Mss.	Winthrop Papers, Massachusetts Historical Society Library, Boston
Winthrop Papers	*Winthrop Papers, 1498–1649*, ed. Allyn B. Forbes. 5 vols. Boston, 1929–1947

N

Portsmouth

Gloucester
Salem

Boston

Plymouth

River

Merrimack

Brookfield

Providence

NARRAGANSETT
INDIAN
COUNTRY

Newport

Brimfield

River

Thames

Stonington

New London

River

Saybrook

Northfield

Sunderland

Deerfield

Hatfield
Hadley

Chicopee

Spring-
field

Brookfield

King's Island
Enfield

Enfield Falls

Fresh Water R.

Connecticut   R.

Poontuck R.

Northampton

Mount
Tom

River

Westfield   River

The Falls

Suf-
field

Windsor

Haddam

Stony   Br.

Hartford
Wethersfield

Middletown

New Haven

Westfield

Housatonic River

Fairfield

L
O
N
G

I
S
L
A
N
D

THE
CONNECTICUT
VALLEY
ca. 1700

miles

50

0

SPRINGFIELD
in the
Seventeenth Century

1 mile

feet
woodland
pine barrens

(Map after Burt, Wright)

CONNECTICUT

CHICOPEE RIVER

Schonunganick
Falls

SKEPNUCK

N

Nonesuch
Meadow

Chicopee
Plain

Chicopee
Plain

Field Brook

Block Brook

End Brook

PINE BARRENS

Sheep
Pasture

Cow
Pasture

The Wood Lots

Garden Br.

Sixteen
Acres

World's
End

Plain Brook

Town Street

Home Lots

Town Br.

MILL RIVER

AGAWAM RIVER

Ashkannunsuck
Falls

THIRD DIVISION

Pickle

Grist
mill

General
Store

Wharf

Three Mile Brook

Pecowsic Brook

TOWN CENTER

½ mile

Tannery

PINE BARRENS

THE WOOD LOTS

Bay

House of
Correction

Cooley Brook

Water Fence
and Gate

Longmeadow

MILL RIVER

Path

Town Br.

Middle Causeway

WET MEADOW

Town Wharf

Meetinghouse

Three
Corner
Meadow

HOME LOTS

Training
Field

Lower
Causeway

to Upper Wharf

to Lower
Wharf

Saw
mill

Cart Bridge

Longmeadow Brook

T. H. Tooley

Causeway

Bridge

CONNECTICUT RIVER

"[T]he growing good of the world is partly dependent on unhistoric acts; and that things are not so ill with you and me as they might have been, is half owing to the number who lived faithfully a hidden life and rest in unvisited tombs."

George Eliot, *Middlemarch*

· *Introduction* ·

Social Diversity and Social Change in Seventeenth-Century New England

FEW TOPICS have rivaled the colonial New England town as an object of fascination for the most recent generation of American historians. Since the simultaneous appearance of important community studies by Kenneth A. Lockridge, Philip J. Greven, John Demos, and Michael Zuckerman in the banner year of 1970, scholars have been reformulating the entire panorama of United States history in the light of the experience of early New Englanders.[1] The studies of Dedham and Andover have been particularly influential, and their portrayal of a communal, egalitarian, harmonious society has not yet been brought into serious question. A new study of Salem, Massachusetts, published in 1980, begins by invoking the current "consensus" regarding the early New England town: "Homogeneous, closed, corporate and cohesive, the pattern has been established and documented."[2] Scholars dealing with topics as diverse as social change during the Revolution and changes in the law of contract and the law of negligence in the early national period have built on the quietistic models of seventeenth-century Dedham and Andover. Historians of the stature of Richard Hofstadter substantially reformulated their own work in response to the findings of the new demographic studies.[3] Building on the communal and "one-class" images of the seventeenth century, these interpretations have linked the apparent disharmony and stratification of the eighteenth century to the coming of the American Revolution. This view sees the rising incidence of land scarcity, religious strife, and "un-

[1] Kenneth A. Lockridge, *A New England Town, The First Hundred Years: Dedham, Massachusetts, 1636–1736*, New York, 1970; Philip J. Greven, Jr., *Four Generations: Population, Land, and Family in Colonial Andover, Massachusetts*, Ithaca, 1970; John Demos, *A Little Commonwealth: Family Life in Plymouth Colony*, New York, 1970; Michael Zuckerman, *Peaceable Kingdoms: New England Towns in the Eighteenth Century*, New York, 1970.

[2] Christine Alice Young, *From 'Good Order' to Glorious Revolution: Salem, Massachusetts, 1628–1689*, Ann Arbor, 1980, p. 1.

[3] *America at 1750: A Social Portrait*, New York, 1971, p. 7.

neighborly" behavior by the villagers as preconditions for the Revolutionary crisis.

In their depiction of the process of cultural change, therefore, the new social historians ironically found themselves in close agreement with the old intellectual historians. For Lockridge and Greven, as for Perry Miller, the story was one of erosion after a heroic first generation—whether the word used to describe this process was "decline" or "declension" or whether the villain was factionalism or secularism. In either case, the end result was the same: the communalistic ideology of Puritanism gave way to the individualistic ethos of republicanism. Insuring godly behavior became less important than protecting private property. Access to markets became more desirable than access to the sacraments. Deferential politics gave way to participatory democracy, and selectmen surrendered up their power to the town meeting. But as politics became more egalitarian, the distribution of wealth became less so, as "the rich" and "the poor" made their first appearance in New England. Well before the first bloodletting at Lexington and Concord, these scholars all agree, Puritans had been transformed into Yankees, and an ascriptive society had given way to one based on achievement.

Surprisingly few historians have questioned this so-called "modernization" thesis, or queried whether the experiences of Dedham and Andover really typified early New England. Particularly striking is the willingness to generalize with such confidence from the examples of two subsistence farming communities, especially since both towns have as many reasons to argue against typicality as for it. The majority of seventeenth-century New Englanders lived either in ocean ports or in major river towns. Dedham and Andover were neither. They were somewhat isolated, backwater farming communities whose very parochialism warns against assumptions of normative behavior.

In point of fact, early New England contained not one but three distinct settlement zones: an urbanized coastal region, typified by Boston and Salem; a subsistence farming region comprised of towns like Dedham and Andover; and an area of highly commercialized agriculture, such as the towns of the colony's breadbasket—the Connecticut River Valley. Each region had different patterns of social relations, economic opportunity, and political behavior. Throughout the seventeenth century, the levels of communal harmony, social stratification, and political elitism displayed a wide diversity in each of the three zones. To use the words of J. M. Cameron, each zone had a distinct "ensemble of social relations."

Scholars have acknowledged this high level of diversity for the eighteenth century, but for the earlier period the Dedham and Andover models continue to command almost universal acceptance. This unanimity is not entirely the result of a dearth of scholarship. Several historians who have closely examined the coastal ports of Boston and Salem have discovered mercantilist, faction-ridden, stratified, and contentious communities rather than peasant utopias. To date, however, there has been no similar treatment of one of the highly commercialized agricultural towns.[4]

This study attempts to remedy that deficiency. It focuses on socioeconomic relationships in Springfield, Massachusetts during the seventeenth century. As a highly commercialized, developmental community, Springfield typified many of the experiences of towns in the Merrimack Valley, in Plymouth, on Cape Cod, and in the remainder of the Connecticut Valley. This study demonstrates that the findings drawn from the subsistence farming regions cannot be generalized to the entire colony. By all measures, Springfield was a more individualistic, less communal and egalitarian place than early New England is usually thought to have been.

Material opportunity, not organic unity, governed the inhabitants' behavior. Men came to the town to seek their fortune—as fur traders, artisans, teamsters, laborers, or farmers—not to establish a godly community. These individualistic goals produced a society where a man's worth was measured largely in economic, not religious, terms. Court records show convincingly that the town's inhabitants were willing to countenance various forms of antisocial behavior, often of a decidedly non-Puritan character, if the culprit was a skilled artisan or a hard-working laborer. The ability to curry leather, join a houseframe, or last a shoe was more highly prized than was personal probity.

These materialistic goals were reflected in Springfield's high level of economic diversification. Here again the town presents a sharp contrast to the Dedham and Andover depiction of a homogeneous society of subsistence farmers. In Springfield, rather than being simply agriculturalists, over two-thirds of the community's men possessed a marketable skill which they used to earn their daily bread. Many inhabitants displayed competence in as many as three or more crafts. Some highly skilled workers rarely, if ever, performed major field labor. These included: carpenters, smiths, coop-

---

[4] Darrett B. Rutman, *Winthrop's Boston: Portrait of A Puritan Town, 1630–1649*, Chapel Hill, 1965; Paul Boyer and Stephen Nissenbaum, *Salem Possessed: The Social Origins of Witchcraft*, Cambridge, Mass., 1974.

ers, tailors, millers, and brickmakers. And almost every man worked periodically as a canoeman, teamster, mill hand, sawyer, stone-mason, drover, or day-laborer.

Equally diversified was the town's manufacturing base. Throughout the seventeenth century Springfield's economy displayed a highly developed commercial orientation. Financed and controlled largely by the town's founding family, the Pynchons, these commercial enterprises encompassed gristmills, sawmills, lead mines, turpentine manufactures, ironworks, and housing construction. These projects provided either full-time or seasonal employment to the roughly one-third of the town's male population who lacked sufficient land to make farming their sole means of livelihood. Such enterprises also served as magnets to draw itinerant artisans and laborers from elsewhere in the valley and colony. Of critical importance here was Springfield's function as what geographers describe as a "central place." It stood at the nexus of an economic region comprised of a network of producing areas and local trading centers which served as feeders to the community's marketing system.[5] Hadley and Westfield were the principal producing areas, Northampton the next largest trading center. The surplus wheat provided by the valley's farmers allowed the Pynchons to export downriver as many as two thousand bushels annually.[6]

Springfield's economic orientation produced a society that was far from being a peasant utopia. It was for many of its inhabitants a depressing place in which to live. Throughout the seventeenth century, it was characterized by inequality, bankruptcy, and social conflict. Two Old World phenomena rarely associated with early New England—land tenancy and wage labor—were everyday realities for half the town's population. In many ways Springfield was not a social community, but an economic community, and the weakness of communal bonds brought a high level of discord. Far from revealing a peasant utopia, court records testify to both the frequency and virulence of antisocial behavior. Throughout the period, the community experienced disruptive levels of physical assault, family feuds, slander, witchcraft accusations, and drunkenness. In their social conduct, as in their economic activities, the inhabitants behaved as self-assertive individuals, not as other-directed communitarians. If a resident found himself enraged at a fellow villager, he was not constrained from venting this anger by an

[5] Edward M. Cook, Jr., *The Fathers of the Towns: Leadership and Community Structure in Eighteenth-Century New England*, Baltimore, 1976, pp. 77–79, 183.

[6] Account Books, 1–6; Howard S. Russell, *A Long, Deep Furrow: Three Centuries of Farming in New England*, Hanover, N.H., 1976, p. 42.

overriding need to preserve communal harmony. In Springfield the most important social bonds were not those of the neighborhood, but those of the marketplace. And the most important market ties were those that led to the Pynchon family.

Nothing illustrates Springfield's contrast with Dedham so vividly as does the position of the Pynchons. Despite Kenneth Lockridge's depiction of seventeenth-century New England as a "one-class" society and Michael Zuckerman's assertion that the development of a distinct social elite was a "virtual impossibility in provincial Massachusetts," Springfield from the beginning was dominated by the Pynchons.[7] William Pynchon founded the town as a fur-trading post in 1636 and soon oversaw the embryonic community much like an English manorial lord. The largest landholder, principal merchant, and employer of almost every citizen, he also held all important civil and judicial power. When he returned to England in 1652, following a theological dispute with the General Court, William's privileges and status devolved upon his twenty-six-year-old son John. The younger Pynchon quickly became the most powerful figure in western Massachusetts. He retained his father's fur monopoly, expanded the family's landholdings, served as the financier for most of the region's settlements, and continued to be the valley's largest employer. In Springfield itself, some forty men worked on an approximately full-time basis for Pynchon, and about half the town's population at any one time was financially dependent in some fashion—rental of land or animals, employment, or debt—on the resources and good graces of Pynchon. As a result of his viselike economic grip on the community, the processes of getting work or getting land routinely began with a trek to the Pynchon general store.[8]

Not surprisingly, by 1665 John Pynchon held virtually every significant leadership position. He was simultaneously magistrate, judge of the county court, permanent moderator of the town meeting, and captain of the militia. Equally important, the townsmen habitually relied on Pynchon's initiative and financial wherewithal, rather than common taxation, for funding community projects. When it came time to build a new gristmill or sawmill, or to purchase a flock of sheep for the community's wool, he supplied the necessary capital and in return received ownership rights as well as toll privileges.

John Pynchon's economic, familial, and political connections with

---

[7] Lockridge, *A New England Town*, p. 76; Zuckerman, *Peaceable Kingdoms*, p. 219.
[8] Account Books, 1–6.

the outside world served as the linchpin to his dominance. This power derived from his position as mediator or "gatekeeper" between the valley and Boston. As Springfield's spokesman in Boston and as the instrument of General Court policy in western Massachusetts, Pynchon commanded enormous influence in both locales. This dominance remained unchallenged until New England's version of the Glorious Revolution dramatically modified the sources of his power. Until this time, Pynchon's economic hegemony, enhanced by his monopoly of political and judicial offices, created a proliferating set of dependency relationships which undermined traditional Puritan concepts of the organic, classless society.[9]

Dependence, of course, does not necessarily connote exploitation. Some men used their association with the Pynchons to improve their standard of living. Joseph Parsons, beginning as a fur agent for the Pynchons, ended his life with an estate valued at £2,088, the second largest inventory probated in seventeenth-century Hampshire County.[10] Others were not so fortunate. They used the resources Pynchon had to offer—work, developmental leases, credit—in an effort to get ahead. The price to *taking* this gamble was dependency on Pynchon, the price of *losing* it was often financial ruin. The tanner Griffith Jones lost his house and lands through indebtedness to the Pynchons, as did the blacksmith John Stewart, the cooper John Mathews, the agricultural laborer and tenant Jonathan Taylor, and the merchant-tailor Samuel Marshfield. Their stories were more typical than was Parsons's.[11]

The particulars of this dependency are laid out in remarkable detail in the Pynchon account books, the principal source used for this study. These volumes reveal how and at what cost men became associated with the Pynchons. When renting land and livestock, buying manufactured goods, or simply transferring credit to a fellow villager, men paid their accounts at the family's general store with the fruits of their labor—whether they were farmers, craftsmen, or laborers. Accordingly, the account books contain a wide variety of information relating to the distribution of goods and services, occupations, credit, indebtedness, prices, tenancy, labor patterns, mortgages, and foreclosures. Better than any similar seventeenth-century documents, the account books illuminate the substance and rhythms of day-to-day existence. They show how often and at what tasks men and women worked in the Pynchons' fields, mills, or canoes.

[9] Lockridge, *A New England Town*, pp. 57–78.
[10] HCPC Rec., 1 (1660–1690), pp. 235–236.
[11] Account Books, 1–6.

By tracing some two hundred individual work careers through the account books, a complex and multifarious portrayal of Springfield's economy emerges—one that calls into question a number of long-standing scholarly assumptions. Among these are: the scarcity of labor, high wage levels, the concentration of skilled artisans in major coastal ports, the ready availability of land, and the universality of fee-simple land tenure. This analysis likewise suggests that the prevailing emphasis on the eighteenth century as a period of declining opportunity and increasing social conflict is in need of modification. In Springfield, it appears, something very near the opposite occurred. Rather than moving toward economic stratification and increased intercommunal strife, the town was growing more egalitarian and harmonious as the Revolution approached. For ordinary inhabitants, access to both land and political power came easier in the eighteenth century than before.

Finally, the account books and the Hampshire court records allow for a humanization of the individual settlers. The new social historians have brought us closer to the everyday life of the "common sort" than most ever imagined possible. But this was often done at the cost of reducing the inhabitants to statistical abstractions, faceless peasants, or Weberian ideal types. The Springfield records reveal that this tendency is not unavoidable. Throughout the seventeenth century the town clearly had its share of vivid personalities, individuals who even at the remove of three hundred years come across in stark and recognizable tones. Theirs is the story this book seeks to tell.

Labor in a New Land

Chapter 1

A Company Town

"Laborare est orare"

SPRINGFIELD began as a commercial enterprise and remained such throughout the seventeenth century. Founded in 1636 by William Pynchon as a fur-trading post, the town quickly became the major merchandising center in the upper Connecticut Valley. The fur trade enriched the Pynchon family and brought large numbers of artisans, teamsters, and laborers to the community. Within a generation of settlement, the relationships between the Pynchons and the laboring classes had produced a society that can best be described as a company town.

The commercial orientation that William Pynchon brought to the Connecticut Valley reflected the economic individualism of his native Essex County. Pynchon had been born in 1590 into a family on the periphery of the English gentry class, and he grew to maturity in the modest Essex County village of Springfield.[1] This was the region to which the enclosure movement had come earliest and, as a result, by the time of Pynchon's youth the manor was "little more than a rent-collecting machine." The growth of enclosed-field farming commercialized land exchange and fostered an environment of economic individualism. Most Essex County landholders—whether of free, lease, or copyhold lands—rationalized their production of cereal grains, wool, and livestock for export to the London market. Augmenting this increased market orientation was the transfer of day-to-day administrative and judicial functions from the courts leet and courts baron to the parish and justice of the peace. By the beginning of the seventeenth century, the manor did not play a significant role in regulating farming activities in Essex and men were left to make their own decisions.[2]

---

[1] *Pynchon Court Rec.*, p. 6.

[2] David Grayson Allen, *In English Ways: The Movement of Societies and the Transferal of English Local Law and Custom to Massachusetts Bay in the Seventeenth Century*, Chapel Hill, 1981, pp. 151–153.

Or at least they were until the centralizing policies of Charles I brought higher levels of taxation, outside control, and religious persecution.[3] William Pynchon, like many of the gentry of the eastern counties, became a zealous convert to the Puritan reform movement, and the King's new policies threatened his religious as well as his economic autonomy. By 1629, with Parliament suspended, higher taxes promised, and wool prices plummeting because of the Thirty Years War, Pynchon decided to leave England. He became one of the patentees of the Massachusetts Bay Company and set sail with the fleet that brought John Winthrop to New England.[4] Accompanying him were his wife Anna and three daughters, and his son John would follow shortly.[5] Already one of the luminaries in the company, William received a midvoyage invitation to dine with Governor Winthrop. The governor entered into his journal that "About eleven of the clock, our captain sent his skiff and fetched aboard us the masters of the other two ships, and Mr. Pynchon, and they dined with us in the round-house."[6]

Upon arrival in America—displaying the energy and purposefulness characteristic of all he did—Pynchon began trafficking in furs, raising livestock, and farming. His boats plied the New England coast as far north as Sagadahock, Maine, sometimes with untoward results. In the fall of 1631, as Winthrop's journal relates, "Mr. Pynchon's boat, coming from Sagadahock, was cast away at Cape Ann, but the men and chief goods saved, and the boat recovered."[7] Such mishaps aside, these voyages brought Pynchon into contact with fur traders and inspired him to concentrate most of his resources on this activity. He remembered the heavy demand for beaver pelts in the London hatmaking industry, and he possessed the right contacts on Fleet Street to begin immediately merchandising furs there. As early as 1621, Pynchon was engaged in a business partnership with Thomas Brocke, "Citizen and Mercer of London," sharing with him a £202 judgment in the Court of Common Pleas against a certain Thomas Elliot of Roxwell.[8] By 1634, with the help of his London agents, Pynchon was the leading fur trader in Massachusetts with a volume of pelts tenfold that of

[3] T. H. Breen, "Persistent Localism: English Social Change and the Shaping of New England Institutions," *WMQ*, 32 (1975), p. 9.

[4] Samuel Eliot Morison, *Builders of the Bay Colony*, Boston, 1962, p. 339; George C. Homans, "The Puritans and the Clothing Industry in England," *New England Quarterly*, 13 (1940), pp. 519–529.

[5] *Pynchon Court Rec.*, p. 9.

[6] *Winthrop's Journal*, 1, p. 14.

[7] *Ibid.*, 1, p. 76.

[8] CVHM Ms.

his nearest competitor.[9] He subsequently moved from Dorchester to the less densely settled town of Roxbury to maximize his advantage.

At the same time, Pynchon entered into a trading consortium with Governor Winthrop and his son John. The London merchant, Francis Kirby, alluded to this connection when he wrote John Winthrop, Jr., on March 26, 1633: "I understand how you have dealt with mr. Pinchen for the Cloth, which bargain is not amisse, but may produce reasonable profit if he deale well with you in the Condicion of the beaver that he shall deliver to you." The magnitude of this trade is suggested by the younger Winthrop's payment to Pynchon of £197 1s. 8d. for imported cloth in March of 1636. Four months later this order was followed by one for 225 yards of cloth valued at £90; and in September of that year Pynchon "Reckoned with mr. John Winthrop Junior . . . for the fraight of 16 Tunn in the [ship] Blessinge at 35 shillings per Tunn . . . [and] for 24 Tunn in the Batchelor for 45 shillings per Tunn."[10]

Yet with the proliferation of traders around Massachusetts Bay, Pynchon recognized that his days of fur trading preeminence were numbered unless he moved west. By far the most promising region for fur trapping was the Connecticut Valley, and the lure of expanding his trade in such a bountiful environment induced Pynchon to move his family for the third time within six years.[11]

The Connecticut Valley had long been known for the abundance of its fur resources. In 1614 the Dutch trader Adrian Block had traveled fifty miles up the river to reconnoiter its commercial potential. So successful was the subsequent Dutch intrusion that during the decade from 1623 to 1633 their traders obtained an average of ten thousand beaver skins annually.[12] The forested valleys of the Connecticut River and its capillary system of tributary rivers and streams provided an ideal habitat for beaver, moose, otter, muskrat, marten, and lynx. Pynchon's decision to tap these resources was made easier by the large migration from Massachusetts Bay of the settlers who established the towns of Hartford, Windsor, and Wethersfield. But while the other migrants made the trek

[9] "Pincheon Papers," *Collections of the Massachusetts Historical Society*, 2nd Ser., 8 (1819), pp. 231–232.

[10] Francis Kirby to John Winthrop, Jr., March 26, 1633, *Winthrop Papers*, 3, p. 116; see also pp. 238, 285–286, 314.

[11] *Pynchon Court Rec.*, p. 11; Ruth A. McIntyre, *William Pynchon: Merchant and Colonizer, 1590–1662*, Springfield, 1962.

[12] Francis X. Moloney, *The Fur Trade in New England, 1620–1676*, Cambridge, Mass., 1931, p. 46.

primarily for religious reasons, Pynchon went to the valley as a merchant, not a Puritan. The community he built reflected this priority.

For his trading post, Pynchon selected a site located immediately above the highest navigable point on the Connecticut River. Not only was it north of the three newly settled towns, but it also stood at the nexus of several major Indian trails. Most important, it bisected the principal Indian path from Narragansett and Pequot country in the southeast to Mohawk territory in the Hudson Valley. His intention to build the settlement on the lush alluvial lands near the confluence of the Agawam and Connecticut Rivers was thwarted when the Indians refused to leave. "[T]he best ground at Agawam [was so] incombred with Indians," Pynchon wrote John Winthrop, Jr., "that I shall loose halfe the benefit thereby: and am compelled to plant on the opposite side to avoid trespassing of them."[13] He thereupon built his settlement on the less promising east side which, while it could not rival the opposite shore in agricultural potential, more than sufficed as a trading post.

In April 1636 Pynchon purchased the site from the Agawam Indians for "eighteen fathams of Wampam, eighteen coates, 18 hatchets, 18 hoes, [and] 18 knives."[14] The deed divided the purchase into three separate sections: (1) the Agawam meadows, located southwest of the Agawam River; (2) the land on the east bank where the Springfield town center was eventually situated; and (3) the "Long Meadow" located four miles to the south on the east bank. The deed allowed that the Agawams, who were hunter-gatherers and primitive agriculturalists, "shal have and enjoy all that cottinackeesh, or ground that is now planted; And have liberty to take Fish and Deer, ground nuts, walnuts, akornes, and sasachiminesh or a kind of pease, And also if any of our cattle spoile their corne, to pay as it is worth; and that hogs shall not goe on the side of Agawam but in akorne time."[15]

The commercial potential of the Connecticut Valley location appeared unlimited. William Pynchon doubtless was struck, as observers have been ever since, by the lushness and natural beauty of the valley. Formed out of the remains of a glacial lake dating back to the late Wisconsin period, the Connecticut basin comprises some 11,320 square miles of fertile and variegated countryside.

[13] William Pynchon to John Winthrop, Jr., June 2, 1636, *Winthrop Papers*, 3, p. 267.

[14] *Springfield Town Recs.*, 1, pp. 17–19.

[15] H. A. Wright, ed., *Indian Deeds of Hampden County*, Springfield, 1905, pp. 11–12.

The river itself meanders along a 410-mile course from the Canadian border down to Saybrook, Connecticut.[16] In the colonial period, the plains and lower terraces flanking the river provided rich alluvial soil, the result of periodic flooding. Rising gently on either side of the valley were the mountainous remains of the perimeter of the lake; these were now covered with both deciduous and evergreen trees. As the first Indian cultivators discovered, the upper terraces of the valley, particularly the bluffs and plateaus extending eastward from the future site of Springfield toward the mountains, offered considerably less promising farmland than did the meadows and plains near the river. The bluffs and plateaus of the east, in addition to their irregular and difficult topography, possessed soil covered by a thin acid litter that severely diminished its fertility.[17] The English settlers later referred to this area as the "pine barrens." The most desirable farmland within the corporate confines of Springfield was found at the confluence of the Agawam and Connecticut Rivers. Here the annual spring floods washed up silt deposits from the rivers to replenish the soil's nitrogen. Not surprisingly, this was the location William Pynchon found "incombred with Indians" upon his initial visit to the valley.

In addition to its obvious potential as a transportation center, the valley location offered the best environment in Massachusetts for cereal grain cultivation. While soil conditions elsewhere in the colony forced the settlers to rely on a combination of rye and Indian corn, in the Connecticut Valley wheat, oats, and barley all flourished. English grains grew successfully in New England only on the alluvial terraces bordering the Connecticut River from Middletown north.[18] Wheat (always the favored grain for bread), barley (needed for bread and broth as well as beer), and oats (for fodder) all were thriving in the upper valley towns well before 1660.[19] The region's climate offered particularly ideal growing conditions for wheat—wet springs followed by long, dry summers. If the climate of twentieth-century Springfield has not changed appreciably over the past three hundred years, the growing season usually averaged between 150 and 170 days, with average annual precipitation of

[16] For an overall description of the Connecticut River, see William F. Steke and Evan Hill, *The Connecticut River*, Middletown, Conn., 1972.

[17] Louis Seig, "Concepts of Change and the Historical Method in Geography: The Case of Springfield, Massachusetts," Ph.D. dissertation, University of Minnesota, 1968, pp. 55–57.

[18] Russell, *A Long, Deep Furrow*, p. 42; Robert A. Gross, "Culture and Cultivation: Agriculture and Society in Thoreau's Concord," *Journal of American History*, 69 (1982), pp. 59–60.

[19] Account Books, 1–2.

just under fifty inches. The first frost rarely came before the mid-October displays of resplendent foliage. The only real drawback for agriculturalists and traders alike was that winters could be severe; and even in normal years, freezing temperatures usually prevailed for at least four months. During particularly frigid winters, even the wide and swift-flowing Connecticut River froze solid. This may have occurred with unusual frequency in the settlement period, as some geographers now believe that the seventeenth century was a quasi ice age, with exceptionally cold and prolonged winters. Under normal conditions, the ground began to thaw after mid-March and the area was usually frost-free by mid-April.[20]

In addition to its potential as a trading post and an environment for raising cereal grains, Springfield offered equally promising conditions for livestock husbandry. The area's extensive pasturage meant that beef, pork, and horses could profitably be raised for the export market. Having grown up in the livestock-orientated wood pastures of East Anglia, Pynchon was determined to recreate in America the dual foundation of English farming: livestock, with grassland to feed it; and bread-grain for the family.[21] Springfield's original incorporation agreement underscored the importance accorded to raising livestock. The first inhabitants alloted two acres of new mowing land for each head of neat cattle and twice that for every horse, "because estate is like to be improved in cattell, and such ground is aptest for theyr use."[22] As with any livestock husbandry, the problems of spring feed, summer grass, and winter fodder all required quick resolution. Wheat and rye straw make excellent cattle fodder, but barley straw does not. Most important of all, however, were the summer grasses. And, as the "starving time" of Springfield's first years revealed, the valley soil's richness would remain largely untapped without the introduction of the superior English grasses.

The paltry harvest of 1637 brought home this lesson to Pynchon. The following spring he described the famine's effect on man and beast alike: "In regard to the great straits the whole population was in, both of persons and cattle for 2 or 3 months together: The wants of the Plantation were such, that som were forced to give malt to piggs to save their lives, and those that had som English meale, and would have kept it, were faine to spend it for want of corne ... and 3 or 4 were in Consultation to leave the Plantation

[20] Government Printing Office, *Climatic Atlas of the U.S.*, Washington, D.C., 1968, pp. 27–31.

[21] Russell, *A Long, Deep Furrow*, pp. 24–25.

[22] Morison, *Builders of the Bay Colony*, p. 345.

for a while, to earne their bread elsewhere, till corne might be had here." Writing in both the third and first persons, he related that: "Mr. Pynchon's wants were often soe great, that divers times he hath not had half a bushell of corne in his house for his family . . . Alsoe, my wife, walking more amongst my Cattle . . . professed that It was her dayly grief to see them in that poore starveing condition."[23] Soon thereafter Pynchon began the process of converting to English grasses. His account books show that he brought up thirty bushels of "Flanders grass seed" from Hartford. This was presumably red clover and it was later supplemented with white clover. (Both were eventually replaced by Timothy grass in the early eighteenth century.)[24]

The successful introduction of English grasses by the early 1650s allowed Springfield to become the first major livestock-producing area in colonial Massachusetts. The Pynchons raised both hogs and cattle for market, stall-feeding the latter.[25] The hogs were usually slaughtered and packed in Springfield itself, while the cattle were taken on the hoof to Warehouse Point at Hartford. The brackish water at Hartford was used to pack the beef for overseas shipment. After midcentury, the Pynchons' drovers also herded cattle from the rich pastures of Hadley and Hatfield and took them overland to markets in Boston.[26]

William Pynchon was equally methodical in building up the town's labor supply. With the departure before 1641 of all but two of the original signatories to the town covenant, he immediately began to recruit indentured servants from Boston and London. Typically these servants arrived under direct consignment to the founder. He thereupon sold their remaining terms of service to one of his fellow villagers, often one of his sons-in-law, Henry Smith or Elizur Holyoke. On September 9, 1650, Hugh Dudley signed an indenture with Pynchon. In the agreement, Dudley, apparently captured in Scotland during the Cromwellian wars, "did covenant promise and grant to and with William Pynchon of Springfield in New England merchant . . . for and duringe the tearme of five yeares."[27] His new master then "assigned and set [Dudley] over to Mr. Henry Smith of Springfield for the said tearme of 5 yeeres." Smith agreed to "allow [Dudley] three pounds and ten shillings per yeare, to find him apparell: and to endevor at the end of his tyme to provide

---

[23] Mason Green, *Springfield, 1636–1886*, Springfield, 1888, pp. 29–30.
[24] Russell, *A Long, Deep Furrow*, pp. 29–30, 130.
[25] *Ibid.*, p. 61.
[26] Account Books, 1, p. 273; 5, pp. 19, 415.
[27] *Pynchon Court Rec.*, p. 224.

him a convenient allottment of land." On the same day another Scot, James Wells, signed an indenture with Pynchon for "the tearme of nine yeares."[28] This contract was likewise turned over to Smith. A third Scot, Edward Foster, was indentured to Pynchon for a term of nine years. Elizur Holyoke received this contract. Pynchon also apprenticed out other servants for the purpose of learning a trade. Hoping one day to become a weaver, on October 15, 1650, Samuel Terry "with the consent of my present master, William Pynchon of Springfield, gentleman, have put my self an apprentense to Benjamin Cooly of Springfield weaver . . . [for] three yeeres 6 months."[29]

Upon completion of their apprenticeships, these men—and most of the town's other inhabitants as well—became employees of William Pynchon. The labor needs of Springfield's founder were manifold. His fur-trading activities demanded the placement of agents throughout the valley, and marketing required extensive use of canoemen, teamsters, coopers, blacksmiths, and common laborers. Almost all men worked at least occasionally at one or more of these tasks. Pynchon constructed a warehouse at Enfield falls immediately below the highest point of navigation on the east side of the Connecticut River, approximately seven miles south of Springfield. He likewise built or rented warehouses in Hartford, Middletown, and New London. [See Connecticut Valley map.] The canoemen who carried goods to and from the warehouses usually traveled by canoes made either from birchbark or a hollowed-out log.[30] Pynchon also needed coopers to build barrels in which to ship furs, pork, and beef, as well as smiths to construct agricultural implements, and common laborers to string the wampum used as Indian currency. Moreover, his burgeoning fields increasingly needed farmhands and tenants, particularly by the late 1640s.[31] Pynchon revealed the scope of his work force in a letter written in 1644 to Stephen Day, who at the time was a mining prospector in the employ of John Winthrop, Jr.: "you write for butter and cheese [but] it is not to be had in all our plantation. I spend it as fast as I make it, because I have much resort and many workmen, which eate it as soone as I have it."[32]

A group profile of the inhabitants entered on the 1646 tax list

[28] *Ibid.*, p. 225.

[29] *Ibid.*, pp. 226–227.

[30] Harold Roger King, "The Settlement of the Upper Connecticut River Valley to 1675," Ph.D. dissertation, Vanderbilt University, 1965, pp. 225–226.

[31] William Pynchon Account Book.

[32] William Pynchon to Stephen Day, October 8, 1644, *Winthrop Papers*, 4, p. 495.

underscores the central importance of William Pynchon to the town's economy. Of the thirty-nine men on this list (out of an overall town population of one hundred men, women, and children), twenty-five remained in Springfield permanently. Three died within the next decade. Of the fourteen who emigrated, one later returned. Fifteen of the twenty-two men who remained in the town derived a substantial portion of their income as employees of either William Pynchon or his son John. Moreover, twelve of those who stayed would at one time or another experience serious indebtedness problems with the Pynchons.

As these men became the Pynchons' employees, they became their customers as well. The general store opened by William quickly became the central wholesale and retail outlet in the upper valley. The store consisted of a palisaded warehouse built on the west side "over agaynst Agawam."[33] Indians canoed down the river and its tributaries with the furs they had trapped to exchange them for wampum, blankets, coats, cotton cloth, axes, knives, and the like. Pynchon's workers then packed the furs into hogsheads, which were either teamed or taken by canoe to the warehouse at Enfield falls. At the falls, coasting vessels picked up the furs for shipment to Boston, whence they were forwarded by sailing packet to the fur market in London. In return, Pynchon imported textiles, tools, and medicines for sale in his general store.[34] As his entrepôt expanded, Pynchon's economic hold over the village's inhabitants grew to the point where, according to Bernard Bailyn, "he could rightly have considered his role that of a manorial lord."[35]

In 1641 this authority was enhanced by Springfield's secession from the colony of Connecticut. Pynchon had been charged by the Connecticut General Court with the task of purchasing badly needed corn from the neighboring Nonotuck Indians. He believed that the Indians' asking price was too high and refused to deal with them until it was lowered. With the colony's half-starved inhabitants clamoring for the corn, the General Court rebuked Pynchon for the delay. Following an opinion the magistrates had solicited from the Reverend Thomas Hooker of the Hartford Church, they fined him forty bushels of corn. The Court also publicly accused him of trying to monopolize the Indian trade. Hooker declared that Pynchon deferred the sale "that he should have all the trade to himselfe, and have all the corne in his owne hands . . . and so rack the country

[33] Morison, *Builders of the Bay Colony*, p. 357.

[34] William Pynchon Account Book.

[35] Bernard Bailyn, *The New England Merchants in the Seventeenth Century*, New York, 1964, pp. 54–55.

at his pleasure."[36] Pynchon defended his actions by citing passages from Sir John Fortescue's *On the Laws of England*. He had earlier attacked the granting of fur monopolies as an unreasonable restraint of trade; now he again preached free market principles in ridiculing the ancient "just price" doctrine. The Indians, he argued, knew full well that the demand for corn was great after the poor harvest in 1637. They intended, therefore, to hold out for as high a price as they thought the market would bear—regardless of the General Court's preoccupation with inherent value and the unlawfulness of usury.[37] But all these arguments were of no avail; the magistrates refused to abate the fine or retract the condemnation. Their rigidity, however, proved costly. It provoked Pynchon into seeking and gaining formal readmission into Massachusetts. On February 14, 1639, "the Inhabitants of Agawam upon Quinnettecot" asserted that they had "by Gode's providence fallen into the line of the Massachusets Jurisdiction."[38] The reentry of Agawam, the settlement's initial name, henceforth gave the community an east-west rather than a north-south axis. Instead of simply being one of several rising towns in Connecticut, Springfield became the westernmost outpost of Massachusetts. This location afforded Pynchon an autonomy he would not have enjoyed in Connecticut and, more significant, conferred new importance on the plantation as the sole representative of Massachusetts in the valley for almost two decades.[39]

The community's first official act after reentering Massachusetts proved prophetic. William Pynchon was named magistrate and given extraordinary powers. The normal authority magistrates possessed included power to probate wills, hold petty sessions, and try all causes not involving loss of life or limb. Magistrates performed the judicial functions of discovery, indictment, trial, and sentencing. They also inflicted corporal punishment and administered oaths. Puritan jurisprudence, like that of England itself, had not yet arrived at a clear-cut distinction between the prosecutorial and adjudicative functions of the bench. And, as John M. Murrin has pointed out, "To judge from their behavior, New England magistrates consciously imitated what they evidently regarded as the

[36] Morison, *Builders of the Bay Colony*, pp. 352–353; William Pynchon to John Haynes, May 2, 1639, *Proceedings of Mass. Hist. Soc.*, 48 (1915), pp. 40–41.

[37] Morison, *Builders of the Bay Colony*, p. 354.

[38] *Pynchon Court Rec.*, p. 203; Simeon E. Baldwin, "The Secession of Springfield from Connecticut," *Publications of the Colonial Society of Massachusetts*, 12 (1908), pp. 55–82.

[39] Seig, "Concepts of Change," p. 96.

most progressive and efficient feature of the whole system, the trend toward summary justice. In a culture as addicted to guilt as Puritan New England, they succeeded overwhelmingly in criminal law, but they had to yield ground over civil disputes which lacked comparable internalized sanctions." While England was "groping toward an adversarial system of justice," in the "strict technical sense of the term, criminal justice in the orthodox colonies was inquisitorial." The criminal law in Massachusetts sought not only to protect against forcible seizure of goods and violence to the person, but to punish sins as well. Seventeenth-century New England jurisprudence, as a conflation of common law and scriptural injunctions (the Ten Commandments), made adultery and blasphemy capital crimes, but not the crimes against property that constituted the overwhelming majority of English capital offenses. Magistrates, accordingly, punished sinners as well as criminals.[40]

In addition to these already impressive traditional magisterial duties, William Pynchon, also received domain over "what ever else may tend to the Kinges peace, and the manifestation of our fidellity to the Bay Jurisdiction and the restraining of any that shall molest Gode's lawes: or lastely whatsoever else may fall within the power of an assistant." Both the execution and substance of this act were illegal under Massachusetts law. According to legal historian Joseph H. Smith, "the sole power to establish courts or grant judicial powers resided in the General Court."[41] Moreover, the enlarging clause, "what ever else may tend to the Kinge's peace," is not customarily included in magistracy authorizations. Pynchon proceeded to hold courts with no *de jure* status for the next two-and-one-half years. In June 1641 the Massachusetts General Court officially validated his actions. In May 1642 he was chosen to be an assistant to the General Court, thereby rendering the town's 1639 commission superfluous.[42] Pynchon had no formal legal training to aid him in fulfilling his judicial functions, and the only law books we know he owned were Michael Dalton's *Country Justice* and Sir John Fortescue's *On the Laws of England*.[43]

Pynchon likewise organized and led the area's militia and served as moderator for all the town meetings of Springfield, as the settlement was officially renamed in 1641. In 1648 the General Court

---

[40] John M. Murrin, "Magistrates, Sinners, and a Precarious Liberty: Trial by Jury in Seventeenth–Century Massachusetts," in David D. Hall, John M. Murrin, and Thad W. Tate, eds., *Essays in Honor of Edmund S. Morgan*, New York, 1983.

[41] *Pynchon Court Rec.*, pp. 90, 203.

[42] *Mass. Recs.*, 1, p. 345; 2, p. 2; 3, p. 230; 4, Part 1, p. 49.

[43] *Pynchon Court Rec.*, p. 31.

authorized him "to make freemen, in the towne of Springfield, of those that are in covenant and live according to their profession." Believing his daily presence necessary for Springfield's survival, Pynchon petitioned the Court to release him from compulsory attendance at its sessions. On May 9, 1649, "Att the request of Mr. William Pinchon, the [General Court] consented with [him] for his dismission from the further attending on the services of this Courte."[44]

Whether or not Pynchon's continued presence was necessary for the town's survival, his taxes were. He regularly paid over half of the annual tax load and also served as the credit agency of first access for the local government. Of the "voluntary rate" of £41 in January 1639, he paid £21. For an additional levy at the same time, he contributed £24 out of £40. He likewise furnished the necessary capital to build the meetinghouse and the gristmills, as well as to pay the Indians for the town plot. In return, he received land grants and other emoluments for persevering "at greate personall adventures" in establishing the town while others "fell off for feare of the difficulties."[45]

By 1646 these grants, in addition to Pynchon's normal allotments, gave him and his kinsmen command over the town's best available land. Although the community possessed some of the most fertile and productive land in the Connecticut Valley, this acreage was concentrated in a few relatively small areas. These included four square miles on the west side of the Connecticut River, two square miles south of the town center, and something less than two square miles north of the center. As we have seen, much of the remainder of the land, especially on the east side, was composed of woodlands, unimprovable pine barrens, marshes, and terrain so rugged as to be useless for farming. Within a decade of the town's founding, most of the acreage that was both tillable and accessible—in particular the lush alluvial meadows of the west side—was in the hands of William Pynchon and his two sons-in-law. The three men held 510 acres, roughly a quarter of the alloted lands. Of the forty-two landowners in Springfield, Pynchon, with 237 acres, had the largest holding. William Vaughan's six acres were the smallest allotment. After the holdings of Pynchon, Smith, and Holyoke, the next largest holding was the Reverend George Moxon's sixty-seven acres. The median holding was less than sixty acres.[46]

William Pynchon's tenure as lord of this emerging manorial economy was cut short by his return to England in 1652. The catalyst

---

[44] *Mass. Recs.*, 2, p. 224; 3, p. 158.
[45] *Springfield Town Recs.*, 1, pp. 157, 160–161.
[46] *Ibid.*, 1, pp. 157, 190–191.

to his departure, surprisingly, was a theological dispute with the Massachusetts General Court. While Pynchon's actions in the New World had been predominantly those of a hard-driving merchant, he returned in the early 1650s to the religious preoccupations of his youth. He penned a tract that was published in 1650 under the title, *The Meritorious Price of Our Redemption*. In it Pynchon attempted to explain his understanding of the atonement, arguing that man's salvation had been achieved through the perfect obedience of Christ, not by the Passion. The crucifixion was the work of men, not a result of the wrath of God. Christ did not, therefore, descend into Hell for the purpose of universal redemption—His perfect life had been sufficient to that end. By emphasizing the redemptive nature of Christ's life instead of His death, Pynchon undercut orthodox Puritanism's central tenet: that by taking men's sins upon himself and dying for them, Christ had saved the elect from Adam's curse. The Springfield leader thus placed himself in accord with the English latitudinarian or "Socinian" writers whose works were widely regarded as antitrinitarian. The Socinians, as Philip F. Gura has recently pointed out, "claimed that trinitarians abused the gift of reason in their arguments for a triune God and insisted that a mind unshackled by ecclesiastical authority would find in the Bible a Christ who, rather than being a part of the godhead, was a mere man, albeit one whom God had greatly exalted so that his moral example would inspire emulation."[47] Pynchon followed the lead of these religious rationalists, demanding greater toleration for heterodox opinions and less stringent tests of faith, tests always rendered suspect by the innate fallibility of all men, ministers and magistrates included. This individualistic and antiauthoritarian biblicism was scarcely calculated to set well with the coastal magistrates, acutely aware as they were about being caught in the crossfire between English Presbyterians and Congregationalists. Immediately upon reading *The Meritorious Price*, the members of the General Court branded it heretical and ordered Pynchon to recant. Publicly declaring that they did "utterly dislike it and detest it as erronious and daingerous," the assistants ordered that the tract be

[47] Gura, " 'The Contagion of Corrupt Opinions' in Puritan Massachusetts: The Case of William Pynchon," *WMQ*, 39 (1982) p. 479. That early New England was religiously, as well as socially, diverse is highlighted by Gura's observation that there is "little doubt that the Connecticut Valley harbored a small but active group of Puritan rationalists . . . whose presence suggests that historians have underestimated the great variety of Puritan thought in New England." *Ibid.*, p. 490. This comment also suggests a link between religious toleration and commercial orientation, two themes that would continue to be linked in Springfield for the remainder of the colonial period.

burnt by the colony's marshal in the Boston marketplace. So implacable was the Court that it refused even to record the objections of Pynchon's few defenders.[48] Attempting to find some common ground, at the next General Court session in May 1651 Pynchon "conferred with the Reverend Mr. Cotton, Mr. Norrice, and Mr. Norton, about some points of the greatest consequence in my booke, and I hope I have so explained my meaning to them as to take off the worst construction."[49] Still not satisfied, the Court deferred judgment, an action which was repeated the following October. At that time the magistrates made it clear that Pynchon would have to recant his views before the May session or be officially censured. Rather than submit to this indignity, the Springfield leader chose to go back to England. His son-in-law Henry Smith and the minister George Moxon made the same decision.[50]

William Pynchon's return to England did not sever his ties with Springfield. His son John remained in Massachusetts and quickly stepped into the leadership vacuum left by William's departure. The valley's fur trade was booming as never before, and the elder Pynchon could now coordinate the merchandising of beaver in the London marketplace. From his new home in the Buckinghamshire County village of Wraysbury, William (while continuing his theological ruminations) worked at the always difficult problem of securing credit.[51] The magnitude of the trade is suggested by a bond signed on May 24, 1662. In it he wrote "I, William Pynchon . . . gentleman, am firmly bound to William Bower of London . . . for three hundred pounds, legal money of England." Two days earlier, Pynchon had given Bower a bond for £80, also for the purpose of obtaining credit on Fleet Street.[52] With William superintending the family's trading activities in England, John Pynchon expanded both his marketing network and his domain over the now nearly 120 Springfield inhabitants. What William sowed, John would reap.

---

[48] *Mass. Recs.*, 4, Part 1, p. 29; Morison, *Builders of the Bay Colony*, pp. 370–373.

[49] *Mass. Recs.*, 4, Part 1, pp. 29–30, 48–49.

[50] *Pynchon Court Rec.*, p. 29.

[51] Morison, *Builders of the Bay Colony*, p. 375.

[52] Bond, William Pynchon to William Bower, May 24, 1662, photoduplicated copy, CVHM; Bond, William Pynchon to William Bower, May 22, 1662, photoduplicated copy, CVHM.

Chapter 2

Dominance

*"Come, come, I'll show unto thy sense
Industry hath its recompense."*
Anne Bradstreet, "The Flesh and the Spirit"

WHEN JOHN PYNCHON died in 1703, the Reverend Solomon Stoddard of Northampton eulogized him as a "Father to the Country." In a moving oration, the Northampton divine lamented that "a great man is fallen this day in our Israel. . . . God has removed one that has been a long while Serviceable. That has been improved about Public Service for above *Fifty Years*: he has been Serviceable unto the Country in general, and in special among our selves. He hath had the principal management of our Military Affairs, and our Civil Affairs: and laboured much in the setling of most of our Plantations, [he] has managed things with Industry, Prudence and Moderation. He hath been careful, in time of War, and as there has been occasion, he has been a Peace Maker among us, and helpfull in composing of differences: he has discountenanced Rude and Vicious Persons, bearing his Testimony against them." Stoddard concluded his memorial by observing that Pynchon "had great influence upon men in Authority Abroad, and upon the People at home, and had more experience by far, than any among us."[1]

Solomon Stoddard's paternalistic metaphor was well-taken. John Pynchon had indeed been a "Father of the Country" during the preceding half-century. While William Pynchon's efforts brought Springfield into being, John's developmental activities did likewise for the remainder of the upper valley settlements. He founded, financed, and helped govern every community established in western Massachusetts during the second half of the seventeenth century. These developmental activities and his generally decent and even-handed treatment of those financially dependent upon him allowed Pynchon to solidify and extend the control over Springfield

[1] Solomon Stoddard, *God's Frown in the Death of Usefull Men*, Boston, 1703, pp. 21–24.

that his father had bequeathed to him. Known to his fellow townsmen as the "Worshipful Major Pynchon," he dominated his town
in ways utterly incompatible with "one-class" and communal images
of early New England. Whether the measure was wealth, power,
and status, or dress, bearing, and world-view, he stood visibly apart
from the remaining inhabitants. The ornate and prepossessing Pynchon mansion gave architectural expression to this disparity. Consciously modeled on the country homes of the seventeenth-century
English gentry, the mansion stood in stark contrast to the modest
two and one-half-room dwellings that most villagers inhabited. As
the town's physical appearance proclaimed, in Springfield the class
structure was essentially two-tiered: John Pynchon and everyone
else.[2]

And Stoddard's Mosaic allusion notwithstanding, Pynchon achieved
this dominance not as a patriarch but as a patron. It was not so
much Elizabethan Puritanism as it was mercantile capitalism that
gave birth to the world of John Pynchon. As the manor economy
was replaced by the market economy, master-servant ties were supplanted by those of employer and employee.[3] The transition from
the world of the manor to the world of the market, as Pynchon's
experience reveals, came through the agency of the patron-client
bond. The patron-client relationship harkened back to the manor
by its emphasis on person-to-person ties, but even more it anticipated the triumph of contractualism and the cash nexus by its
preeminently economic nature. Patron-client ties occupied the middle ground between feudalism and capitalism, and they allowed
the peasants of the sixteenth century to become the wage-earners
of the eighteenth.

John Pynchon's success derived from his ability to forge both
corporate and private patronage bonds. He simultaneously dominated public life in Springfield (and in the upper valley generally)
while establishing strong financial claims over more than half the
town's individual citizens. In 1652, after he assumed ownership of
his father's approximately three hundred acres and lucrative fur-
trading network, the General Court selected Pynchon to serve on
the magistrate's commission.[4] By 1665 he had parlayed these early
advantages into positions of economic and political dominance. He

---

[2] The most palpable expression of this disparity was the £8,446 estate left by
Pynchon at his death in 1703. As we will see below, almost half of Springfield's
17th-century decedents left estates valued at less than £100; for Pynchon's estate,
see HCPC Rec., Box 19, no. 40.

[3] Allen, *In English Ways*, p. 151.

[4] *Pynchon Court Rec.*, pp. 227–228.

simultaneously filled the positions of magistrate, judge of the county court of Hampshire, permanent moderator of the town meeting, and captain of the militia. First elected as Springfield's deputy to the General Court in 1659, Pynchon followed this selection with appointment as judge of the newly created Hampshire County court in 1662. Three years later he was elected magistrate and held that position until the colony's first charter was suspended in 1684. In 1661, during their annual meeting to choose officers for the forthcoming year, Springfield's inhabitants selected Pynchon as "Moderator for all Towne meetings the yeare ensueing"—a procedure that continued without break until 1694.[5] In equally rapid succession he received commissions in the militia: lieutenant in 1653, captain in 1657, sergeant major in 1671, and elevation to the rank of colonel during King Philip's War (1675–76).[6]

Militia leaders in the Connecticut Valley commanded much greater authority than they did in eastern towns. Because of the almost continuous threat of Indian attack after 1675, the decisions of militia officers directly affected the safety and well-being of all inhabitants. In a letter requesting gunpowder from Boston in 1690, Pynchon emphasized that "we are dayly alarmed of" possible Indian assaults. In a similar letter eight years later, he underscored the extent to which the Indian threat disrupted the rhythms of daily existence: "we Cannot with safety follow out ourselves in the Fields. We dare not live upon our Lands that lie a little Remote from the body of our Towne; the Countrye is putt to Great Charge in maintaining Garrison Souldiers, and also for pursueing after them when they have done hurt."[7] The Indians and their French allies were fully aware of the valley settlers' reliance on Pynchon's leadership. He told his cousins in Hartford, Samuel Willys and John Allyn, that "Stephen Lee reported here that the French and Indians had a special aime to this Towne and a particular designe against me."[8]

The Indians' view of Pynchon's importance was not misplaced. He was the essential cog in the governmental machinery of western Massachusetts. This role derived from Pynchon's position as mediator or "gatekeeper" between the Connecticut Valley and Boston.

[5] *Springfield Town Recs.*, 1, p. 281; 2, pp. 197, 339. Michael Zuckerman explores the moderator's power over town meetings in *Peaceable Kingdoms*, pp. 162–165.

[6] *Pynchon Court Rec.*, p. 37.

[7] John Pynchon to Major General Wait Winthrop, July 17, 1690, Winthrop Mss.; John Pynchon and Samuel Patrigg to Governor Bellomont, July 26, 1698, British Public Record Office, C.O. S/1041 1 (1v) 639, typescript copy, CVHM.

[8] John Pynchon to Samuel Willys and John Allyn, February 24, 1690, Edes Ms., Mass. Hist. Soc.

Mediators, according to anthropologists, are those who link the local world to the outside world, guarding and controlling access each way. Those in the locality desiring access to the metropolis, or those at the provincial level needing to implement public policy in the village, must deal through—and reward—the mediator. Much like the gentry of seventeenth-century England, land magnates in nineteenth-century Italy, or "padrones" in twentieth-century Andalusia or Castile, John Pynchon served as the indispensable middleman in implementing public policy. As magistrate, he held the highest position in the local community and also sat on the governor's council in Boston. Local and provincial power reinforced each other. Because he alone occupied the formal offices that linked the local and provincial systems, Pynchon functioned as a mediator between the community and the rest of New England until the Crown suspended the first charter in 1684.[9]

This role was available to Pynchon because of the parochial nature of seventeenth-century New England towns, even those as highly commercialized as Springfield. The locus of men's daily actions—and thoughts—rarely extended beyond the community's boundaries. Few villagers who were not teamsters or canoemen had reason to travel to other towns, newspapers were few, and communications by letter were usually the prerogative of the gentry. As Kenneth Lockridge's study of literacy in colonial New England has revealed, less than 60 percent of men in seventeenth-century Massachusetts could read fluently. Moreover, less than 60 percent could write, 20 percent were semiliterate, and 20 percent were illiterate. Commenting on the implications of these findings, Lockridge emphasizes that access to the written word allowed elites to act as intermediaries between their illiterate fellow villagers and the outside world: "These data open the way to a new understanding of the respect shown for the sermon, for the minister, and indeed for any highly literate man in seventeenth-century New

---

[9] The anthropological literature which deals with mediators is extensive. See Sydel F. Silverman, "Patronage and Community-Nation Relationships in Central Italy," *Ethnology*, 4 (1965), pp. 172–188; Eric R. Wolf, "Aspects of Group Relations in a Complex Society: Mexico," *American Anthropologist*, 58 (1956), pp. 1065–1078; Clifford Geertz, "The Javanese Kijaji: The Changing Role of a Cultural Broker," *Comparative Studies in Society and History*, 2 (1960), pp. 228–249; also see T. H. Breen, "Persistent Localism," *WMQ* (1975), p. 9; Peter Laslett, "The Gentry of Kent in 1640," *Cambridge Historical Journal*, 9 (1947–1949), pp. 148–164. For an analysis of the magistrate's power, see John M. Murrin "Anglicizing an American Colony: The Transformation of Provincial Massachusetts," Ph.D. dissertation, Yale University, 1966; and Barbara A. Black, "The Judicial Power and the General Court in Early Massachusetts, 1634–1686," Ph.D. dissertation, Yale University, 1975.

England. They suggest that New Englanders once lived closer than we have imagined to the credulous word-of-mouth world of the peasant, closer to its absorbing localism, closer to its dependency on tradition and on the informed few."[10] In addition, because it was separated from Boston by over one hundred miles of forested, often inaccessible terrain, Springfield's isolation from its colonial government was even more complete.

John Pynchon, and mediators like him elsewhere in the colony, bridged this distance by personal communications as well as official correspondence with other gentry leaders. Unlike most villagers, whose perceptions of their world were shaped by the immediacies of what they saw and heard, the gentry actively followed and reported on colony-wide and even international developments. In February of 1668 Pynchon thanked Connecticut Governor John Winthrop for several (borrowed) London newspapers which Winthrop had sent the Springfield leader to apprise him of affairs in the mother country. During the 1680s Pynchon and Robert Livingston of Albany exchanged information on the military exploits of Prince Louis of Baden, commander of the armies of the Holy Roman Empire in Hungary against the Turks in 1689–1690. Praising Prince Louis's daring, Pynchon noted that "The Imperialists have taken Belgium and other places so that the Turks are almost outed of Hungaria," which was "A Notable exploit of Prince Louis, who with 3,000 horses attacked the Turks that Proved to be . . . 15,000."[11] In like manner, Springfield learned of wars with the Dutch and the machinations of rival political groups in London from letters Pynchon received from Winthrop and Captain Sylvester Salisbury, Commander-in-Chief at Fort Albany.[12]

In concepts as basic as time, a perceptual gap stood between the informed few and the remainder of the inhabitants. The annual cycles of planting and harvesting grain governed most villagers' comprehension of time. When Sarah Clark, unwed, testified before the magistrate during an inquiry aimed at discovering the paternity

[10] Kenneth A. Lockridge, *Literacy in Colonial New England*, New York, 1974, p. 15.

[11] John Pynchon to Robert Livingston, January 16, 1689, Livingston Family Papers, Franklin Delano Roosevelt Library, Hyde Park, New York.

[12] John Winthrop, Jr. to John Pynchon, November 9, 1674, Winthrop Mss.; John Pynchon to Captain Sylvester Salisbury, July 20, 1678, in E. B. O'Callaghan and J. H. Brodhead, eds., *Documents Relating to the Colonial History of the State of New York*, Albany, 1881, 13, p. 511. Darrett B. Rutman examines the problems of vertical and horizontal spheres of integration in "The Social Web: A Prospectus for the Study of the Early American Community," in W. L. O'Neill, ed., *Insights and Parallels: Problems and Issues of American Social History*, Minneapolis, 1973, pp. 57–88.

of her child, she declared that Richard Barnard had "carnall knowledge of her Body last English harvest at the very beginning of Reaping Ry."[13] By contrast, specific months, days, and even hours—rather than agricultural seasons—formed John Pynchon's concept of time. He invariably wrote the exact calendar date and sometimes the time of day on all his correspondence. In Springfield, he was usually the only link between the Sarah Clarks and the outside world.[14]

John Pynchon's position of mediator was the necessary precondition for his role as patron. He became the instrument of General Court policy in western Massachusetts and his community's agent in Boston as well. When the Court wanted new plantations established in the Connecticut Valley, negotiations with Connecticut or the Mohawk Indians, or boundaries perambulated, John Pynchon was inevitably its choice. When, for example, the General Court voted to construct a new highway to Connecticut, the magistrates "refferd to Major Pynchon to order the said way to be laid out and well marked."[15] Similarly, in Boston, Pynchon articulated local issues. His townsmen knew that his access to provincial authorities could be translated into palpable benefits for Springfield in the form of land grants, tax abatements, or favorable rulings on boundary disputes. And because the colonial officials in Boston recognized Pynchon's influence in the Connecticut Valley, they heeded his recommendations.

In his memorial oration, Solomon Stoddard underscored the fundamentally reciprocal nature of Pynchon's mediating role as well as the enormous influence it brought at both the provincial and local levels. He asserted that Pynchon "had great influence upon men in Authority abroad, and upon the People at home." Men like Pynchon are "well respected, and upon that account capable to do abundance of Service; their proposals are much hearkened to by those that are in Supream Authority in the Country." The eulogist emphasized that this influence directly benefited all of the valley's inhabitants: "If [useful men] make a motion for the good of the places where they live, they are readily hearkened unto, their judgment and fidelity is relied on; they can do a man a kindness with their word" because "They can have access to those in

---

13 *Pynchon Court Rec.*, p. 272.

14 Pynchon lost this exclusivity of access after the Glorious Revolution. See Chapter 6.

15 *Mass. Recs.*, 5, p. 394.

Chief Authority when others cannot; their word will be regarded when the word of others will not."[16]

Pynchon's principal task as the instrument of General Court policy in the valley—the coordination of relations with Connecticut—was greatly facilitated by his close friendship with Connecticut Governor John Winthrop. Pynchon's wife Amy, the daughter of former Connecticut Governor John Willys, spent over a year in Winthrop's care while recovering from an illness during the early 1650s. In expressing his gratitude for Winthrop's services as a physician, Pynchon wrote "my wife hath now been a Tabler with you above a yeare, besides all your Phisick and paines, I pray Sir let me know what the one and the other is worth, that I may sattisfie accordingly, and yet shall acknowledge my selfe as long as I live ingaged to you."[17] Pynchon continued in the following decades to turn to his friend for medical help. On December 19, 1660, he wrote that "my Son Joseph . . . is much trobled with a kind of hoarsness and dryness in his throate and yet not with any Cold that we can preceive. But a continuall kind of hemming and harsh dryness." In May 1661 the Springfield leader needed orthopedic advice regarding his daughter and the son of one of his workers. He asked Winthrop what to do about the "Lame boy" and "my daughter . . . [to] bring her legg to rights and straite."[18] Sometimes a note of grave concern accompanied these requests. On July 24, 1663, he wrote, "Sir we are bold to crave your advice concerning our young daughter about or neere one yeare and three quarters old, God having pleased to visit her with Illness: shee hath not been very well these 3 or 4 days but especially yesterday morning was taken with a greate looseness and vomiting which doth Continue much and exceedingly weaken her."[19]

John Pynchon and Governor Winthrop were also trading partners and often pooled their resources on joint economic ventures. Winthrop, along with Pynchon's influential cousins in Hartford, Samuel Willys and John Allyn, oversaw the transshipment of the Springfield merchant's grain and livestock. On April 6, 1658, Pynchon wrote Winthrop, "If Goodman Rogers should send any vessell for Corne before I returne hom, that you would please to direct them to have recourse to my Cousin Allyn."[20] On another occasion,

---

[16] *Usefull Men*, pp. 12–13.
[17] John Pynchon to John Winthrop, Jr., May 28, 1655, Winthrop Mss.
[18] John Pynchon to John Winthrop, Jr., May 23, 1661, Winthrop Mss.
[19] John Pynchon to John Winthrop, Jr., July 24, 1663, Boston Medical Library, typescript copy, CVHM.
[20] John Pynchon to John Winthrop, Jr., April 6, 1658, Winthrop Mss.

Pynchon expressed enthusiasm over a pending livestock deal, but, having no marketable animals, he told Winthrop that "for your position about Calves, I like well of it, if I could procure any worth the sending."[21]

These personal and commercial ties between Pynchon and Winthrop, combined with geographic proximity and the common threat of Indian danger, made the two men the spokesmen of their respective colonies. The Massachusetts General Court habitually called on Pynchon to act as an intermediary between the two governments. In March 1674 the Springfield leader wrote Winthrop for the purpose of "conveying it to you whereby you will understand what our Court [has] done."[22] Pynchon also personally oversaw negotiations aimed at resolving long-standing boundary disputes. Most important of all, when beleaguered Massachusetts needed military assistance from Connecticut during King Philip's War, it was "left with Major John Pynchon to treat with the Governour and council there for effecting the same."[23] The ferocious Indian assaults of the 1690s brought another request from the General Court for Pynchon to appeal to Connecticut's "friendly neighbourlyness" in an effort to secure more military aid. He wrote the Connecticut General Court that his government had "direct[ed me] to apply to your Honors . . . to supply with 60 men."[24]

Pynchon likewise served as the General Court's principal emissary to New York. In August 1664 he received a commission from the Court to travel to New York in order to coordinate military activities against the Dutch.[25] In 1689 he made a "long and tedious" journey to Albany, this time for the purpose of coordinating the New England and New York explanations of the overthrow of Governor Edmund Andros during the Glorious Revolution. Upon returning to Springfield, Pynchon informed the officials in Boston that "We have Indeavoured with al faithfulness to Manage the Negotiation you Imployed us about" and presented the colony with a bill for expenses of £219.[26]

Pynchon was equally indispensable as the Massachusetts colony's agent to the western Indians. Springfield's location and Pynchon's commercial ties with the Indians again made him the natural choice

[21] John Pynchon to John Winthrop, Jr., June 24, 1656, Winthrop Mss.

[22] John Pynchon to John Winthrop, Jr., March 23, 1674, Winthrop Mss.

[23] *Mass. Recs.*, 5, p. 171.

[24] John Pynchon to the Governor and Council of Connecticut, January 18, 1692, Edes Ms., Mass. Hist. Soc.

[25] *Mass. Recs.*, 4, Part 2, pp. 123–125.

[26] Mass. Archives, 35, p. 32.

for this position. As with Connecticut, whenever the Court needed to negotiate with the Indians, it turned to Pynchon. Most important in the wake of King Philip's War was the need to secure an alliance with the Mohawks against the hostile Wampanoags and Narragansetts. In April 1677 Pynchon and James Richards embarked on a "long, troublesome and hazardous journey" to Albany to negotiate with the Mohawks on behalf of both Massachusetts and Connecticut. Pynchon calculated his service and expenses to be valued at £128 and charged the colony accordingly.[27] By 1680, the Mohawk alliance still unconsummated, the Springfield leader once more travelled to Albany, "in order to the stopping of any invassions, depredation, and insolencys toward our neighbors, Indians and friends, that live within this jurisdiction."[28]

While negotiations with neighboring colonies and with the Indians were Pynchon's major diplomatic responsibilities, his principal domestic task was plantation-founding. In his eulogy of the Springfield magistrate, Solomon Stoddard emphasized that Pynchon had "laboured much in the setling of most of our Plantations," and rightly so. The General Court appointed him to head the commission of every town founded in western Massachusetts during the period from 1653 to 1702. In May 1653 the Court empowered Pynchon and two other men to organize the town of Northampton.[29] Six years later he formed a commission to establish the new settlement of Hadley.[30] During the same period, he also organized a commission to oversee settlement at Woronoco, the future Westfield. In May 1667 the magistrates called on Pynchon to superintend the founding of a new community, this time at Quabaug.[31] In similar fashion he was empowered to organize the settlements of Suffield in 1670, Northfield in 1671, Deerfield and Sunderland in 1673, Enfield in 1683, and Brimfield in 1701.[32]

The powers of these founding commissions were considerable. The commission members received authority to lay out the new settlements, admit inhabitants, grant lands, appoint selectmen, administer the freeman's oath, and govern the community until it was officially incorporated by the General Court. In 1656 Westfield's founding commission received authorization to "dispose of the land . . . to such men as they Saw fit, and what quantity they

[27] *Pynchon Court Rec.*, p. 43; *Mass. Recs.*, 5, pp. 138, 165–168.

[28] *Mass. Recs.*, 5, p. 299.

[29] *Usefull Men*, p. 22; *Mass. Recs.*, 4, Part 1, p. 136.

[30] *Mass. Recs.*, 4, Part 1, p. 368.

[31] *Ibid.*, 4, Part 2, p. 342.

[32] *Ibid.*, 4, Part 2, pp. 469, 528–529, 557; 5, pp. 410–411.

should give to any person whomsoever they in theire best discretion saw fit."[33] The Quabaug (Brookfield) commission likewise was empowered to "admitt inhabitants, grant lands, and to order all the prudentiall affayres of the place" until "the place shall be so farr setled with able men as that this Court may judge meete to give them full liberty of a township."[34] Of all these powers, easily the most significant was the authority to grant land to the prospective inhabitants. By determining the amount of acreage each man would receive, Pynchon and his fellow commission members directly fashioned the social structure of each new community.

The lifespans of the founding commissions, the interval between a town's settlement and its incorporation, averaged approximately ten years. When the General Court received an official petition for incorporation, the magistrates sought John Pynchon's opinion of its merits and, if he acquiesced, the petition was approved.[35]

While Pynchon was organizing the new valley towns in his public capacity, as a private citizen he was financing them. The only valley resident with significant credit resources, Pynchon routinely was called upon by prospective inhabitants to buy land from the Indians. He paid for this acreage with wampum, textiles, or tools from his general store. In turn, the patentees gave him a conveyance of lands in trust until they repaid the principal. More important, for his services, each new community also granted the Springfield entrepreneur extensive lands and allowed him to erect gristmills and sawmills within the settlement. In this manner Pynchon financed the establishment of the towns of Northampton, Hadley, Westfield, Deerfield, Northfield, Brookfield, Enfield, and Suffield.[36]

Many communities remained in Pynchon's debt for extended periods. He did not formally assign a settlement title to its land until he had received payment in full. Accordingly, it was in the settlers' best interest to repay their debt as quickly as possible—or risk erosion of their corporate autonomy. The fact that the period in which the loans were outstanding was usually coterminous with the life of the founding commissions made this autonomy especially precarious. Many communities were simultaneously economically and politically dependent on Pynchon for over a decade. He bought lands for Westfield during the mid-1660s, paying £50 to an Indian squaw named Paupsunnick for acreage on the south side of the

[33] *Springfield Town Recs.*, 1, p. 245.
[34] *Mass. Recs.*, 4, Part 2, p. 342.
[35] *Ibid.*, 4, Part 2, pp. 469, 528–529, 557; 5, pp. 410–411.
[36] *Ibid.*

Woronoco River.[37] An interval of twenty years passed, however, before the loan was repaid. On February 11, 1685, he formally assigned the title to the Westfield inhabitants: "I John Pynchon . . . Several yeeres since made a purchase of Lands at Westfield of the Indians for the Inhabitants of Westfield . . . to Paupsunnick I did truly pay for the same about fifty pounds which sum . . . I have [now] received of the Inhabitants . . . according to Each man's Proportion."[38] In September 1653 Pynchon paid 150 fathom of wampum, ten coats, and assorted small gifts for the purchase of Northampton's land. A decade later, the settlers having completed repayment, he assigned them title.[39] On three separate occasions between 1658 and 1662, the inhabitants of Hadley called on Pynchon to buy Indian lands. His expenses, totalling £78, were not fully repaid until eleven years after the initial transaction. It took Suffield's settlers fifteen years to complete their repayment. In 1670 Pynchon paid the Indian owner £40 for six square miles of land. It was not until April 10, 1685, however, that he closed out the account book entry: "For al Lands which I [bought] for the Inhabitants of Suffeild [for] forty pounds, and do hereby acknowledge . . . to be fully satisfied."[40] Nearly eleven years passed between purchase and assignment of the land for the town of Enfield. Pynchon bought the land for the settlers in 1683, but by 1694, £3 10s. of the £30 principal remained unpaid.[41]

In addition to his specific responsibilities as diplomat and plantation-founder, the General Court expected Pynchon to act on his own initiative on any issue touching the colony's interest. These initiatives often included a wide array of problems: supplying provisions for the royal fleet, paying bribes to Indian informants, or hiring mercenaries in time of war. In 1667 during the Anglo-Dutch wars, "by his oune voluntary contribution," Pynchon expressed "his sence of the then present distressed condition of his majestie's fleet in his plantations in the [Caribbean] Islands" by "put[ting] on board [an embarking ship] sixteen barrells of pork."[42] In 1673, in order to elicit intelligence on possible hostilities from neighboring Indians, Pynchon gave "[re]wards . . . [among] our Indians to Effect

[37] Wright, ed., *Indian Deeds*, p. 97; Hampden County Deeds, Volume AB (1636–1704), p. 53, Hampden County Court, Springfield.

[38] Hampden Co. Deeds, Volume AB, p. 53.

[39] *Ibid.*, Volume A (1638–1699), p. 15.

[40] Account Books, 2, p. 248.

[41] *Ibid.*, 6, Index, p. 15.

[42] *Mass. Recs.*, 4, Part 2, pp. 547–548.

it."[43] When faced with an insufficient number of troops to meet the Indian threat in the 1690s, he was "forced to Imploy . . . private Soldiers."[44] On a more prosaic level, when a carpenter proposed to build a bridge over the Quabaug River in Brookfield, Pynchon and John Winthrop collaborated in arranging its construction. Pynchon informed Winthrop that the carpenter "desired me to write to your Worship about it," as "he will Ingage to make a good Bridge for £20 . . . if he may be sure of his pay." In a request that emphasizes the conflation of public and private spheres in early New England, Pynchon asserted that "for my owne part I will willingly give 4 or 5£ toward it" if Winthrop could come up with a similar amount.[45]

John Pynchon did not go unrewarded for these services. Because both the local community and the provincial hierarchy saw Pynchon as the indispensable man, they rewarded him with land—the most highly prized commodity in seventeenth-century Massachusetts. This in turn increased his power, in both the local community and beyond. Local and provincial power reinforced each other, and the result was a spiral effect where power brought land and land brought more power. When Pynchon's home town allocated new acreage to its inhabitants, for example, he invariably received a disproportionate share. In a typical allotment, for the "inner commons" in 1699, Springfield awarded Pynchon 133 rods of mile-long strips; the next largest grantee, his nephew John Holyoke, received only 26 rods.[46] Through these land grants and by private purchase and mortgage foreclosures, Pynchon expanded his family's monopoly over Springfield's best land. He eventually owned over two thousand acres, including most of the town's genuinely first-rate land.[47] Similarly, other Connecticut Valley towns indebted to Pynchon for services rendered paid him back in lucrative land allotments. Usually, but not always, these grants were a direct result of his organization of the respective founding committees. And, as we saw earlier, these grants were often made in tandem with privileges for building gristmills and sawmills within the new community. In the

[43] John Pynchon to Gerrt Van Slichtenhorst, December 12, 1673, Livingston Family Papers, Roosevelt Library.

[44] Mass. Archives, 36, p. 439.

[45] John Pynchon to John Winthrop, Jr., December 24, 1666, Winthrop Mss.

[46] "Coppy of Mens' Lots in the 2d Division," April, 1699, Manuscripts Collection, Springfield Public Library.

[47] 1685 tax list, inscribed "Anno Dom. 1685. An Estimate of the Plantation, both of Mens' Houses and Lands, in Springfield," Tax Collector's Office, Springfield City Hall, hereafter cited as 1685 Tax List.

1680s the town of Enfield granted Pynchon 314 acres of land "for Severall years pains and Services as Committee for said Enfield."[48]

At the provincial level, Pynchon found the General Court equally generous. During the period from 1659 to 1685, he received over 8,170 acres from the Court for mediating services performed by him or his father William.[49] On November 12, 1659, "In answer to the petition of Capt. John Pynchon, the Court judgeth it meete to grant him one thousand acres." Seven years later, "for severall services past," he received an additional 500 acres.[50] On October 17, 1681, "in consideration of his paines formerly in runing our patent line," the Court awarded Pynchon an island on the Connecticut River below Enfield falls.[51] The fourth of June, 1685, was a particularly good day for the Springfield leader. First, the Court granted William Avery, Hezekiah Usher, and Pynchon 1,000 acres in the Connecticut Valley. Later that day, in answer to his petition, the Court granted "the quantity of eight miles square [5,120 acres] to Major John Pynchon."[52] Pynchon eventually owned extensive tracts in every Massachusetts town in the Connecticut Valley. In addition to his 2,000 acres in Springfield itself, he held 510 acres and both a sawmill and a gristmill at Suffield, 200 acres and a gristmill at Brookfield, 314 acres and both a sawmill and a gristmill at Enfield, and 120 acres at Deerfield.[53] Outside of the colony, Pynchon owned 2,788 acres at Groton, Connecticut, and part of the island of Antigua in the West Indies.[54]

After land grants, the most valuable emoluments available to mediators were trading monopolies, and one of these—the fur-trading franchise—played a decisive role in Pynchon's stunning

---

[48] Hampden Co. Deeds, Volume AB, p. 86.

[49] *Mass. Recs.*, 4, Part 1, p. 402; Part 2, p. 306; *ibid.*, 5, pp. 482–486; Mass. Archives, 45, p. 82. Pynchon also may have received an additional 1,000 acres from the Court after his extensive losses sustained during King Philip's War in 1675; see J. G. Holland, *History of Western Massachusetts*, Springfield, 1845, 1, p. 309. Moreover, Pynchon and two other men received a grant of ten square miles in 1659 during the abortive effort to establish a fur-trading post 40 miles west of Springfield; see Arthur H. Buffington, "New England and the Western Fur Trade, 1629–1675," *Transactions of the Col. Soc. Mass.*, 18 (1917), pp. 176–177. Theodore B. Lewis underestimates Pynchon's landholdings in "Land Speculation and the Dudley Council of 1686," *WMQ*, 31 (1974), pp. 255–272.

[50] *Mass. Recs.*, 4, Part 1, p. 402; Part 2, p. 306.

[51] *Ibid.*, 5, pp. 329–330.

[52] *Ibid.*, 5, pp. 482, 486.

[53] Hampden Co. Deeds, Volume AB, p. 86.

[54] Account Books, 2, pp. 238–239; Samuel Willys to Connecticut General Court, October 1687, "Private Controversies, 1642–1716," Ser. 1, Volume 3, Document 258, Connecticut State Library, Hartford.

commercial rise. Before the depletion of beaver in the late 1660s, the most lucrative monopoly in the Connecticut Valley was the fur trade. Because of their influence in the colonial government, William Pynchon and later John received fur monopoly rights. They in turn farmed out these privileges to selected agents at various locations throughout the valley.[55] Furs received by the agents were then sent to the Pynchon general store for eventual shipment to London.

John Pynchon's account books testify to the extraordinary magnitude of the fur trade. During the period from 1652 to 1674, he transshipped over 23,930 pounds of beaver to the London market. With the price of beaver skins averaging ten shillings per pound, he realized gross receipts during these years of approximately £11,965. Calculating his profit margin at one shilling per pound, John's total earnings for this period exceeded £1,196. In a society where the daily wage for a farm laborer averaged between sixteen and twenty pence, these profits represented an enormous sum. In addition to the beaver, Pynchon shipped over 7,000 pounds of moose skins, 400 otter skins, 718 muskrat, 315 "Foxes and Raccons," and lesser amounts of mink, marten, and lynx. In 1654 alone, Pynchon sent 3,723 pounds of beaver to his London agents—giving him gross receipts that year of £1,860.[56]

The halcyon days of the fur trade in the Connecticut Valley were over by the late 1650s. The volume of the trade declined somewhat sporadically thereafter, until King Philip's War brought an abrupt end to all commercial exchange between whites and Indians. Again, statistics tell the story. Between 1652 and 1658, John Pynchon shipped 13,917 pounds of beaver, or 58.2 percent of the total amount he merchandised. By 1663, he had exported 19,778 pounds or 82.6 percent of all the beaver he sent to England in the seventeenth century.[57]

Pynchon, as magistrate, enforced the monopoly rights he enjoyed as a private trader. Poachers risked the exceedingly punitive fines that the law allowed for these infractions. Samuel Fellows and Joseph Leonard learned this lesson to their dismay on March 28, 1671. Pynchon brought the two men before the county court over which he presided as quorum judge. He accused Fellows and Leon-

---

[55] Ruth A. McIntyre, "John Pynchon, Merchant and Colonizer of the Upper Connecticut Valley in the Seventeenth Century, A Study of the Business Practices of John Pynchon," unpublished Ms., CVHM.

[56] Account Books, 3, pp. 319–321.

[57] *Ibid.*

ard of two offenses: "buying of the Indians One Skin of Beaver against [the] Law" and selling the Indians "Strong Liquors." The respective punishments for the two offenses underscore the severity with which Pynchon and the General Court viewed unlicensed fur trading. The defendants received fines of £10 for violating the ordinance against selling liquor to the Indians—always considered a grave offense because it was "famously known how the Indians abuse themselves by excessive drinking of strong liquors." For "buying One Skin of Beaver" without a license, however, the two men were fined the immense sum of £100. Joseph Leonard may have pointed out Pynchon's conflict of interest in the proceedings, as the court slapped him with an additional £5 fine for his "contemptuous carriage particularly towards the Worshipfull Captain Pynchon."[58]

By the late 1650s, fur merchants in Massachusetts recognized that long-term survival of the trade depended on expansion into the Hudson Valley. With the eastern rivers almost entirely depleted and the Connecticut Valley nearly so, the New Englanders would have to tap the fur domains then controlled by the Dutch. No one understood this reality better than did John Pynchon, and he set out to do something about it. In 1659 he and Major William Hawthorne of Salem and a number of merchants in Boston formed a company designed to establish overland trading routes to the upper Hudson Valley. The company attempted to combine Boston capital with Pynchon's trapping network, friendly relations with the western Indians, and proximity to Fort Orange (Albany). Expecting opposition from the Dutch fur traders, the Hawthorne Company, as it was eventually named, resorted to subterfuge. They told the (presumably incredulous) Dutch that the company intended to settle a small plantation midway between Springfield and the Hudson River for the sole purpose of raising cattle to supply the Dutch at Fort Orange. In August 1659 Pynchon accompanied Hawthorne to Fort Orange in a vain attempt to convince the Dutch of their good intentions. In 1662 the company made an abortive effort to revive the plan, and this time they succeeded in constructing a small trading post on the Housatonic River. But the Dutch were still unyielding and again made clear their determination to keep New England merchants out of New Netherland. By this time Pynchon had wearied of his fellow members' general lack of resolve, and he withdrew from the project. He charged the company £60

[58] *Pynchon Court Rec.*, pp. 235, 271.

for his journey to Fort Orange and for the "loss of tyme and disappointment."[59]

England's conquest of New Netherland in 1664 removed the threat of Dutch opposition to the expansion of the Massachusetts fur trade, and in the early 1670s Pynchon tried again. He joined forces with Governor John Leverett and William Paine, one of the Boston merchants involved in the Hawthorne project, and petitioned the General Court for an extensive land grant in western Massachusetts. The Court ruled favorably on the petitioners' request, granting them ten square miles of land near the colony's western border. But with the fury of King Philip's War about to explode on the New Englanders, the time was not propitious for new fur-trading schemes.[60] The failure of the Hawthorne and Paine projects to secure entry into the Hudson Valley sounded the death knell for the Massachusetts fur trade.[61]

The abrupt termination of the fur trade wreaked havoc with John Pynchon's economic enterprises. Because most of his wealth was in the form of fixed capital investments—land, mills, ships, mines—he relied on the fur trade for needed liquid assets. Pelts could quickly and easily be converted into specie, wampum, or bills of exchange and thus represented the seventeenth-century equivalent of ready cash. In February 1672 Pynchon emphasized the severe limitations on his trading imposed by this money shortage. In a letter to his son Joseph, then beginning a career as a physician in Uxbridge, England, he wrote: "I am forced not to send to England for any goods this yeare: I have noe trade as formerly and am altogither out of that capacity of helping with Monny."[62] Three years later, his commercial affairs still in disarray, Pynchon again wrote his son, reiterating that he was unable to send any money and in fact might need to borrow some: "it may be you are in expectations of some help from me, which I should readyly afford If I could, but am noe ways able to doe any thing, having been wholy out of Trade ever since you went from this Country [and I] am now reduced to our best Contrivance for our Comfortable Living and much adoe to make things hold out. So that I am sometimes almost ready to send to you for some of that I reserved

[59] McIntyre, "John Pynchon," pp. 55–57.

[60] Douglas Edward Leach, *Flintlock and Tomahawk: New England in King Philip's War*, New York, 1966.

[61] Bailyn, *New England Merchants*, pp. 54–55.

[62] John Pynchon to Joseph Pynchon, February 1, 1672, Wetmore Family Papers, Yale University Library.

to be paid me yearly."[63] But while the fur trade was gone, Pynchon still had his landholdings and the general store. As things turned out, these would be more than enough.

Even before the final depletion of the beaver, Pynchon had made a major decision—to shift the basis of his exports from furs to agricultural products. By the mid-1660s, because of its capacity for large-scale production of both wheat and livestock, the Connecticut Valley was becoming the breadbasket of New England. And because of his extensive commercial network, it was Pynchon who did most of the merchandising of these foodstuffs. Farmers from as far north as Deerfield, as far east as Brookfield, and as far west as Westfield brought their surplus pork and grain to his general store. He also accumulated the pork, wheat, and barley from his own farms and from the fields of his tenants. Unlike his earlier tendency to send most of his exports to Hartford or Boston, Pynchon now increasingly turned toward the sugar islands of the West Indies.[64]

The explosive growth of the British West Indies—Barbados, Jamaica, and the Leeward Islands—allowed Pynchon to reestablish his commercial preeminence by trading foodstuffs for rum. The radically labor-intensive nature of sugar cane cultivation induced planters to import massive quantities of flour and livestock rather than detailing precious slave labor for raising food. The rum, molasses, and sugar Pynchon received in exchange for his foodstuffs likewise afforded him a monopoly of these products back in the Connecticut Valley.[65]

Recognizing that the profits to be made from rum rivaled those made earlier in the fur trade, Pynchon attempted to establish his own sugar colony in the early 1680s. Together with his Hartford associates, Samuel Willys and Richard Lord, Pynchon founded what was called the "Cabbage Tree Plantation" on the island of Antigua.[66] The three men went to considerable pains in setting up their incongruously named colony with slaves, foodstuffs, and livestock. Antigua had long been among the least promising of the Leeward Islands, both because of its aridity and proximity to the French sugar islands.[67] These barriers, along with some internecine quarreling over financing between Willys and Lord, eventually

[63] John Pynchon to Joseph Pynchon, June 30, 1675, Historical Society of Pennsylvania, Philadelphia, typescript copy, CVHM.

[64] Account Books, 3, 5.

[65] Richard S. Dunn, *Sugar and Slaves: The Rise of the Planter Class in the English West Indies, 1624–1713*, New York, 1973.

[66] Wyllys Ms., 2, p. 60, Connecticut Historical Society, Hartford.

[67] Dunn, *Sugar and Slaves*, pp. 117–148.

doomed the colony's prospects.[68] But despite this setback, the West Indies market remained a bonanza for New England merchants, and by the mid-1680s the sugar islands were the destination for the major portion of John Pynchon's exports.[69]

Land speculation was an equally attractive source of revenue for Pynchon in the waning days of the fur trade. Here he engaged in speculative ventures with men as highly placed in the Massachusetts political structure as Governor John Leverett. Together the two men purchased extensive tracts in the Connecticut Valley for subsequent resale to private individuals.[70] Dealings between the two men were doubtless eased by kinship ties. Pynchon's son John married Margaret Hubbard of Ipswich, whose brother had married Ann Leverett, the governor's daughter.[71] In Connecticut, Pynchon and James Rogers collaborated in purchasing between three thousand and five thousand acres in Rogers's home town of New London during the mid-1660s.[72]

But it was the control of both Springfield's export trade and its domestic economy, particularly the mills, that provided John Pynchon with his most secure and predictable sources of income. As on the English manor, the most symbolic expression of local preeminence was ownership of the community's mills. In an agricultural society that relied heavily on cereal grains for food, gristmills were especially important. Because grain was a staple in the diet of all early New Englanders, mill owners were invariably powerful figures within the township. Unlike Virginians, who relied on mortar and pestle well into the eighteenth century, northern settlers ground almost all their grain in gristmills from the mid-seventeenth century onward. Springfield's dependence on its gristmill is highlighted by the often calamitous consequences brought by breakdowns. In August 1675, Pynchon dispatched a frantic note to the General Court asking that provisions immediately be sent to the town because "our Mill having been out of order renders it extreame difficult here."[73] When the Indians attacked two months later, their most devastating blow was putting Pynchon's gristmill to the torch. The hardships imposed by living without a mill brought some inhabitants to the brink of despair, with talk of abandoning

[68] Wyllys Ms., 2, p. 60, Conn. Hist. Soc.
[69] Account Books, 3, 5.
[70] Hampden Co. Deeds, Volumes A, AB.
[71] *Pynchon Court Rec.*, p. 42, n. 34.
[72] *Ibid.*, pp. 47–48.
[73] John Pynchon to unknown, August 7, 1675, Long Island Hist. Soc., Brooklyn, typescript copy, CVHM.

the town rampant. Pynchon wrote Leverett that "our People are under great discouragement, Talke of Leaving the Place . . . [We need] Provisions, I meane Bread, for want of a Mill is difficult." He emphasized the primacy of grain in the villagers' diet: "we have flesh enough . . . [but] noe Mill will drive many of our Inhabitants away, especially those that have noe Corn."[74]

Mill ownership, of course, brought profit as well as social influence. Millers were entitled to a fixed percentage of the corn they processed. For his gristmill, John Pynchon received "the eleventh partt of the bushell, for all Sorts of graine that shall be heere ground."[75] Characteristically, Pynchon sublet his mills to a tenant who tended the mill in exchange for a third of the annual tolls. On November 28, 1672, he agreed with Goodman Aires "to keepe the mill at Quabaug [Brookfield] and tend it to grind the Corne brought to it for one yeare: he to take the Tole allowed, viz. ½ a peck out of a bushel . . . and for his tending the Mill, he is to have one 3d of the Tole."[76]

The manner in which Springfield constructed its mills reveals both the weakness of corporate and the importance of patron-client ties. When the town was unable to secure sufficient funds to build a new mill, John Pynchon stepped in and provided the requisite funding. In exchange for these outlays, the town granted him land, mill ownership, toll privileges, and voluntary labor from the citizens. In 1666 a town *ad hoc* committee appointed to "consider what course they judge best to be taken for the supply of the Towne" recommended the construction of a new gristmill. The town meeting, however, soon found itself deadlocked over how to raise the necessary funds. Whereupon, "the case being long debated, Capt. Pynchon did promise . . . that Hee will be at £200 charge for the building of a new mill." Pynchon offered to finance the project, "Provided the Towne will disburse what estate more must be laid out which £200 will not discharge for the effecting such a worke." Despite his willingness to defray most of the expenses for the mill's construction, Pynchon's fellow villagers balked at paying the remaining costs. After an extended and frequently acrimonious debate, "the Plantation [was] not cheerfull to engage therein." Pynchon thereupon agreed to build the mill using his own resources and the voluntary labor of any willing inhabitants on condition that he receive in perpetuity a toll of one-twelfth of all grain ground at the mill. Their inability to cooperate on funding the mill resulted

[74] Mass. Archives, 67, p. 290.
[75] *Springfield Town Recs.*, 1, p. 247.
[76] Account Books, 5, p. 325.

in the inhabitants' forfeiture of control of their community's single most important capital investment.[77]

Construction of Springfield's first sawmill followed a similar pattern, with an additional inducement of 150 acres for the entrepreneur. In January 1663 the town meeting voted to grant Pynchon "thirty acres of land . . . and . . . the priviledge of the said brook . . . on Condition that he build a Saw Mill . . . within five yeeres."[78] Three years later, the mill still unbuilt, the town tried to sweeten the pot by deciding that "Captain Pynchon shall have 50 acres of Upland and 30 acres of Meddow . . . Provided that he build a Saw Mill . . . within three yeeres from this tyme." As these grants failed to spur him to action, the town acted again six months later: "whereas Capt. Pynchon hath had and still hath intentions to sett up a Saw Mill within this Township . . . for his encouragement in the said work . . . To all other former grannts made to the said Capt. Pynchon in reference to such work, There is further granted unto him by the Plantation the free use of the said Streame . . . also free Liberty for felling and Sawing what trees he shal please that are upon the Comons . . . [also] thirty acres of land."[79]

Throughout the seventeenth century, Springfield turned to John Pynchon for its major capital improvements. When it came time to build a new mill, school, or house of correction, or when the inhabitants wanted to erect a storage chamber over the meetinghouse or establish sheep-raising or swine-raising projects, Pynchon acted as both financier and construction supervisor. Land grants, preemption rights, monopoly privileges, and free usage were the emoluments he received in return. When the town's population more than doubled during the two decades after midcentury—from just over one hundred to nearly three hundred people—construction of a new seating gallery in the meetinghouse became imperative. Pynchon agreed to "defray all the charge that concerns the work" if the town allowed him to sell seatrights in the proposed gallery. After a discussion, the town meeting acceded to his proposition, ordering that "Captayn Pynchon shal be paid by Such as shal be Seated there [at] 4s. a person."[80]

The action of Springfield in contracting with Pynchon to build a gallery in the meetinghouse and then charging for seatrights is richly emblematic of the community's system of values. The contrast is obvious between the accustomed practice in the communal towns

[77] *Springfield Town Recs.*, 1, pp. 352–355.
[78] *Ibid.*, 1, pp. 303–304.
[79] *Ibid.*, 1, pp. 354–355.
[80] *Ibid.*, 1, p. 303.

where everyone was assigned a place by virtue of membership in the community and the selling of seatrights in Springfield, where essentially users paid for the benefit and Pynchon profited from his service to the town. Similarly, when Springfield needed additional storage space for its corn, the meeting voted that "if mr. John Pynchon will make a [storage] chamber over the meeting howse and board it: he shall have the use of it Intirely to himselfe for Ten yeares." After the expiration of the ten-year period, "then if the Towne neede it and require it they may have it, Provided they allow the said mr. John Pynchon the charge that he hath [paid for] it."[81] Seeing need for a local smeltery in the mid-1690s, the town again turned to Pynchon. On December 5, 1696, he and Joseph Parsons "made some proposals in order to the setting up and carrying on an Iron Mill." After considering "the great benefitt [the iron mill] will bee to this place," the town granted Pynchon and Parsons monopoly rights over all iron ore within the township.[82] Continuing its deliberations the following month, the town granted the two men an eighty-acre site on which to locate the ironworks.[83]

Pynchon was also called upon to build up the town's vital livestock herds—particularly the sheep necessary to free the colonists from reliance on English woolen imports. As with livestock production generally, the Connecticut Valley pasturage was unsurpassed in Massachusetts for grazing sheep. In emphasizing the valley's unique congeniality for sheep-raising in New England, agricultural historian Howard S. Russell points out that "Sheep raising is a specialized calling. Sheep require good pasturage free from thickets and briers likely to catch and tear their wool coats, protection from predatory animals, and careful knowledgeable attention on the part of man. Much of New England's surface, even in the 1700s, was still too untamed for their somewhat fastidious appetites."[84] Recognizing their region's potential, in 1654 the town voters granted Pynchon twenty-one acres of the town's most highly assessed land on condition that he purchase "40 sheepe within the space of Six months." He agreed to "use his best endevoure to bring [the sheep] into Towne and there to dispose of them as hee shall se cause."[85] In 1660 the community resorted to similar procedures to augment its dwindling supply of hogs. Pynchon and two other well-heeled

[81] *Ibid.*, 1, p. 200.
[82] *Ibid.*, 2, p. 346.
[83] *Ibid.*, 2, p. 288.
[84] Russell, *A Long, Deep Furrow*, p. 154.
[85] *Springfield Town Recs.*, 1, p. 232.

inhabitants received forty acres of land "according as they carry on theire designe of keeping swine there."[86]

Reliance on John Pynchon's enterprise and resources became a habit in Springfield, and it could include the most routine obligations. In 1670, learning that the town's representative had not received his commissary payments, Pynchon again stepped in. The town meeting acknowledged its "neglect in providing for the deputy . . . to the General Corte . . . whereof many tymes his diet at Boston is too long unsatisfyed." Because of "the Towne's want of pay in hand, Capt. Pynchon proffers to give 20s. towards it."[87] When Springfield's gunpowder stocks became dangerously depleted in 1668, Pynchon "propounded to the Town, That if the Towne would grannt him [a] house lott . . . he would lett them have one halfe of [a] barrell of powder, which the Towne did yeeld unto."[88]

By "yeelding unto" John Pynchon with such frequency, the inhabitants of Springfield forfeited control over their own economic destinies. When corporate remedies failed, the residents looked to Pynchon rather than themselves to find a way out. Throughout the seventeenth century, when they asked him to finance new capital improvements, he usually agreed to do so—but always at a price. The concessions he exacted, in the forms of land grants, monopolies, and special privileges and immunities, ultimately served to enrich him at the expense of his fellow villagers. Without corporate self-reliance, it became only too easy to keep calling on Pynchon, even at such an obvious cost. The weakness of the town meeting was the mirror image, as well as the product, of the economic individualism typical of early Springfield. Reliance on Pynchon came easier than cooperation with one another, and his dominance of the public economy was the result.[89]

And while John Pynchon's sway over the public economy was considerable, his private power as an employer, landlord, and creditor was even more complete. During the period from 1652 to 1703, over two hundred men were personally dependent on Pynchon for employment, land, or credit—or some combination of the three. These dependent men usually included half of the adult male population at any time. Of the seventy-two men on the 1665 List of Springfield Inhabitants, forty (56%) were wage-laborers, tenants, or debtors of Pynchon. Of the seventy-six inhabitants entered on the 1672 List of Springfield Town Meeting Voters, thirty-two (42%)

[86] *Ibid.*, 1, p. 280.
[87] *Ibid.*, 2, p. 106.
[88] *Ibid.*, 2, pp. 95–96.
[89] See Chapter 5.

fulfilled one or more of these categories. Fifty-six (47%) of the 120 taxpayers in 1685 can be so classified.[90]

These men came to Pynchon on their own volition and with their eyes open. He had the land, the tools, the draft animals, and the jobs that they needed. This was particularly true for the large numbers of single and semi-impoverished men who had made their way to Springfield with little more than the clothes on their back. Pynchon offered them a chance to get established, to secure a leasehold, employment, and a line of credit for buying the first piece of land. Word doubtless got around that Pynchon had these things to offer, and many men whose indigence would have invited a warning-out from the covenanted communities hoped for better prospects in Springfield. In this expectation, they were rarely disappointed because Pynchon needed them as much as they needed him.

The dependency bond between Pynchon and these men was a dual one. Just as the word "bond" has a double meaning—a connection and, as in "bondage," a restraint—so too was this, as all relationships, subject to influence and constraints.[91] The authority figure, in this case John Pynchon, is never an autonomous figure. Neither the authority figure nor his dependent in Springfield was a free actor. Both in fact were dependent. Each exercised some measure of initiative.[92] Tenants, as well as landlords, had bargaining powers. Both understood that authority always has limits that are particular to place, person, and time. What, Pynchon might have asked, is a landlord without his tenants, a boss without underlings, a creditor without debtors? Tenants might have no choice but to rent, but they could go elsewhere. The same was true for those looking for work or credit. As Richard Hofstadter observes, "raw, idle land could be made profitable only when settlers were brought in to work, rent, or buy it." Hofstadter cites Sir Josiah Child's assertion that "Lands, though excellent, without hands proportionable will not enrich any kingdom."[93] It was Pynchon's recognition of this mutual dependence that gave the system its motive force. As the account books reveal, he actively sought out men and attempted to establish patron-client relationships.

These individual patron-client ties may be defined as an "informal contractual relationship between persons of unequal status and

[90] *Springfield Town Recs.*, 2, pp. 76–77, 115–116; 1685 Tax List.
[91] I am grateful to Thomas Slaughter of Rutgers University for emphasizing this point for me.
[92] Richard Sennett, *Authority*, New York, 1980, Chapters 1 and 2.
[93] *America at 1750*, p. 10.

power, which imposes reciprocal obligations of a different kind on each of the parties."[94] As patron, John Pynchon exchanged the fruits of his status, power, influence, and authority for the loyalty and political support of the client. Men sought out Pynchon because he was the only one who could help supply their economic needs. He rented them land, provided employment, or lent money. Most important, he showed selective flexibility in hiring, firing, and foreclosing. Clients could count on keeping their jobs, lands, or housing when others could not. In response, the clients accepted certain restrictions on their behavior. Those tenants whose rent was in arrears, men chronically indebted to Pynchon, or wage laborers dependent on him for long-term or seasonal employment were not likely to oppose his wishes in the town meeting, on the muster green, or anywhere else.

The Pynchon account books show vividly the myriad forms of the patron's favoritism. Pynchon often ignored contractual deadlines if the client found himself unable to meet them. Mortgages were not foreclosed, lands and housing were not seized, debts were not called on the day or even the month or year of maturity. Laborers, too, were hired when Pynchon had no genuine need or desire to take them on. Likewise, he seldom pursued his technical legal rights as a creditor, landlord, or employer in cases relating to clients. The strength of the particular patron-client bond determined whether Pynchon would modify, renegotiate, or postpone collection of debts. For the same reasons, some renters were able to secure significantly better terms than others. Some, for example, were entitled to one-half of all offspring born to cattle rented from Pynchon. Lesser clients or non-clients were contractually obliged to raise all calves to the age of two years and then forfeit them to Pynchon.

Because clientage, by its nature, is an informal, oral (even unspoken) relationship, it does not yield to easy identification. In many

---

[94] Silverman, "Patronage and Community-Nation Relationships," *Ethnology* (1965), p. 176. See also George M. Foster, "The Dyadic Contract: A Model for the Social Structure of a Mexican Village," *Am. Anthropologist*, 63 (1961), pp. 1173–1192, and "The Dyadic Contract in Tzintzuntzan, II: Patron-Client Relationships," *ibid.*, 65 (1963), pp. 1280–1294; Julian A. Pitt-Rivers, *The People of the Sierra*, Chicago, 1961, pp. 154–155; Morton H. Fried, *Fabric of Chinese Society: A Study of the Social Life of a Chinese County Seat*, New York, 1953, pp. 224, 227; Michael Kenny, "Patterns of Patronage in Spain," *Anthropological Quarterly*, 33 (1960), pp. 14–23, and *A Spanish Tapestry: Town and Country in Castile*, Bloomington, Ind., 1961, pp. 154–155. For a particularly suggestive discussion of the relationship of cliency to the formation of village factions, see Edit Fel and Tamas Hofer, "Tanyaket-s, Patron-Client Relations, and Political Factions in Atany," *Am. Anthropologist*, 75 (1973), pp. 787–800.

ways it is only discernible by an apparently routinized disruption of normal patterns of association that *may* be verified. To employ a metaphor from astronomy, clientage is very much like a black-hole argument. It must be there because of the strange way every-thing else behaves when passing through its orbit. Yet it itself re-mains invisible. An examination of John Pynchon's dealings with his tenants, workers, and debtors shows an inescapable pattern of separating these men into two camps: those for whom he would walk the extra mile, and those for whom he would not. For those whose skills he needed, and whose support in public affairs he could count upon, Pynchon showed a pronounced indulgence, par-ticularly regarding debt collection. For others, too busy to help him at harvest, too irregular in their work habits, or simply too per-sonally independent, he stuck inflexibly to the sovereign letter of the contract. The difference, for many men, ultimately was between success and failure.[95]

Pynchon's negotiations with William Brooks in early 1667 illus-trate the bargaining process between patron and client. Brooks had approached his landlord to request a second year's grace on his mortgage. As Pynchon related in his account book: "William Brooks desyred me not to advantage against him of this agreement but to let him enjoy his [land] one yeare longer, he desyred but a yeares tyme more . . . though this tyme was out above a yeare since, and I might . . . now challenge the land for newly owned." But after this assertion of his legal rights, rights that both men recognized would be enforced in Pynchon's courtroom, the landlord relented. He vouchsafed that "yet I would settle to his desires in it and grant him one yeare's tyme longer to pay the debt per contract, and if he payd it not by this tyme 12 months then the land to be mine." This kind of ameliorating behavior paid dividends to both parties. Brooks gained still another year in which to raise the necessary funds; Pynchon secured the loyalty of the client.[96]

The trade-offs for this kind of favor, of course, were rarely stated explicitly. Contractually, Brooks offered Pynchon nothing in return for the foreclosure's extension. But as both the court records and account books reveal, Pynchon's subsequent claims on Brooks's loyalty could not be easily denied. When the magistrate needed support in the town meeting, help at harvest time, or intelligence regarding illegal gaming activities in the community, he could usu-

[95] I am obliged to John M. Murrin for helping me to refine these points, and for suggesting the metaphor.
[96] Account Books, 2, p. 215.

ally count on William Brooks.[97] Equally important, neither patron nor client found this kind of asymmetrical relationship unusual or demeaning. Brooks knew that he was joined by roughly half the town's men in dependency on Pynchon. All Springfield inhabitants recognized that those who hoped to establish a secure economic foothold usually found John Pynchon more forthcoming in meeting their material needs than was the town meeting.

But, as with the town meeting's habitual reliance on Pynchon's entrepreneurial resources, individual reliance on patron-client rather than corporate ties came at a price. Dependency relationships with Pynchon tended to become permanent and often, in the long run, disabling. William Brooks, for example, eventually lost his 150 acres to the creditor and ended up quitting the town.[98] As he learned, the dependency ties in Springfield—despite appearances—were not those of the medieval manor, but of the company town.

Springfield was an almost textbook example of the "hegemony" described with such brilliance by Antonio Gramsci, and used by Eugene Genovese to highlight the reciprocal obligations characteristic of slave society. As in the company towns of the postbellum South, the bottom line of paternalism was profit, not protection. Springfield was an avatar of the new capitalist world, for which the patron-client bond would serve as midwife. Clientage was a relationship that permitted the entrepreneur to rationalize production and maximize returns partly by relying upon premodern patterns of behavior among subordinates. Those with skills who responded in the expected way could expect indulgence. Those who behaved differently might get away with it, but if they foundered, they could expect no mercy. As Pynchon's use of clientage reveals, the emergence of a true capitalist type depended partly upon the continuing existence of others less modern than he. And the future would belong to the market, not the manor. For Pynchon, patron-client ties were preeminently a means of organizing labor, and, as Robert L. Heilbroner observes, "the driving force of capitalism [is] the accumulation of capital by means of wage labor." Heilbroner's definition of capitalism helps place Pynchon's use of patronage ties in context: "Capitalism . . . is quintessentially a means of organizing labor to produce a social surplus. By a surplus I mean the production of material wealth over and above whatever is needed to maintain ordinary life at its existing level. The line between surplus and mere replenishment is always blurred, as are most social dis-

[97] See Chapter 5.
[98] Account Books, 5, p. 27.

tinctions, but in the large there is no difficulty in distinguishing the form and extent of surplus in all surplus-producing systems."[99] Nothing betokens this surplus-orientation more vividly than does the highly commercialized nature of both land and labor. To invoke the Aristotelian distinction between "use value" and "exchange value" to determine whether an economy is capitalized or not, Springfield's was clearly in the latter camp. And it was so from the beginning.[100]

[99] Robert L. Heilbroner, "The Demand for the Supply Side," *The New York Review of Books* (June 11, 1981), pp. 37–41.

[100] E. J. Hobsbawm, "Pact with the Devil," *The New York Review of Books* (December 18, 1980), p. 3.

• Chapter 3 •

Land

*"Somebody once said that capitalism
without bankruptcy is like Christianity without hell."*
Frank Borman, chairman and president of
Eastern Air Lines, *Forbes* (June 8, 1981)

LAND in seventeenth-century Springfield was less a communal bond than it was a fungible commodity. Unlike the subsistence farming communities, land in the Connecticut Valley town changed hands early and often. As the "Records of Possession" make clear, Springfield had an active land market as early as 1650. The weakness of corporate ties resulted in the town meeting's loss of primary control over land allocation. Rather than carefully rationing acreage in order to preserve social harmony and protect future generations, Springfield allowed most of the town's genuinely first-rate acreage to pass quickly into private hands. And, by a combination of allocation, purchase, and foreclosure, most of it ended up with John Pynchon. The result was twofold: a high level of social stratification and the prevalence of land tenancy.[1]

The amplitude of land and the absence of tenancy in seventeenth-century New England towns have become articles of faith among historians. The ready availability of land, we are told, minimized inequality and muted social tensions. In Dedham, Massachusetts, the "incomparable abundance of land" enabled sons to "expect a patrimony which would keep [them] from having to rent land or work for another man or beg in the streets."[2] In Andover, by 1662, land allotments provided the town's earliest settlers with "land on a scale impossible for most of them to have anticipated . . . in England."[3] A resident of such communities could expect to

[1] "Records of Possessions," 1651–1699, City Clerk's Office, Springfield.

[2] Lockridge, *A New England Town*, pp. 70–71.

[3] Greven, *Four Generations*, p. 59. For a sophisticated treatment of the relationship between land availability and communal solidarity, see Robert A. Gross, *The Minutemen and Their World*, New York, 1976, pp. 68–108.

receive approximately two hundred acres during his lifetime, and overall, according to Kenneth Lockridge, "an estimate of 150 acres for the typical early inhabitant of an eastern Massachusetts town is a reasonable figure."[4] Consequently, in these towns the "distribution of wealth [was] relatively even and the spectrum of social rank narrow." Or, to use Lockridge's forthright characterization, they composed a society of "One class, one interest, one mind."[5]

Springfield, however, was anything but a one-class society. Patterns of unequal land distribution appeared with the town's founding and intensified as the century progressed. The 1646 tax list, as we have seen, shows William Pynchon and his two sons-in-law monopolizing the best acreage in the community's three planting fields. Their combined holdings of 510 acres comprised 25 percent of the total land allocated.[6] By 1655 there were already so many landless men in Springfield that the meeting devised a separate system for taxing them.[7] In addition, unlike the subsistence towns where inhabitants were discouraged from leaving the village center, Springfield passed legislation designed to facilitate out-migration and thereby reduce the demand for land.[8] As early as 1664, the town meeting unhappily concluded that "there are diverse Persons in this Town who have but little land." Three years later, the meeting appointed a committee to "consider of the necessitous Condition of some familyes in the Plantation," who needed relief.[9] Fathers complained, presumably with some warmth, that they had insufficient acreage to provide an inheritance for their sons. In drawing

[4] Kenneth A. Lockridge, "Land, Population and the Evolution of New England Society, 1630–1790; and an Afterthought," in Stanley N. Katz, ed., *Colonial America: Essays in Politics and Social Development*, Boston, 1971, pp. 469–471. See also Greven, *Four Generations*, p. 59; Christopher Jedrey, *The World of John Cleaveland: Family and Community in Eighteenth-Century New England*, New York, 1979, pp. 58–94; Sumner Chilton Powell, *Puritan Village: The Formation of a New England Town*, Middletown, Conn., 1963, Appendices 6 and 7; Charles S. Grant, *Democracy in the Connecticut Frontier Town of Kent*, New York, 1961, pp. 97–103. For comparisons with English landholding practices, see Mildred Campbell, *The English Yeoman Under Elizabeth and the Early Stuarts*, New Haven, 1942, Chapters 3 and 4; Lawrence Stone, *Family and Fortune*, Oxford, 1973, pp. 288–291; W. G. Hoskins, *Provincial England*, London, 1963, pp. 151–160; Brian Manning, *The English People and the English Revolution, 1640–1649*, London, 1976, pp. 112–162; and Peter Laslett, *The World We Have Lost: England Before the Industrial Age*, New York, 1965, pp. 22–52.

[5] Lockridge, *A New England Town*, p. 76.

[6] *Springfield Town Recs.*, 1, pp. 190–191.

[7] *Ibid.*, 1, p. 245.

[8] *Ibid.*, 1, pp. 248–249. To encourage settlement of Woronoco (Westfield), then under Springfield's control, the town rebated one-half of the rates assessed there.

[9] *Springfield Town Recs.*, 1, pp. 318, 359.

up a petition for rate relief, the town asked the General Court to "consider our poverty."[10] Even Springfield's minister, Pelatiah Glover, wondered if the level of privation in the community would make it impossible for the residents to pay his salary. In discussing Glover's plans to move elsewhere, the selectmen observed that "he apprehends that Wee are not able comfortably to maynteyne him."[11] Because this privation was rooted in the inequitable land distribution, the committees responsible for land grants were in constant disarray. During its first three decades the town repeatedly vacillated over the question of which institution—the board of selectmen, a special *ad hoc* committee, or the entire town meeting—should control land allocation.[12]

This progressive stratification is plainly revealed by the remarkably detailed 1685 tax list. Drawn up amid the uncertainty over land titles arising from the Crown's *quo warranto* proceedings against Massachusetts, this list shows the size, location, and valuation of all land holdings. Anxious to demonstrate incontrovertible proof of ownership, the assessors designated which land already had been "broken up" for tillage, and they computed the overall worth of each tract of woodland, pasture, and upland. The 1685 list thus affords an unrivaled look at both the distribution of acreage and the relative worth of various holdings. Not surprisingly, on both counts—particularly the latter—John Pynchon comes out on top by a wide margin. Of a total of approximately 9,000 acres held by some 120 persons, Pynchon owned 1,800 (20%). The acreage of the next largest landowner, Japhet Chapin, was 365. Pynchon held more land than the collective acreage of the fifty-two smallest owners, or 43 percent of the total number of male freeholders. The bottom 10 percent possessed less than 1 percent of all the acreage; the bottom 20 percent, 4.2 percent; and the bottom 30 percent, 8.6 percent of the land granted. With Pynchon's holdings subtracted from the whole, the mean acreage was 60. Forty-nine men held estates smaller than 50 acres, and sixteen owned fewer than 25 acres. Still more important, these landholdings, in addition to being small, were often infertile or remote. Like his father before him, John Pynchon monopolized the holdings in the rich alluvial third division adjacent to the Agawam (Westfield) River. [See Springfield map.] Here land valuations averaged up to sixty shil-

---

[10] *Ibid.*, 2, p. 166; *Mass. Recs.*, 2, p. 270; 3, p. 154; 5, pp. 483–484.

[11] *Springfield Town Recs.*, 2, pp. 101–102; also see Chapter 5.

[12] *Springfield Town Recs.*, 2, p. 81.

lings per acre, in contrast to median valuations of twenty shillings per acre elsewhere.[13]

The distribution of wealth revealed by the 1685 tax list is paralleled to a striking degree in estate inventories. From 1650 to 1705 the town (or Hampshire County) probated the estates of seventy Springfield inhabitants. With adjustments made for encumbrances, the total value of probated estates was £22,843. Of this amount John Pynchon's estate totaled £8,446 (37%). Largely because of his extensive property, the top 5 percent of the decedents held £11,721, or 51 percent of the inventoried wealth. At the other extreme of the social spectrum, things were radically different. The bottom 20 percent held estates valued at a total of £243 (1%), and the bottom 50 percent owned £1,951 (8.5%). The poorest sixty-two men (89% of the decedents) held a total of £8,547 (37.4%). It took the combined holdings of almost 90 percent of the deceased townsmen, therefore, to equal the property owned by John Pynchon. Only three men other than the magistrate held estates valued in excess of £800. Ensign Benjamin Cooley owned holdings worth £1,241 when he died in 1684. Pynchon's brother-in-law, Elizur Holyoke, died eight years later leaving his heirs property worth £1,187. Quartermaster George Colton owned assets valued at £847 at his death in 1690. At the opposite end, thirty men (43%) died with estates worth less than £100; fifteen of these were valued below £50. Six men died owning assets amounting to less than £25, four of whom died as town charges. Only 24 percent of the decedents, seventeen men, left estates within the supposedly normative £200 to £400 range.[14]

These figures reveal that the specter of intermittent poverty stalked at least half of Springfield's seventeenth-century population. Estimates of the number of acres necessary to provide adequately for a family's needs vary greatly, largely because the relevant evidence is fragmentary and often ambiguous. Speculations regarding the requirements for the typical family of seven range from twenty-eight to one hundred acres, depending on such variables as soil

[13] 1685 Tax List.

[14] HCPC Rec., 1–4 (1660–1780). Many Springfield decedents never had their estates inventoried. Most quantitative historians believe that those dying young or poor were the most likely to be excluded. For a comparative view of another Connecticut Valley town, see Linda A. Bissell, "From One Generation to Another: Mobility in Seventeenth-Century Windsor, Connecticut," *WMQ*, 31 (1974), pp. 79–110. For a portrayal of similar divisions in Plymouth Colony, see John J. Waters, "The Traditional World of the New England Peasants: A View from Seventeenth-Century Barnstable," *New England Historical and Genealogical Register*, 129 (1976), pp. 3–21.

fertility, agricultural techniques, access to markets, and dietary habits.[15] The Springfield data suggest that a minimum of sixty accessible acres was needed to support a family of seven if the householder lived exclusively by farming.[16] Skilled artisans, depending on the profitability of their craft, could make do with somewhat less. But while they may have required less planting ground than did full-time farmers, artisans, like everyone else, needed a homelot, pasturage, and woodlots. Each household in colonial New England, for example, needed between fifteen and twenty cords of wood to get through an average winter.[17] Likewise, all inhabitants shared the common necessity of providing a patrimony for their male children.

For that half of Springfield's population with fewer than sixty acres, and much of this infertile or distant, the choice was to get a lease from John Pynchon or get out. Most chose the former. During any one year between 1650 and 1703, over one-third of the town's adult males were renting some or all of their land, housing, or livestock from Pynchon. In 1685, 49 out of the 120 inhabitants entered on the tax list leased land or livestock from Springfield's seigneur. Of that same 120, fully 113 rented from Pynchon at some point during their stay in the town. During the half-century after 1650, approximately 140 renters paid him over £4,000 for fifteen hundred contract years.[18] The landlord's annual income from rent receipts during this time ranged from £100 to £150, in addition to value derived from tenants' improvement of his property. Men

---

[15] A careful evaluation of land requirements for family subsistence is found in James T. Lemon, "Household Consumption in Eighteenth-Century America," *Agricultural History*, 41 (1967), pp. 59–70. For the land needs of communities primarily devoted to stock-raising, see Jedrey, *The World of John Cleaveland*, pp. 58–64.

[16] 1685 Tax List.

[17] Russell, *A Long, Deep Furrow*, p. 175.

[18] 1685 Tax List. The number of contract years has been calculated by totaling each contract year paid for every rental, even if some were coterminous; that is, if a man rented a 30-acre lot for 6 years and a yoke of oxen for the same 6 years, his total contract years would be 12. It is probable that the rental periods were considerably longer than the statistics cited suggest, because only the years in which Pynchon actually entered the payment for the rent in his account books were used in the sample. Repeatedly, in the account book, a contract was signed for a lease of 5, 7, 11 years, etc., but no subsequent payments are recorded. Although Pynchon was, for the period, an assiduous bookkeeper, it is likely that many payments were not recorded—or were recorded in day books that have not survived. To ensure the integrity of the statistics in this analysis, all contracts without recorded payments have been ignored. In addition to the 140 Springfield tenants, some 60 residents of other valley towns also rented from Pynchon. Usually they leased lands or housing within their own communities, although some rented within Springfield itself.

rented from Pynchon largely because he owned a disproportionate share of the town's alluvial meadows and bottom land in the third division. Men without allotments in these fields were usually consigned to pine barrens, rocky woodlands, and marshlands. Consequently, rather than work infertile lands or make the daily trek to distant fields, many approached Pynchon for a lease. In a telling 1676 petition to the General Court for relief from garrison duties, the town declared that "many are forced to hyre land here, there own being so remote."[19]

Tenancy in seventeenth-century Springfield, however, was often a swift route to economic hardship; and the reasons for this hardship are found in the complexities of the English common law notion of waste. In America, in sharp contrast to the mother country, the rule of waste was used developmentally. In England, the common law notion of waste barred the tenant from making any alterations of the leasehold, whether these changes involved clearing the land for cultivation or erecting buildings. At common law, "any fundamental alteration by a tenant of the condition of the land constituted waste for which he was liable."[20] And "a tenant who erected buildings on land had no right to remove them at the end of his term."[21] Legal historians have long mistakingly viewed the English law of waste as a dead letter in colonial America. Justice Joseph Story's famous ruling in *Van Ness v. Pacard* (1829) is the most frequently cited justification of this view. According to Story, the common law rule of waste had never been accepted in America because "The country was a wilderness, and the universal policy was to procure its cultivation and improvement. The owner of the soil as well as the public, had every motive to encourage the tenant to devote himself to agriculture, and to favor any erections which should aid this result; yet, in the comparative poverty of the country, what tenant could afford to erect fixtures of much expense or value, if he was to lose his whole interest therein by the very act of erection?"[22] But as the contractual terms of John Pynchon's ground rents make clear, the rule of waste *was* received—although used very differently—in America. In the New World, the rule of waste appears to have been stood on its head. Many of Pynchon's leases

[19] Springfield Petition to the Massachusetts General Court, August 30, 1676, CVHM; 1685 Tax List.

[20] Morton J. Horwitz, *The Transformation of American Law, 1780–1860*, Cambridge, Mass., 1977, p. 54; see also S.F.C. Milsom, *Historical Foundations of the Common Law*, London, 1969, pp. 252, 255.

[21] Horwitz, *Transformation of American Law*, p. 55.

[22] Cited in *ibid.*, p. 55.

required the tenant to clear and break up new land, and often included provisions for erecting buildings as well. But the tenant received neither equity nor the right to remove the buildings upon termination of the lease. Tellingly, the only area where the English use of waste did prevail in America was in regard to equity. Waste, as a time-honored landlord's remedy, protected against tenants' suits to recover equity by making the lessee in fact liable for such changes. Tenants in Springfield cleared and built only for the landlord's ultimate benefit.[23]

The rule of waste deprived the Springfield tenants of their most valuable capital asset—their labor. As Stuart Bruchey points out in his seminal *The Roots of American Economic Growth, 1607–1861*, the value of improved land was "by far the most important constituent of capital" in the colonies.[24] And according to economic historian William N. Parker, "Land clearing was the heaviest of the tasks [confronted by the colonists]. . . . Altogether it took a man as many as twenty to thirty-five days to make an acre of land reasonably free of its original cover and ready for first cultivation."[25] In a frontier agricultural society, the labor involved in clearing the land, erecting fences, and nurturing livestock was the most available means of capital formation. Only by this daily investment of time and sweat could most men appreciably better their standard of living. But labor for someone else's benefit was counterproductive, for if,

[23] Account Books, 6, p. 229. Because of the importance of contractual obligations in Springfield (see Chapter 4), when a contract existed, its terms would govern a dispute over property removal, not the doctrine of waste. But John Pynchon sometimes issued leases without a contract, or with an agreement so vague in its construction as to be open to conflicting interpretations. In disputable cases, and for those without written contracts, the cardinal function of waste was to frame men's *expectations*. The doctrine of waste as it was used in England, the only legal culture most colonists knew, predisposed them not to expect equitable recovery for improvements of the leasehold. In regard to the apparent unfairness of the developmental leases, Pynchon doubtless would have pointed to their modest rents and the large assumption of risk in being a frontier landlord. The fact that he supplied some of the construction materials would likewise support his position. Paradoxically, the modern law of contract, in some ways, has come full circle and returned to the "just price" theory so odious to the Pynchons. Today, a defendant might raise the argument that the lease/contract was unfair and a contract of adhesion. Thus it must be voided as "unconscionable." I am indebted to Rayman L. Solomon of the American Bar Foundation for these observations.

[24] Stuart Bruchey, *The Roots of American Economic Growth, 1607–1861*, New York, 1965, p. 23. This reference was brought to my attention by David Thomas Konig, *Law and Society in Puritan Massachusetts: Essex County, 1629–1692*, Chapel Hill, 1979, p. 65, n. 4.

[25] William N. Parker, "The American Farmer," in Jerome Blum, ed., *Our Forgotten Past: Seven Centuries of Life on the Land*, London, 1982, pp. 182–183.

after clearing, stubbing, and plowing the land, constructing fences and sometimes buildings, raising stock, and paying rent and taxes, a tenant surrendered up his lease, all money and labor were lost. One of the principal grievances in the Tenant Rising of 1766 in Dutchess County, New York, was the ejection of the tenants without "any manner of recompense for their labour, fatigue, and expense in cultivating, manuring, clearing, fencing, and improving said lands, nor for their buildings thereon erected."[26] A still more graphic indictment of tenancy's capacity to rob a man of the fruits of his labor is provided by Cadwallader Colden. He ascribed the depopulation of the Hudson Valley patroonships to this theft of a tenant's labor: "every year the Young people go from this Province and Purchase Land in the Neighbouring Colonies, while much better and every way more convenient Lands lie useless to the King and Country. The reason for this is that the [owners] themselves are not, nor never were in a Capacity to improve such large Tracts and other People will not become their Vassals or Tenants for one great reason, as people's (the better sort especially) leaving their native Country, was to avoid the dependence on landlords, and to enjoy in fee [simple] to descend to their posterity *that their children may reap the benefit of their labor and Industry.*"[27]

Tenancy in America only made sense for those who had nothing to lose to begin with. Men without sufficient capital to purchase the land, provisions, and equipment required to start their own freehold doubtless saw tenancy as an attractive alternative to the life of a wage laborer. There can be little question that many men came to Springfield specifically in order to rent from John Pynchon. In so doing, of course, they were simply following everyday practices in England where tenants constituted 80 percent of the working agricultural population. The Pynchon account books show that tenancy in Springfield enabled men to move up from laborer to husbandman—itself no small achievement. But because renters were not recompensed for their labor, their long-term prospects were limited by an inability to gain enough wealth to become independent. Tenancy in Springfield, therefore, was usually a dead-end street. It offered a certain kind of mobility to the landless, but only at the price of dependence on John Pynchon. For those tenants who were landholders, their labor for Pynchon precluded improvement of their own freeholds. Many in both categories became chronic

---

[26] Cited in Staughton Lynd, *Anti-Federalism in Dutchess County, New York: A Study of Democracy and Class Conflict in the Revolutionary Era*, Chicago, 1962, p. 47.

[27] Cited in Irving Mark, *Agrarian Conflicts in Colonial New York, 1711–1775*, New York, 1940, p. 14; emphasis mine.

debtors; some forty men lost sizable amounts of land, housing, or livestock to Pynchon for their debts.[28]

The forms of tenancy in Springfield varied greatly. Some tenants leased eighty-acre farms, complete with housing, orchards, livestock, and tools, for twenty years or longer—at rents sometimes exceeding £22 annually. Others rented a single acre of meadow for one year at six shillings. Most leases fell between these extremes. A typical renter might hold fifteen acres, some housing, and a yoke of oxen for between twelve and sixteen years. In addition to oxen, tenants rented draft horses, cows, sheep, pigs, and the stud services of Pynchon's bulls.[29] Other men leased gristmills and sawmills from the landlord, at charges up to £18 a year.[30] Heavy artisans such as blacksmiths, tanners, and millwrights leased the tools of their trade from him.[31] Those without a plow did likewise. To his more affluent tenants, Pynchon rented out fur-trading rights, warehouse space, and shares in ocean-going vessels.[32]

In addition to their rent, which was paid at "Michaelmas" in late September, tenants were usually responsible for fence maintenance, local taxes, and, as we have seen, the clearing of part of the leasehold.[33] Often, Pynchon required his tenants to "stub, clear, and bring to plowing" designated portions of the holding. Some contracts likewise specified the exact dimensions of any housing, barns, or out-buildings to be erected by the tenant. Livestock rentals provided that Pynchon receive half and sometimes all of the offspring—a significant requirement in that cows, horses, pigs, and sheep were valued as much for their ability to reproduce as for their daily utility.[34]

---

[28] For a discussion of the importance of rent in the transfer of wealth in preindustrial economies, see Eric R. Wolf, *Peasants*, Englewood Cliffs, N. J., 1966, pp. 9–10. Wolf also discusses caloric minima and villagers' efforts to curtail consumption. These problems are likewise explored in G. M. Foster, "Peasant Society and the Image of Limited Good," in J. M. Potter, M. N. Diaz, and G. M. Foster, eds., *Peasants: A Reader*, Boston, 1967, pp. 300–323.

[29] Account Books, 5, pp. 548–549.

[30] *Ibid.*, 5, p. 170.

[31] *Ibid.*, 2, p. 283.

[32] *Ibid.*, 6, pp. 230–231.

[33] Pynchon's willingness to retain the usage of such "popish" terms as Michaelmas, Whitsuntide, and Eastertide is itself instructive. Massachusetts Governor John Winthrop and most other coastal magistrates, by contrast, did their best to banish such terms, regarding them as relics of superstition. I am grateful to John M. Murrin for this observation.

[34] Account Books, 5, pp. 161, 307. For comparisons with tenancy practices elsewhere in the colonies, see Mark, *Agrarian Conflicts*; Gregory A. Stiverson, *Poverty in a Land of Plenty: Tenancy in Eighteenth-Century Maryland*, Baltimore, 1977; Aubrey

John Pynchon's account books make it possible to identify six classes of renters in Springfield: (1) fifteen tenant farmers (characterized by Pynchon as "My Farmers"); (2) fifty dependent renters; (3) thirty short-term dependent renters; (4) nine long-term independent renters; (5) thirty-one short-term independent renters; and (6) five who rented only animals. Of these, the tenant farmers were the most dependent.[35]

The tenant farmers leased self-contained, fully equipped farms for extended periods at high rents. Their only contribution to the arrangement was labor.[36] John Pynchon supplied the lands, housing, barns, dairy and draft animals, and tools. The cost was accordingly high: £18 yearly was the most common sum, an amount often equal to the value of half or more of the tenant's harvest. Collectively, the tenant farmers paid for a total of 226 contract years, with payments of £1,903. The average duration of their rental period was fifteen years. Most began renting from Pynchon while in their late twenties or early thirties, presumably after it had become evident that other avenues for obtaining land were closed. Virtually to a man, the tenant farmers continued in some kind of contractual relationship with him as long as they remained in Springfield.

Isaac Morgan's experience can stand as typical. The son of a Welsh immigrant who had been John Pynchon's most active canoeman, Morgan first rented land in March 1672. He started off with a lease for three and one-half acres in the Chicopee section

---

C. Land, "Economic Base and Social Structure: The Northern Chesapeake in the Eighteenth Century," *Journal of Economic History*, 25 (1965), pp. 639–654. The most benign portrayals of American tenancy are found in Sung Bok Kim, *Landlord and Tenant in Colonial New York: Manorial Society, 1664–1775*, Chapel Hill, 1978; Patricia U. Bonomi, *A Factious People: Politics and Society in Colonial New York*, New York, 1971, pp. 179–228. For continental and Latin American parallels, see Thomas F. Sheppard, *Lourmarin in the Eighteenth Century: A Study of a French Village*, Baltimore, 1971, Chapters 1 and 6; Laurence Wylie, *Chanzeaux, A Village in Anjou*, Cambridge, Mass., 1966; and William B. Taylor, *Landlord and Peasant in Colonial Oaxaca*, Stanford, 1972, pp. 67–163, 195–202.

[35] In his description of tenancy in a 20th-century Japanese village, Ronald P. Dore proposes the following categories: "*Landlords*—renting out more land than they farmed. *Owner-farmers*—owning at least 90 per cent of the land they farmed and some of them also renting out an acre or two. *Owner-tenants*—owning 50–90 per cent of the land they farmed. *Tenant-owners*—owning 10–50 per cent of the land they farmed. *Tenants*—owning less than 10 per cent of the land they farmed." See *Shinohata: A Portrait of a Japanese Village*, New York, 1978, p. 46. Such categorization makes sense for 17th-century Springfield as well, although insufficient data on yearly percentages of owned vs. leased land prevents the outright adoption of this scheme for the Massachusetts community.

[36] Account Books, 5, p. 524.

of town. The following year, at age twenty-one, he married Isabel Gardner and quickly sought additional land with which to support his new bride. On Christmas day he signed an agreement with Pynchon to lease a forty-two-acre farm for a term of eleven years. The obligations of both men were considerable. Pynchon bound himself to bog and clear five acres of land, to provide "sixty load of dung to mend the land," and to "Build at the round hill this next Summer, a house for the said Isack Morgan to dwell in to the End of the terme." The landlord also supplied "a Barne . . . Three cows, a yoake of oxen and a horse . . . togither with a Cart and wheeles, yoake, Plough and chaine, and all irons for the Teames" and "80 Apples trees for the said Isack's use." The tenant, for his part, agreed to clear and plow the remaining upland and to pay both the town rates on the livestock and rent graduated up to £22 yearly.[37]

The account books show that Morgan worked hard to make a go of his leasehold. In addition to raising his own crops, he also performed a variety of manual labor for Pynchon. Indeed, so active was Morgan after taking over the forty-two-acre farm that his labor credits rivaled the annual £15 salary Pynchon paid his farm hands. Morgan specialized in heavy field work and, like his father Miles, slaughtering. Most of his labor credits were for such tasks as digging ditches, draining marshes, gathering stones, carting goods, and either gelding or slaughtering livestock. In November 1672 he received credit for "mowing, haymaking . . . 58 Rod ditching [and carting up from Enfield falls] 17 bushels ½ Salt." The year Morgan took the farm, Pynchon paid him £9 for "Bogging And the 3 acres he formerly engaged to doe . . . and 2 acres he engaged to cleare . . . and for 35 Rod of ditching." The next year he earned £13 for a wide array of tasks: "digging stones . . . cutting calves . . . carting 2 load stone . . . raising house, Nayling up Bords . . . cutting a Bull . . . 7 load wood . . . 8 days [work] . . . Setting up Rayles . . . Mowing . . . carting clay and daubing, fencing . . . carting 1 load Posts . . . killing sheep . . . winter[ing] of 7 cattle and killing 2 [cattle] . . . killing hoggs."[38]

King Philip's followers destroyed most of the farm when they attacked Springfield in 1675, but they did not sever Isaac Morgan's ties to John Pynchon. During his sixteen-year rental career, he leased additional plowland, meadow, and oxen before he emigrated to Enfield in the early 1680s. There he also continued to work for

[37] *Ibid.*, 5, pp. 422–423.
[38] *Ibid.*, 5, pp. 189, 420–423.

his former landlord. On December 31, 1681, Pynchon "Agreed with Isack Morgan well to stub and break up with Plough 2 acres of land in my lot at Enfield. That is to say all the bredth of my lot there and 14 rod in the length of it and the place where he is to doe this is agreed to be about 40 rod from the front of my home lot there . . . [for] Three Pounds and a stubbing hoe." A year later Pynchon asked Morgan "to do 20 rod of good 5 Raile fence at fresh water [for] 37 shillings."[39]

Jonathan Ball's career illustrates a similar dependence on Pynchon. It also shows how day-laborers used tenancy as a vehicle for upward mobility. Ball was born in Springfield in 1645 and began working for John Pynchon as a field hand at the age of nineteen. Pynchon wrote in 1665 that "Jonathan Ball came to me the 21 March 1664/65 and he is to be with me 2 months for which I am to allow him 20s. per month." Ball continued to work primarily for Pynchon for the next dozen years, receiving payments for "carting dung 6 days . . . 2 months work in 1665 . . . a Journey to New London, and looking up cattle . . . 15 days worke . . . 11 days worke at the Mill . . . 2 days worke sawing . . . fencing at woronoke, Rayls 25s., ditching 9s., Log fence 10s."[40] During the early 1670s, Ball began to concentrate increasingly on canoe work, as account book entries credit him for "carrying Corne downe the falls May 22 1671, your share of all is £3 2s. . . . By bringing up wine, sugar, Cords and etc. . . . By goeing down the falls and bringing up goods with Goodman Miller [in] May and June 1675, your part is . . . £3 5s. 4d." Not giving up field work completely, however, Ball took 10 shillings in 1675 for "50 Rod of ditch[ing]."[41]

In 1677, at the age of thirty-two, Ball leased Pynchon's eighty-acre farm in joint tenancy with Samuel Taylor. Rent was set at £18. As the account books reveal, the tenants were starting from scratch. They brought almost nothing of their own to the farm and relied on the landlord to supply even the most elemental necessities, including fodder, foundation stock, and planting seed. On April 13, 1677, Pynchon sold them "[7] bushels pease . . . 1 load of hay, 19 bushels of oates, 1 pair of Cart wheels . . . Cart irons . . . [and] 6 rubstones." Presumably to celebrate their new lease, Ball and Taylor also bought "2 pints of Liquors." A year and a half later, Pynchon "put to my farmers besides a yoak of steeres which I let to Sam Taylor and 2 steers I had of Henry Chapin." After the tenants complained that they lacked sufficient pasturage, Pynchon also

---

[39] *Ibid.*, 5, p. 421.
[40] *Ibid.*, 3, pp. 128–129.
[41] *Ibid.*, 5, pp. 40–41.

"agreed with my farmers, they desyring . . . to fence in some ground for a pasture."[42]

As the prominence of oats in the planting seed suggests, Ball and Taylor planned their enterprise around animal fodder production. In the seventeenth century, as today, wheat, barley, and rye were for human consumption; oats were used as winter feed for livestock.[43] In this expectation, the two tenants were apparently successful. During their first year of operation, Pynchon paid them £12 for "80 bushels of oates [and another] 20 bushels of oates." Likewise, two years later he credited them £8 for "80 bushels of oates." To help meet operating expenses, both men continued to perform field labor for their landlord worth roughly £12 annually. But, despite these efforts, Ball and Taylor could not generate enough income to cover their overhead, particularly the £18 rental fee. After holding the farm seven years, they gave it up in 1684. Ball, however, continued to lease his meadowland and plowground from Pynchon. That year he rented two acres of meadow at sixteen shillings, and in 1688 he leased eleven acres of prime upland for £3 8s. yearly. Ball held this land until the landlord's death fifteen years later. By that time he had paid for a total of twenty-five contract years, with cumulative payments in excess of £145.[44] This period of extended tenancy, as the 1685 valuation list reveals, is attributable to insufficient lands. In that year Ball owned only twenty-nine acres, despite the fact that he was at that time over forty years old and had been married twelve years. Moreover, sixteen of his twenty-nine acres were located in a marshy and unproductive section of Springfield known as the "Pickle."[45]

---

[42] *Ibid.*, 5, p. 524.

[43] Russell, *A Long, Deep Furrow*, p. 42.

[44] Account Books, 5, pp. 524–525; 6, pp. 18–19.

[45] 1685 Tax List. The fact that Jonathan Ball was a tenant farmer did not bar him from full participation in the community's social and political life. He held a number of town offices, including those of both selectman and tithingman. His illiteracy was no barrier to service as a selectman. Boards of selectmen in 17th-century Springfield often included at least one member unable to read. Ball's selection as tithingman, however, may have raised a few eyebrows. Tithingmen were charged by the General Court with the responsibility for ensuring domestic peace and maintaining Puritan norms of personal rectitude within the villages. And on occasion, it seems, Ball's behavior was something less than exemplary. In the spring of 1667 he was fined five shillings for "unseasonable Night Metings." Typically these offenses related to Ball's penchant for nightly bouts of drinking with his friends Sam Owen and Josias Leonard. On one such occasion, in early January of 1686, Owen apparently had a bit too much, and Ball and Leonard failed to see that he got home safely—with somewhat calamitous consequences for the widow Sarah Barnard. Two weeks later, Mrs. Barnard stood before the court and testified that

With his tenant farmers paying annual rents as high as £22, John Pynchon fully appreciated their worth. In a letter to his son describing the devastation brought by the Indian attack, Pynchon underscored his growing reliance on income derived from tenants (and debtors as well). After relating the town's and his own losses, he cited the destruction visited on his tenants, especially the farmers: "Four of those houses and barns . . . which were burnt in this towne belongeth to me also. So God hath laid me low. My farmers are also undone, and many in this town that were in my debt utterly disabled, so that I am really reduced to great straits."[46] In a similar letter to the Reverend John Russell of Hadley, Pynchon again lamented the burning of the "houses and barnes I had let out to tenants."[47]

But it was the second class of tenants, the dependent renters, that provided Pynchon with his greatest sources of income. The fifty men in this group paid for some 890 contract years, with total recorded payments of £2,133. Their rental careers lasted an average of seventeen years, their average lifetime payments were £43—in addition to taxes and labor. Each dependent renter was in

---

the inebriated Owen had on that night invaded both her home and her bed. She told the court that "the 7th of this . . . January shee was much afrighted by a mans coming in to her House in the Night when she was in Bed and lying downe on her Bed wherupon shee gat up and called when presently Thomas Lamb came in and speaking to him he gave noe answer to said Lamb till he Pulled him about to the fire and saw that it was Samuell Owen . . . at first [he] only opened his eyes and shut them again: I decerned that he had bene Drinking and smelled of it." Lamb and David Morgan attempted to resuscitate Owen, at first unsuccessfully. After an interval of fifteen minutes, Owen revived and "Labord to get up though he staggered a pritty while before he could recover himself, but at last he stood up." At this point Lamb proceeded to admonish the still-bewildered Owen: "I asked him Samuell what will your wife say to this that you come to another womans Bed." Under this questioning, Owen "made no answer for some time." As his head cleared, however, he began to wonder about the whereabouts of his drinking companions, and he then "askt after Josias Leanord and Jonathan Ball." When Lamb inquired "were they of your company," Owen again "made noe answer." Lamb then took it upon himself to see that Owen was started toward home: "Samuell: said I Come goe hom, and leading him as far as my House He Inquired the way Hom; I showed him and set him in it, and so parted." This parting was apparently premature, as "Goodman Foster told [Lamb] he gat but to his House that Night, and that with some difficulty having fallen in the Snow as he saw next morning." Jonathan Ball did make it home safely that night, possibly because his strong physical constitution allowed him to carry his liquor more easily than did Owen. His robustness enabled Ball to outlive his two drinking companions, his landlord, and most of the rest of his neighbors as well. He finally died in 1741, at the age of 96. Account Books, 3, p. 128; *Pynchon Court Rec.*, pp. 310–311.

[46] John Pynchon to Joseph Pynchon, October 20, 1675, CVHM.
[47] Mass. Archives, 67, p. 282.

some vital way reliant on his lease for economic sustenance. Unlike the tenant farmers, who were drawn almost entirely from the town's most marginal families, the dependent renters represented a broad spectrum of the population. They included both respected and venerable selectmen and the dispossessed. The career of Edward Foster illustrates the experiences of the latter.

Foster began and ended his stay in Springfield as a client of the Pynchon family. He was brought to the community from Scotland under an indenture to William Pynchon. Upon arrival, Foster's nine years of service were assigned to Elizur Holyoke.[48] After gaining his freedom, he went to work in John Pynchon's lead mine (which up until that time had been more promise than fulfillment). On March 30, 1659, Pynchon wrote that "The £3 which Edward Foster owes me below he engages to pay me out of his worke in the lead mines . . . noe pay to be made to [Foster] . . . till the debt is Satisfied." By the end of the decade of the 1650s, Foster had committed himself to full-time work for John Pynchon. After mining, his principal areas of concentration were canoe work, agricultural labor, and sawing. Various account book entries during the period from 1659 to 1674 credit him for "goeing downe the falls and carying 77½ bushels wheat with Goodman Mirick," "26 days ½ worke at the Mill Trench at 2s. 6d. [is] £3 6s.," "127 foote of boards," "making 8 rod of fence against the River," "By worke this Last Summer Mowing and about my Mill Dam and carting [12] days."[49]

Foster first rented land from Pynchon in 1668, and remained a tenant almost continuously until 1703. During this time, he paid for thirty-six contract years, with total payments of £153. In the late 1660s and early 1670s, Foster leased a 3½-acre homelot and 4½ acres of bottom land. His rent for these holdings was over £5 yearly—approximately half his former annual income as a laborer. In one of the leases, signed in March 1668, Pynchon "Lett out to Edward Foster my land in the Spring Bottom being about 4 acres for which he is to allow and pay me for this yeare coming the sum of thirty shillings . . . he is to take care of and repair the fence for the security of the field. Also let out to Edward Foster the hom lot of 3 acres and ½ . . . for 3 yeares, for which Edward Foster is to allow me 28s. per anum and repair the fence." The lease also included a proviso that if Pynchon decided to sell the land, "he shall have it before another at a meate price." In 1673 Foster signed

[48] *Pynchon Court Rec.*, p. 225.

[49] Account Books, 1, p. 217; 2, p. 209; 3, pp. 184–185, 247; 5, pp. 58–59, 474–475; 6, pp. 54–55; 1685 Tax List.

a contract with Pynchon that significantly altered his tenancy status. Now, rather than a two- or three-year lease, Foster agreed to a ten-year rental period. If he had envisioned his earlier leases as temporary expedients until he secured an adequate freehold, Foster evidently abandoned that hope in 1673. The new contract consolidated all the tenant's existing leases, along with additional meadowland, and called for rents of £7 yearly. He held this lease for the next eighteen years, until 1690. Foster subsequently rented five more acres in the rich Cold Spring bottom for thirty shillings annually, which he paid for the next seven years. Like the tenant farmers, he apparently rented because his own holdings were insufficient. In 1685 he owned only twenty-five acres, six of which were located in a distant and barren section with the ironic name of None Such. Because of these acreage deficiencies, Foster continued to rent from the third generation of Pynchons.[50]

The provisions of John Kilum's lease show graphically how tenancy could deprive a man of the fruits of his labor. The January 1689 contract committed Kilum to what in ordinary circumstances would be nearly a decade's worth of work. Pynchon "Agreed with John Kilum to have some of my Land over Agawam River for fifteen yeares . . . five acres . . . also he is to have my forty acres of upland in the Feild." The tenant was required to "cleare and break up at least fifteene acres," build "a good Timber House . . . at least 23 foote long [and] 18 foote wide," and "Plant an orchard." He also agreed to build and maintain all fences and pay rates up to ten shillings. The landlord agreed to provide boards for the floors and the exterior of the house. After Kilum fulfilled these obligations and paid an annual rent up to £5, he was expected to "Leave it . . . Tennentable" at the expiration of the lease.[51] Likewise, Philip Matoone's obligations in leasing Pynchon's eighteen cow commons and four sheep commons in Deerfield were considerable. In addition to a rent graduated up to £4, the tenant agreed to pay all rates, maintain the fences, and build "a good dwelling house strong substantial and well Built and Compleately furnished," with dimensions of 30-by-20-by-10 feet as well as a barn of at least 48-by-24-by-14 feet. The contract bound Matoone to "compleate and

---

[50] *Ibid.*

[51] Account Books, 6, pp. 228–229. Kilum held this land for 9 years, during which time he and Pynchon renegotiated the rent from £5 to £7 10s. annually. Kilum subsequently leased a total of over 30 acres of plowland and meadowland, some at joint tenancy. In 1693 he leased 11 acres in joint tenancy with Thomas Jones for £3 8s. yearly. By the time of John Pynchon's death in 1703, Kilum had paid for 16 contract years with lifetime payments of £66.

finish the same before the end of the terme, then leave and deliver all in good repaire."[52] Working on others' lands left men little time to work on their own. When Indians took his life in 1696, Philip Matoone's estate was valued at but £87, £23 of which was in real property.[53]

Such leading figures as selectmen and deputies to the General Court were numbered among the dependent renters. John Dumbleton, selectman for sixteen terms as well as a militia officer, paid £117 for sixty-six contract years during the period from 1652 to 1692. He leased at various times over fifty acres, oxen, bulls, and horses.[54] Lieutenant Abel Wright, selectman and representative to the General Court, paid £56 for leases of plowland, meadow, oxen and bulls during the years from 1668 to 1686. In 1668 Wright rented land which Pynchon two days earlier had taken for debts from Benjamin Dorchester. The contract provided that if, at the expiration of the term, Wright "can attain to buy the land he is to have it before another." Unfortunately for the tenant, he failed to come up with the purchase price and ended up paying the thirty-eight-shilling rent for the next eighteen years.[55] Wright owned 160 acres in 1685 and would appear, therefore, to be an unlikely candidate for tenancy. But, again, his holdings show the fallacy of equating land *ownership* with land *use*. Because of a combination of remoteness and infertility, Wright's 160 acres were valued at £47, an average of only six shillings per acre, roughly one-tenth of land valuations in the third division.[56]

Although the dependent renters included men drawn from both the town's leadership elite and the servant class, most tenants came from a large middle group composed of men who were usually freemen but rarely civic leaders. Lazarus Miller was typical of these men. During a rental career that was cut short by his death at the age of forty-two, he leased over seventy-seven acres of upland and meadow as well as housing, orchards, and oxen. As with Abel Wright, a lack of decent, accessible acreage led Miller to rent. The sixty-four acres he owned in 1685 were located several miles from the town center in "Block Bridge" where land values averaged five shillings per acre. In 1680 Miller rented an eleven-acre lot, an

[52] Account Books, 5, pp. 536–537.

[53] HCPC Rec., 3 (1692–1713), p. 27.

[54] *Pynchon Court Rec.*, p. 266; Account Books, 1, pp. 67–69; 2, p. 164; 3, p. 181; 5, pp. 50–51, 182–183, 540; 6, p. 196.

[55] *Pynchon Court Rec.*, pp. 313, 387; Account Books, 3, pp. 116–117; 5, pp. 102–103; 6, p. 174; 6, Index, p. 4.

[56] 1685 Tax List.

orchard, and a house in Chicopee plain for two years at £3 10s. annually. This lease was followed by one in 1684 for a twenty-four-acre lot in Chicopee field. In 1694, he leased a thirty-acre lot, ten acres of which had already been plowed. His rent was £1 15s. yearly, as well as fence maintenance and town rates; in addition the tenant was required to stub and clear all the remaining unbroken land and build a shelter.[57] Largely because he had spent his life's labors improving Pynchon's leaseholds, instead of his own, Miller left very little except debts when he died in the mid-1690s.[58] In a scene replete with patron-client overtones, his brothers Obadiah and John approached Pynchon to seek forgiveness of part of the balance. As Pynchon recounted the conversation after the two men had left: "Obadiah Miller and John Miller seeing this account and being satisfied in it: proposed that I would abate something or give something to the widdow: which I yielded unto and we readyly and freely give to Lazarus Miller's widdow Thirty shillings out of this Debt and so reduce the Debt to £8 12s." Pynchon appended this entry with the comment that "This was in case the Estate proved Solvent to Incourage them to administer and for their benefit."[59] The estate, however, did not prove solvent. Miller's total assets were valued at £38, his debts at £39, of which—after a final recalculation—£18 were owed to Pynchon.[60]

The third class of tenants was the short-term dependent renters—men who relied on leases from Pynchon to help them through brief periods of economic dislocation. These thirty renters paid approximately £240 for 218 contract years. The average duration of their rental period was seven years; the average total payment was £8. Their dependency on Pynchon is illustrated by the scope and diversity of their contracts. Some men, clearly of adequate means, used short-term tenancy as the most expeditious way of getting a start in Springfield. Joseph Marks, for example, although he paid for only seven contract years, rented a twenty-acre lot in Chicopee field for £3 10s. yearly, as well as a shed, yoke of oxen, mare, and a gun.[61] Likewise, Miles Morgan's nine contract years included leases for a house, twenty-five acres, oxen, a bull, and a cow.[62] Men with the necessary skills sought to lease Pynchon's mills, doubtless aware of the highly remunerative tolls earned by millers.

[57] Account Books, 5, pp. 490–491; 6, pp. 190–191; 6, Index; 1685 Tax List.
[58] HCPC Rec., 3, p. 38.
[59] Account Books, 6, p. 190.
[60] *Ibid.*; HCPC Rec., 3, p. 38.
[61] Account Books, 6, pp. 130–131.
[62] *Ibid.*, 1, pp. 77, 265; 3, pp. 142–144, 240; 6, p. 26.

Thomas Copley rented both a sawmill and a gristmill between 1681 and 1685. The contract specified that the mills were to be held "at halves." Copley tended and maintained the mill, while Pynchon helped defray the cost of upkeep. The two men divided the tolls equally at year's end.[63] Other millers simply paid an annual rent of £16 and kept all the tolls to themselves.[64]

The short-term dependent renters included a high percentage of joint or multiple tenancies. Under these leases, the tenants divided expenses, profits, and labor according to a prearranged formula. John Burt, Benjamin Knowlton, and Thomas Mirrick rented an eleven-acre lot in the third division from 1689 to 1693 "at thirds."[65] Victory Sikes and George Granger leased meadowland over the Agawam River for £4 10s. yearly. Pynchon required the two tenants to "clear off all trees and bush from the mowing land."[66] Ebenezer Graves rented a twenty-one-acre lot in Chicopee in joint tenancy with his brother Daniel in 1689.[67] Because joint tenancies allowed marginal men to pool their meager resources, they were commonly utilized by Springfield's more impoverished inhabitants.[68]

The fourth category of tenants, the long-term independent renters, included nine men who leased moderately sized plots of land for extended periods, usually twelve to fourteen years.[69] In contrast to the dependent renters, leasing for this group was a supplemental activity. They rented because it was convenient and profitable, but not necessary, to do so. Many of these contracts suggest what anthropologists describe as "collegial relationships." These are largely symbolic economic ties between relative social equals whose purpose is to solidify friendship and loyalty.[70] For example, Henry Chapin, the son of Springfield's first deacon, leased 7½ acres of wet meadow from Pynchon for a period of twenty-two years.[71] Chapin, who

[63] *Ibid.*, 5, pp. 170–171; 6, p. 48.
[64] See Chapter 4.
[65] Account Books, 6, p. 178.
[66] *Ibid.*, 6, p. 106.
[67] *Ibid.*, 6, pp. 156, 172.
[68] It is not possible, however, simply to equate joint tenancies with impoverishment. The Graves brothers were clearly among Springfield's more marginal inhabitants. Both were landless on the 1685 Tax List. Similarly Benjamin Knowlton who, married for ten years by 1685, owned only 16 acres. At his death in 1690, Knowlton's land was valued at £13. HCPC Rec., 2 (1678–1716), p. 61. John Burt and Thomas Mirrick, by contrast, were obviously not among the town's poor. Burt owned 72 acres of prime land in 1685, Mirrick, 110 acres. 1685 Tax List.
[69] As a group, these renters paid for 118 contract years, with average payments of £11.
[70] Foster, "The Dyadic Contract," *Am. Anthropologist* (1961), pp. 1173–1192.
[71] Account Books, 3, pp. 156–157; 5, pp. 22–23, 208; 6, p. 44.

bought two hundred acres from Pynchon in 1659 and was the third largest landholder on the 1685 tax list, rented out of choice, not necessity.[72] So did Joseph Ashley, who leased three wharf lots between 1678 and 1687, two of them for at least nine years each. Ashley was a part-time merchant and rented primarily to foster his trading activities. He already had sufficient land on which to raise his crops. In 1685 Ashley owned eighty-six acres in the most highly assessed section of the town, and, at his death in 1711, his real estate was valued at £209.[73]

The fifth set of tenants, those least reliant on Pynchon, were the short-term independent renters. These were individuals who, like the long-term independent renters, leased for reasons of choice, not necessity. The thirty-one tenants in this group rented for limited periods, usually three years or less.[74] Predominantly from Springfield's more affluent families, they likewise possibly hoped to establish a symbolic bond with John Pynchon.[75] Japhet Chapin, a brother of Henry, held 365 acres in 1685, second only to Pynchon's 1,800 acres. During an intermittent rental career that extended from 1665 to 1695, Chapin leased a 5½-acre lot, a 4-acre lot, a meadow, and a bull.[76] George Colton, quartermaster in the militia, selectman, and representative to the General Court, died in 1690 leaving an estate worth £847. But he too rented, a "little red stonehorse" in 1654 and meadow on Freshwater River between 1663 and 1667.[77]

The sixth and last group of renters, those who leased animals exclusively, was composed predominantly of non-Springfield residents. Of the twenty-six men in this category, only five lived in John Pynchon's home town. Draft animals—oxen or stone horses— were the most frequently rented livestock, though leases of short-horned cattle, mares, swine, and sheep were not uncommon. Renters in this group were usually drawn from poorer families. Judah Trumble, for one, was a subsistence farmer who tilled his small plot with a yoke of oxen leased from Pynchon for £2 annually for

[72] Deed, John Pynchon to Henry Chapin, March 9, 1660, CVHM.

[73] Account Books, 5, pp. 444–445; 6, pp. 28–29; 1685 Tax List; HCPC Rec., 3, pp. 243–244.

[74] The short-term independent renters paid for a total of 85 contract years. In addition to the 31 Springfield renters, there were 20 short-term renters from other valley towns.

[75] Foster, "The Dyadic Contract," *Am. Anthropologist* (1961), pp. 1173–1192.

[76] 1685 Tax List; Account Books, 3, pp. 58–59; 5, p. 13; 6, p. 44.

[77] HCPC Rec., 3, pp. 68–70; Account Books, 1, p. 140; 2, pp. 246–247; 3, pp. 60–62.

seven years.[78] As with all livestock leases, Trumble paid all the rates and charges on the oxen and was responsible for replacing them if they were injured or destroyed while in his service. The option of what to do with the offspring—allow the renter to keep all or part of them, take them after two years while indemnifying the renter, or simply take them without compensation—made livestock leases fertile ground for patron-client relationships. John Crowfoot, for example, apparently was not a client. He leased a young mare for three years during the 1680s and was required to give Pynchon all foals that reached two years of age. Symon Rumnel, by contrast, rented a "sanded sow" for three years "at halves," and the owner received only one-half of the new piglets.[79] While most livestock leases stipulated three-year terms, some were for as many as seven. In 1692, Pynchon let out a cow to William Booth for seven years at ten shillings annually.[80] Because it was not possible for a family to subsist long in the absence of draft and dairy animals, (witness "Jack and the Bean Stalk") a note of urgency sometimes accompanied lease requests. After John Woodward had approached him several times during the early 1690s, Pynchon yielded to Woodward's "entreaties" for a yoke of oxen.[81] Both men recognized that Woodward had few alternatives. In Springfield, those who needed livestock, like those who needed land, turned to John Pynchon.

But for all these groups, the risk posed by increased dependence on Pynchon was serious and sometimes crippling indebtedness. The debit entries in the account books lay bare the process of wealth transfer in early Springfield. Because Pynchon's control of the local economy was so extensive, all residents found at least occasional indebtedness to him inescapable. Tenancy was the principal cause, but even those who avoided becoming indebted as tenants often saw their economic fortunes imperiled through chronically unbalanced ledgers at the store. Not all debt is detrimental, of course. In a barter economy, people became indebted to each other for the day-to-day exchange of goods and services, or for loans made for capital improvements. The critical distinction here, however, is between this constructive indebtedness and the kind of chronic, disabling indebtedness which is not redeemed through regular transactions. For those without clientage ties with Pynchon, chronic

[78] Account Books, 5, pp. 342–343.
[79] *Ibid.*, 5, p. 307; 6, p. 122.
[80] *Ibid.*, 6, p. 91.
[81] *Ibid.*, 6, p. 35.

indebtedness was likely to result in loss of lands, home, or live-stock—or possibly even debt peonage.[82]

Debt peonage, as Pete Daniel observes, "flourishes best in a primitive capitalistic economy that is adjusting its labor system." Daniel points to such transitional periods as the abolition of the *encomiendas* in South America and of chattel slavery in North America. In addition to a labor system in transition, he finds peonage resulting from "high illiteracy rates, a rural and isolated environment, an inviolate power structure, and corrupt or corruptible local law-enforcement officers." With the exception of official corruption, all of these elements apply with some degree to Springfield.[83] What the town didn't have, of course, was the *institutionalized* deprivation of disprivileged groups such as Indians or blacks by vagrancy laws, labor-contract statutes, criminal-surety systems, and convict leasing. In the post-Civil War South, the engine to the system of peonage was not paternalistic persuasion, but rather legal enforcement. As Daniel asserts, "The line that divided the cropper from the peon was a thin but crucial one. It depended on the compulsion that forced a man to remain on a plantation year after year," a compulsion provided by sheriffs, constables, local police, justices of the peace, and state legislators. "Peonage occurred," Daniel reports, "only when a planter forbade the cropper to leave the plantation because of debt." If, when the account books were balanced, "the planter told his cropper that he remained in debt and could not move from the plantation, then the system became peonage." Peonage resulted from indebtedness, "but the debtor had to be restrained for the legal definition to be fulfilled." When a peon fled, the creditor called on local law enforcement officials, who would "arrest [the] black laborers, hold them in jail until the planter arrived, and then allow the employer to deal with the prisoners as he would."[84] No such institutionalized collusion between the creditor and the law existed in Springfield. Equally important, the town lacked the general climate of violence, intimidation, and terrorism that provided the crucial extra-legal enforcement of the planter's will in both the post-bellum South and Latin America. Debt peon-

---

[82] Debtors could not expect much protection from colonial courts. As William E. Nelson observes, "Debtors in general were almost powerless" while "Creditors had broad remedies not only against their immediate debtors but against others as well." *Americanization of the Common Law: The Impact of Legal Change on Massachusetts Society, 1760–1830*, Cambridge, Mass., 1975, pp. 42–43.

[83] Pete Daniel, *The Shadow of Slavery: Peonage in the South, 1901–1969*, New York, 1973, p. x. See also William Cohen, "Negro Involuntary Servitude: A Preliminary Analysis," *Journal of Southern History*, 42 (1976), pp. 31–60.

[84] Daniel, *Shadow of Slavery*, pp. 24–25.

age in Springfield, as elsewhere, was a form of manipulating laborers; but John Pynchon called on personal obligation instead of the constable to achieve this end. Peonage in Springfield, as with tenancy and work, was a personal, not institutionalized, experience. Here again the key transitional device from manorial to capitalistic relationships was the patron-client bond. Nothing shows this so vividly as do the contrasts between John Pynchon's treatment of those debtors who were clients and those who were not.

For those men with whom Pynchon had forged a patron-client relationship, indebtedness was restrictive but not destructive; it curbed their political autonomy but it did not drive them under. The account books are replete with instances of long overdue debts. The carpenter Joseph Leonard, for example, owed Pynchon the sum of £98 in 1680. Seven years later the figure had grown to £116, and the creditor expressed his growing impatience but did not threaten or take legal action. In February 1689 the two men made an accounting and found £79 "of old account which hath been long due."[85] Leonard was the most highly skilled joiner in Springfield and was usually the first man Pynchon turned to when the landlord needed new houses constructed. Moreover, a large part of the reason Leonard was so indebted was the annual rent of £10 10s. the carpenter paid for five and a half acres of Pynchon's land in the third division.[86] Leonard, who died with an estate valued at £640, *needed* neither employment nor a lease from Pynchon in order to survive.[87] His skills and his lands gave him sufficient bargaining power. And Pynchon's recognition of this power made it prudent to forestall collection of Leonard's debts for so long. The same was true for the tavern-keeper Nathaniel Ely, whose ordinary served as the courtroom where Pynchon sat as magistrate.[88] Ely, who rented his house and lands from Pynchon for £8 yearly, was indebted to his landlord for more than £130 by 1664. Rather than hectoring Ely or threatening litigation, he allowed the tavern-keeper to get by simply by paying a 5 percent annual interest on the principal.[89] Possibly the most dramatic example of Pynchon's willingness to long defer debt collection was Thomas Cooper. A twenty-term selectman as well as one of Pynchon's fur agents, Cooper was in-

[85] Account Books, 5, pp. 66–67, 532; 6, pp. 62–63.

[86] *Ibid.*, 5, pp. 66–67, 532.

[87] HCPC Rec., 4 (1708–1780), pp. 14–15.

[88] John F. Whicher, "Criminal Procedures before the County Court for Hampshire County, Massachusetts, From 1658 to 1685," unpublished paper, January 6, 1947, CVHM.

[89] Account Books, 3, pp. 108–109.

debted to Pynchon for £1,000 in 1656. But despite the magnitude of the debt, Cooper was allowed to bring it down gradually; he had not fully repaid it by the time Indians killed him in 1675.[90]

For those men who were not clients of Pynchon, however, the consequences of indebtedness were often calamitous. For them, he showed little inclination to long ignore deadlines or forgive a portion of the balance. The choice was either to pay up or forfeit part of their freehold. Many were forced to take the latter route. Between 1655 and 1703, over forty Springfield residents lost a total of some one thousand acres, in addition to houses, mills, and livestock, for debts to Pynchon amounting to £1,134. Many who lost property in this way subsequently rented it back. The unhappy experiences of Jonathan Taylor, Obadiah Miller, and Samuel Marshfield illustrate this process. In October 1656, Taylor's debt to Pynchon stood at £19 19s. and he set his mark to a formal acknowledgment of this sum. Two years later, Taylor's mounting debt compelled him to give his "yoake of steeres" to offset £12 10s. of the balance due. As a replacement for his team Taylor purchased an ancient steer, well past the age when most draft animals had been put out to pasture. Broke, Taylor paid for the animal with a promise of future labor: "Sold to Jonathan Taylor 12½ [-year-old] flax steere for which he Ingages and promises me to reape and shock 2 acres of wheate and to cut one acre of pease when I call for it to be done next harvest and to doe it upon 2 days [notice]." Despite surrendering his oxen, and performing a wide array of tasks for Pynchon—"21 days worke . . . carting dung . . . haymaking . . . 10 days at the mill . . . milking my Cows this yeare 6 weeks"— Taylor failed to reduce his debt. Moreover, on March 10, 1668, he increased his financial dependence on Pynchon by leasing a house and 7½ acres of land. The landlord "Let out to Jonathan Taylor my house (on the west side of the River) and 7 acres and ½ of Ground . . . for 35s. and to repair the house by thatching it and etc. . . . and he is to repair all the fencing."[91]

Two days after signing the house lease Taylor dropped by the smithy, presumably to share a pipe and some conversation with the blacksmith, John Stewart; but he got more than he bargained for. John Pynchon arrived in the shop and straightaway lit into Taylor for non-performance. As the account books relate it: "meeting with Jonathan Taylor at the smith's shop I spake to him to bring in the Indian Corne and the wheate which he promised for the Sugar

[90] *Ibid.*, 1, p. 326; 5, pp. 258–259; HCPC Rec., 1, p. 167.
[91] Account Books, 1, pp. 125–126, 314; 2, pp. 228–229; 3, pp. 174–175.

per Contract: and told him that when he had all which was 2 Months agoe he promised Corne Spedyly and twas tyme now to pay it, which he Granted and so he would bring it in quickly." He then proceeded to admonish Taylor for also allowing his debts to remain unpaid: "I then wished him to pay what he owed me, viz. that per Contract and in old booke and told him it had bin due a great while and now it was tyme to pay it." Taylor agreed that the debt was well past due but "propounded noe way of pay." When the creditor proposed to "take your 4 acres of land which you offered me a while agoe," Taylor replied that he "knew not how to part with it." Pynchon's entry in his account book reveals the precarious state of Taylor's finances: "Noe said I, are you not willing to pay the debt[?] He said he could not doe it till next yeare: said I, I think it tyme you should pay it now, and though you have bin on my debt a long time yet, I will give you £12 for that land; he said he thought it was too little and would not let it goe so, and said he could not tell how to pay me till next yeare."[92]

Returning home with celerity to discuss the family's plight with his wife, Taylor decided that he had no alternative but to give up the land. One week later, Pynchon "Agreed with Jonathan Taylor for his land over the River by my meddow . . . by the black Pond, all which (as he says) it is above 5 acres and ½ for which I am to give him £13 17s. and the use of it this summer coming." The landlord also consented to "give him in 20 pounds of Sugar which he was to have into the bargaine."[93] Taylor continued to rent Pynchon's house and land until his death in 1681. Problems with indebtedness plagued him until the end. By March of 1680 his balance owed to Pynchon stood at £46.[94] Again, as with the earlier debt of £14, this was not an abnormally high sum. Pynchon habitually allowed clients with debts in excess of £100—and in Thomas Cooper's case in excess of £1,000—extraordinary flexibility in the repayment schedules. Not so for Taylor, however. Not having forged the necessary patron-client bond, he continued to forfeit land. The year before he died, Taylor lost an additional seven acres in Chicopee plain for debts of £36.[95] When his estate was probated in 1683, it was valued at £40, only £5 of which was in land. The estate's encumbrances amounted to £47.[96]

[92] *Ibid.*, 3, pp. 174–175.

[93] *Ibid.*; Deed, Jonathan Taylor to John Pynchon, March 22, 1682, Hampden Co. Deeds, Volume AB, pp. 61, 167.

[94] Account Books, 5, p. 53.

[95] Deed, Jonathan Taylor to John Pynchon, March 30, 1698, Hampden Co. Deeds, Volume AB, p. 167.

[96] HCPC Rec., 2, p. 39.

The experiences of Obadiah Miller are reminiscent of those of Jonathan Taylor to a striking degree. Like Taylor he worked as a day-laborer and rented from John Pynchon from the mid-1650s onward. In 1656, in what would be the first of many such accountings, Pynchon "Received by one acre and halfe of meddow" from Miller for debts. Seven years later the creditor wrote that "rests due to mee from Obadiah Miller the sum of Eight Pounds Ten shillings foure pence which is all now due to be paid in wheate at 3s. 6d. [per] bushel." But Miller could not come up with the necessary funds and told Pynchon that "he is unable to pay all this yeare and therefore only engages 20 bushels of wheate this yeare . . . and [the] rest he promises to pay some short tyme after." However, after the projected interval had passed, "he [had] failed of payment so owes me the whole [sum]." Part of Miller's problem resulted from the fact that his work for Pynchon was more than offset by his food purchases from him. In early January 1663, Pynchon wrote that "what worke he did for me this yeare 1662 was set off for corne he had of me." Moreover, in the spring of 1668 Miller decided that it was time for a new house, and he went to see what Pynchon had to offer. The entrepreneur had a frame ready for sale, and he agreed to subcontract the remaining work. On June 27, Pynchon "Sold to Obadiah Miller the Timber for a house frame over the River . . . for which he is to pay me the Sum of £3 10s. And I am to help him toward the getting it done, viz. to procure Thomas Coply to saw it which Obadiah is to pay me for as also I am to Sattisfie John Baker £3 for his worke to frame the house which Obadiah is to repay me."[97]

But even as Miller made plans to move into his new house, the family's indebtedness problems continued to mount. In December of 1665 he lost his "Sixe acres of Land which lys neere the cold Spring Bottom." Pynchon agreed to allow Miller "Liberty for this year to Mow that acre and ½ by my house which I bought of him in case John Henryson doth not hold it and he is Ingaged for this yeare to come to Looke to set up and sufficiently repair all the fencing which belongs to this 6 acres of land." In March 1668, Miller lost nine more acres for debts of £17. A month later, the process continued. Wearied by the accelerating erosion of the family's fortunes, Miller's wife Joanna decided to take matters into her own hands. According to the account book entry: "Goodwife Miller came to mee with her husband and said she was willing I should have the land. But she thought I gave too little, and in further

[97] Account Books, 1, p. 302; 2, pp. 134–135; 3, pp. 178–179; *Springfield Town Recs.*, 2, pp. 605–606.

discourseing and owning my debt to have been long due, she was willing to agree to the sale, if I would allow her 11s. she owes for kersey, which I yielded to, and so both of them were willing, and the price for the land is £18 1s."[98] Such modest favors failed to bring the Millers to solvency and their indebtedness problems became worse, not better. Finally, in 1682, they lost an additional eighty acres and a yoke of oxen to Pynchon "for the debts [of] £54."[99] Left with little more than a few household belongings, the Millers packed these up and departed the town forever.

The most spectacular example of the destructive effects of indebtedness was Samuel Marshfield. Born in England and one of the earliest settlers in Springfield, Marshfield quickly became a prosperous and esteemed member of the community. He served as the town's representative to the General Court for three terms and was a selectman for no less than thirteen years.[100] Something of a jack-of-all-trades, Marshfield earned his livelihood as a merchant, tailor, canoeman, teamster, drover, carpenter, sheep-shearer, smith, and agricultural worker.[101] He also kept the town ordinary from 1660 to 1665.[102] He first became a tenant of John Pynchon in 1665, leasing for varying periods thereafter 9 acres, a 7½-acre lot with an attached orchard, a 3½-acre lot, land in the "Pickle," and plowland over the Agawam River. He also periodically rented a yoke of oxen. By the late 1680s, Marshfield's annual rental payment stood at £7. In an apparent paradox, the number of his leases multiplied as he entered his declining years. Rather than moving from tenancy to freehold, he was doing the reverse. The explanation is found in his indebtedness records.[103]

By 1667, Marshfield's debt to John Pynchon stood at £54 and the creditor called it in. As with Taylor and Miller, the magnitude of the debt—when compared with the sums owed to Pynchon by many of his clients—was in no way excessive. But the flexibility over payment schedules enjoyed by clients did not extend to Marshfield. The creditor demanded immediate payment on pain of forfeiture of all of the debtor's land and housing on the east side of the Connecticut River. Marshfield confessed his inability to pay, and Pynchon thereupon took "his howse and land, viz. all his howsing and all his land on this side of the great River . . . To Cleare

98 *Springfield Town Recs.*, 2, pp. 605–606.
99 Account Books, 5, p. 543.
100 *Pynchon Court Rec.*, p. 381; *Springfield Town Recs.*, 1, pp. 26–39.
101 Account Books, 1, pp. 108, 110; 2, p. 109; 3, p. 111; 6, pp. 188–189.
102 Whicher, "Criminal Procedures," p. 30.
103 Account Books, 1, p. 108; 3, pp. 110–111; 5, pp. 36–37, 471; 6, pp. 188–189.

the debt."[104] Still a man of considerable means because of his property holdings on the west side, Marshfield appeared likely to survive even such a major land forfeiture. But the past was prologue. Two decades later, Marshfield's debts having grown to over £150, Pynchon demanded a similar reckoning. Again Marshfield could not raise the necessary funds and in September of 1686, the creditor took the surety of 124 acres and part ownership in a sawmill: "I accept as followeth: 15 acres of Land in the Medow over Agawam River more or less, 12 acres in the Pikle over the River more or less, 7 acres and ½ by my orchard over the River, 10 acres of Meddow and 10 acres of upland at Nonsuch: 20 acres more or less his due at Enfeild, 50 acres at the falls joining to that Land which I had of William Brookes. His part of the sawmil at Schonunganock . . . with the Saw wholy to be mine."[105] Even this transaction did not extricate Marshfield from the noose of indebtedness. At his death six years later, landless and with total assets of but £66, he still owed John Pynchon £72.[106] The debt was then remanded to Marshfield's son Josiah. Three years later, with an outstanding balance of £23, the creditor offered to abate the amount to £18 if it was paid "within 10 or 20 days."[107]

The lessons of these land forfeitures presumably were not lost on the rest of Springfield's inhabitants. Without a strong, communally oriented town meeting to protect their interests, the best route to survival in the town's perilous economy was a patron-client bond with John Pynchon. The experiences of Taylor, Miller, and Marshfield—and many more like them—could serve as cautionary tales, whether intended as such or not. In the company town that was Springfield, the financial destinies of half the population were sealed over the counter of the Pynchon general store. Those who needed land—and wanted to keep it—had to make an accommodation with John Pynchon. This also applied to those who needed work.

[104] *Ibid.*, 3, p. 111.
[105] *Ibid.*, 6, pp. 188–189, 230–231.
[106] *Ibid.*, 6, p. 188; HCPC Rec., 3, p. 2.
[107] Account Books, 6, pp. 230–231.

- *Chapter 4* -

Work

"You see a man skillful in his craft:
he will serve kings, he will not serve common men"
Proverbs, XXII, 29

FOR MOST of the inhabitants of early Springfield, the process of "getting work" began with a trek to the Pynchon general store. Over half of the town's population at any given time was working a month or longer each year for John Pynchon, and for approximately forty seventeenth-century inhabitants he was their primary source of income. Men worked for Pynchon either by choice or necessity. Those who worked by choice were the skilled artisans—blacksmiths, coopers, tailors, and the like—who found in Pynchon a man eager for their services and well able to pay for them. Those who worked by necessity were the landless laborers or marginal tenant farmers, individuals who were forced to supplement their meager incomes by toiling in Pynchon's fields for sixteen to twenty pence per day.[1]

The necessity for a large and reliable labor force was Pynchon's chief incentive for forming patron-client ties with so many of the town's men. Throughout the seventeenth century, his new fields needed to be cleared, stubbed, and plowed. Likewise, weather permitting, few days passed without the continuous ringing of hammers as a town was formed out of a wilderness. Pynchon's mills needed to be tended, and so did his herds of livestock. When his wheat grew golden in the fields, he needed to be able to count on the labor of some forty-odd reapers during the always hectic days of harvest. Men who owned canoes or oxcarts found Pynchon always in need of their services, hauling goods to and from Enfield falls, carting logs to his sawmills, or gathering dung from the pasture. Those who had a way with animals broke his oxen to the yoke

[1] Still the standard work on labor and wage patterns in early America is Richard B. Morris, *Government and Labor in Early America*, New York, 1946; see also, Carl Bridenbaugh, *The Colonial Craftsman*, New York, 1950.

and his horses to the saddle. Those with sufficient barn space stall-fed his livestock from late November to early March, earning up to twenty shillings per head for their efforts. Finally, the Springfield entrepreneur needed men for his various extractive projects, including lead, iron ore, tar, turpentine, and resin.

While an age profile of John Pynchon's work force would reveal a preponderance of men between the ages of eighteen and thirty, most inhabitants continued to do at least occasional labor for him throughout their productive lives. It was not uncommon for fathers and sons to work side-by-side harvesting Pynchon's crops, clearing his upland, or tending his mills. Occupation patterns, like patterns of tenancy, tended to perpetuate themselves over several generations.[2]

Most work agreements were contracted orally, with payment coming upon completion of the task. Typically these were regularized procedures, with workers approaching Pynchon with similar job requests year after year. A predictable yet flexible system, it allowed the employer and his workers to adjust to the requirements of any particular year. Larger projects that would make a prolonged demand on either a worker's time or Pynchon's resources required written contracts. The same was true for contracts for the performance of highly specialized tasks. Contracts for carpentry work were the ones most often committed to writing. On December 2, 1657, for example, Pynchon "Agreed with Thomas Barber to Build me a Barne over the great River [of] 50 foote long and 24 feete wide with a leantoe, all along the back side." The project was "all to be compleated [by] Harvest next" for which "I am to allow him £21."[3] Similarly, in January 1677 Pynchon contracted with Jonathan and David Morgan "to Build me a house of 24 feet Long [and] 18 feet wide . . . they to doe all the worke from falling to finishing Except the Sawing . . . for which I am to allow and pay them fourteen Pounds; they well clapboarding the whole House ale Timber worke as well as above."[4] Likewise, an agreement signed with Sam Gaines in 1688 stipulated that the carpenter-millwright was "To

---

[2] The Strong family, tanners all, is one such example. In 1671 John Strong, Sr., received £8 3s. for "Taning per agreement (ox hides at 13s. and Cow hides at 8s. apeace) 7 Sole hides at 13s. pce . . . [and] 9 upper leather hides at 8s." His son Returne was credited at various times in John Pynchon's account books for "dressing 13 hides and 2 small ones . . . to 7 hides [and] taning 4 hides and a horse skin [and] by taning 6 hides." Another son, Ebenezer, received payments for "4 hides att 24s. apce, 1 ox hide 36s., the bull hide 27s. [is] £7 19s." Account Books, 3, pp. 205, 209, 219½.

[3] Account Books, 1, p. 176.

[4] *Ibid.*, 5, pp. 384–385.

Build my Mills at Suffeild New and compleate and substantial both Corne mil and Saw mil and Dam for them . . . in all respectes workmanlike done and after the securest manner, I am to allow and pay him the full Sum of Seventy-five Pounds."[5] Agricultural tasks that promised a prolonged expenditure of time also demanded written agreements. In December 1673 Pynchon "Agreed with Richard Waite to Bogg and cleare my meddow on the other side of the hill by the old ditch 8 rod broad."[6] On May 16, 1656, he contracted with Thomas Mirrick "for 30 load of dung, he promised me I should have good dung . . . (as good as any in New England) at 8d. per load."[7]

Pynchon paid his workers both by the day and by the project. Rowland Thomas received £8 2s. 6d. for "63 days worke . . . at 2s. 6d." for "stonning the celler" of the employer's son-in-law Joseph Whiting. But on another occasion he was paid by the load, receiving thirty-six shillings for carting "36 load of stone . . . at 12d." Back on a per diem basis in a subsequent account book entry, Thomas took twenty-seven shillings for "3 days Trimming Trees" and 8½ days "Levelling my ground and goeing after the Mares."[8] For major construction projects, Pynchon sometimes took on workers for up to a year or more at a predetermined salary. On August 27, 1677, he "Agreed with John Artsell . . . [to] serve me one yeare at Stony River about [righting] up my Saw mill setting it to worke sawing and etc., [and] doeing my corne mill." He promised to pay Artsell "Twenty Pounds and let him have Sixe weeks tyme to help out of it on the yeare."[9]

Regardless of the method of calibrating earnings, wages in Springfield—particularly for the unskilled—remained surprisingly low throughout the seventeenth century. Early American labor historians have long contended that wage levels were much higher in the colonies than they were in England. In his authoritative *Government and Labor in Early America*, Richard B. Morris writes that "The colonial workman commanded real wages which exceeded by from 30 to 100 per cent the wages of a contemporary English workman." But without a study of the relative wage levels and living costs in each society, such assertions are not persuasive.[10] More to

[5] *Ibid.*, 6, pp. 271, 273.
[6] *Ibid.*, 5, p. 391.
[7] *Ibid.*, 1, p. 100.
[8] *Ibid.*, 3, p. 197.
[9] *Ibid.*, 5, p. 205.
[10] Morris, *Government and Labor*, p. 45. What comparative data does exist fails to support contentions that American workmen received substantially higher wages.

the point, however, the Pynchon account books reflect low rather than high wage levels throughout the seventeenth century. They fail to support the universally cited contemporary assertion that "labor is deare [in Massachusetts], viz., 2s., and sometimes 2s., 6d. a day for a day labourer."[11] Rarely, in Springfield, did day-laborers average more than eighteen to twenty-four pence for summer work, and fourteen pence or sixteen pence for winter work. Likewise, we have been told that the abortive attempts by the Massachusetts General Court to establish wage and price controls during the decades of the 1630s and 1670s foundered because workers were accustomed to getting much higher wages than the guidelines prescribed—two shillings daily for common laborers, for example. But when wage levels of the 1630s ordinance and the proposed bills of the 1670s are compared with the payment schedules in the Pynchon account books, the Springfield levels are often *below* the standardized rates.[12] Workers in the American colonies did make more than English laborers, but they did so because they worked longer and harder, not because they received higher wages. As the conspicuous absence of the countless English feast days attests, work—not rest— was normative in America.[13]

As James E. Thorold Rogers's exhaustive study of wages and prices in preindustrial England reveals, English laborers during the second half of the 17th century received from twelve to fifteen pence per diem; craftsmen took between two shillings sixpence and three shillings. Day-laborers in Springfield received between eighteen and twenty-four pence for summer work during the same period. Craftsmen normally took between three shillings and four shillings sixpence, depending on their skill level. Because Massachusetts currency was inflated in relation to English currency in the ratio of £125 to £100 for most of the 17th century, the apparently higher wages in the colony, are brought closer to parity if inflation is allowed for. The fact that the Pynchons nearly universally paid wages in country pay (credit for goods and services) instead of specie—which usually exchanged at a rate 10 to 20 percent higher—likewise brings Springfield's wage levels more in line with those in England. James E. Thorold Rogers, *A History of Agriculture and Prices in England*, Oxford, 1887, 5, pp. 668–669, 817; John J. McCusker, *Money and Exchange in America, 1600–1775: A Handbook*, Chapel Hill, 1978, pp. 146–147. From comparisons with Essex County, Massachusetts, the Pynchons' accounts apparently exhibited considerably less fluctuation over time than did prices in the coastal towns; see William I. Davisson, "Essex County Price Trends: Money and Markets in 17th Century Massachusetts," *Essex Institute Historical Collections*, 102 (1967), pp. 144–185; see also Terry Lee Anderson, *The Economic Growth of Seventeenth Century New England: A Measurement of Regional Income*, New York, 1975, pp. 44–81.

[11] *Morris, Government and Labor*, p. 45.

[12] For the wage levels of the 1630s ordinance and the bills of the 1670s, as well as attempts at wage and price controls elsewhere in New England, see Morris, *Government and Labor*, pp. 55–84.

[13] E. P. Thompson, "Time, Work-Discipline, and Industrial Capitalism," *Past and Present*, 38 (1967), pp. 56–97. For a suggestion that the lack of sufficient work

The Pynchon account books show plainly that the settlers were persevering and tenacious in building their community. While, as in any agricultural society, there was always time for sitting in the sun, enjoying a pipe, or stealing a nap, the men and women of Springfield spent more time on the job than off it. Theirs was a frontier society, and the demands of building, cultivating, and repairing were unrelenting. The destruction of some fifty-odd buildings during King Philip's War merely called for a redoubling of these daily efforts. By way of contrast, historians such as Edward P. Thompson have emphasized the irregular work habits of the contemporary English population, with "alternate bouts of intense labour and of idleness [common] wherever men were in control of their working lives." He asserts that "Saint Monday . . . appears to have been honoured almost universally wherever small-scale, domestic, and outwork industries existed."[14] As the author points out, the reason for the working population's irregularity was lack of opportunities as well as lack of incentive. Richard Hakluyt observed in 1584 that the poor laws and proclamations against vagabonds had failed "for want of sufficient occasion of honest employment."[15] Gregory King's estimate that half the families in England did not earn enough to support themselves (without public relief) reveals the severity of the problem of underemployment. As Joyce Appleby asserts, "Capitalism required unrelenting personal effort in the market place" and could only work "if the poor, like the rich, were converted to possessive individualism and economic rationality." The laboring poor of England needed new opportunities *and* new aspirations. They needed more days in which to work than the disjointed English economy allowed them, and they needed to adapt the notion of expandable spending. In short, they had to experience "the propulsive power of envy, emulation, love of luxury,

opportunities provoked the massive emigration of indentured servants from early 17th-century England, see James Horn, "Servant Emigration to the Chesapeake in the Seventeenth Century," in Thad W. Tate and David L. Ammerman, eds., *The Chesapeake in the Seventeenth Century*, New York, 1979, pp. 51–95, esp. pp. 75–80. See also Edmund S. Morgan, "The Labor Problems at Jamestown, 1607–1618," in T. H. Breen, ed., *Shaping Southern Society: The Colonial Experience*, New York, 1976, pp. 17–31. For a general consideration of the relationship between preindustrial and industrial patterns of work, see Herbert G. Gutman, *Work, Culture, and Society in Industrializing America*, New York, 1976, esp. pp. 3–78; and Daniel T. Rogers, *The Work Ethic in Industrial America, 1850–1920*, Chicago, 1978, pp. 1–29.

[14] Thompson, "Time, Work-Discipline, and Industrial Capitalism," *Past and Present* (1967), pp. 73–74.

[15] Richard Hakluyt, "Discourse on Western Planting," in E.G.R. Taylor, ed., *The Writings and Correspondence of the Two Richard Hakluyts*, London, 1935, 2, p. 234.

vanity, and vaulting ambition."[16] But in England the idea of universal economic rationality always came to grief over the shortage of available land. England was not a frontier society, and few day-laborers or small craftsmen could realistically aspire to become freeholders or even husbandmen. Saving their meager wages would not lead to land ownership, so they patronized the grog shops instead.

In the American colonies, however, aspirations toward land ownership were not chimerical for laborers—even in such restrictive environments as seventeenth-century Springfield or Virginia.[17] As the Pynchon account books reveal, the laboring men and women of early Springfield hoped one day to become freeholders. The road to this goal was often fraught with peril and sudden reverses and chronic indebtedness always threatened to reduce the labors of a lifetime to ashes. But the vision lingered nonetheless, and the prospect of working for themselves made the town's laborers willing, even eager, to work for others. For those who were marginal, getting ahead meant getting work.[18]

[16] Joyce Appleby, "Ideology and Theory: The Tension between Political and Economic Liberalism in Seventeenth-Century England," *American Historical Review*, 81 (1976), pp. 500, 505, 515.

[17] For the charnel house that was early Virginia, see Edmund S. Morgan, *American Slavery-American Freedom: The Ordeal of Colonial Virginia*, New York, 1976, pp. 71–179.

[18] For a description of the negative attitudes toward work found in an environment with exceedingly limited opportunities for upward mobility, see David D. Gilmore, *The People of the Plain: Class and Community in Lower Andalusia*, New York, 1980, pp. 54–56. The author points out that in the rigidly stratified agricultural towns of southern Spain, "work is a curse." The laborers "view work not as a means for social mobility or personal satisfaction, but as a hateful burden to be avoided at all costs." This attitude arises "from the fact that trabajo [work] is thought to produce not wealth, but only *miseria*, or poverty; that is, the more you work, the poorer you become." As the townspeople explain to their American visitor: "if a man must work to live, then obviously, he owns no land and is thus dependent upon the vagaries of agrarian wage-labor. This dependency, in turn, means that this unfortunate is necessarily unemployed for half the year. Informants conclude, with unshakably circular logic, that when this man *does* work, his wages are used only to pay off old debts; he can never save and thus improve himself. The proceeds from work are immediately depleted and the round of debt and impoverishment begins anew. Or, as the laborers say proverbially, 'lo comido por lo servido'—'No sooner served than eaten.' The laborers express their intense hatred for work succinctly in statements like the following:
'The only man who *doesn't* earn money is the laborer!'
'The only way you *can't* get rich is by working!' " p. 55.
The 17th-century Springfield economy, of course, possessed all these perils and more. But it also offered real possibilities for advancement as well, a small but psychologically critical distinction.

The importance of work in Springfield was reflected in a contractually oriented legal system. For labor, as with land, the town adopted a philosophy of economic individualism. Court decisions in Springfield call into question recent claims that judges and juries in colonial Massachusetts did not order compliance for non-performance of contractual obligations.[19] Both the magistrate's court and the Hampshire County court systematically enforced contractual rights. Surprisingly, plaintiffs in special assumpsit cases did *not* have to plead performance (show that they had already fulfilled their part of the agreement by paying a consideration) to recover damages for either misfeasance or nonfeasance. All that needed to be demonstrated was a witnessed oral contract or a written instrument (covenant). In Springfield throughout the seventeenth century, a bargain made was a bargain enforced. Both judges and juries (the latter used with surprising infrequency in contract disputes) ordered that the terms of the agreement be upheld. Notions of a "just price" did not invalidate a bargain once made. In some cases, the court even went so far as to order specific performance for personal service contracts (believed unenforceable in colonial America). On April 2, 1655, Thomas Cooper brought an action against John Bliss for "non-performance of a bargayne of fetchinge the said Thomas some fencinge stuffe." Despite Bliss's denial, the commissioners ruled that "synce the bargayne is proved, the said John Bliss shall carry this fencinge stuffe soe soon as the way is fitt for cartinge, and whereas the tyme is come that fences should be sett up; it was adjudged that John Bliss should be liable, to pay such damages as accrew for want of the fencing beinge done, because he neglected to cart the stuffe when there was convenient opportunity to cart it."[20] Likewise, in 1660 Hugh Dudley brought suit against Thomas Mirrick for "not performinge Covenante in plowinge up ½ an acre of new ground, which should have been done in May last . . . the said Hugh pleadinge great damages and still expectinge the ploughinge of the ground." After hearing the plaintiff, commissioners John Pynchon and Samuel Chapin ruled that "Thomas Mirack was adjudged to have damnified the said Hugh ten shillings, which he is to pay him, and also to plow up the ½ acre of ground by the first of May next."[21]

In a still more involved case of specific performance litigated in May 1661, Henry Burt complained "against John Henryson for

[19] Nelson, *Americanization of the Common Law*, p. 6; and Nelson, *Dispute and Conflict Resolution in Plymouth County, Massachusetts, 1725–1825*, Chapel Hill, 1981.

[20] *Pynchon Court Rec.*, p. 236.

[21] *Ibid.*, pp. 246–247.

not paying of Three bushells of wheate according to promise for spinning and knitting of Stockens." Henryson's defense was that "the debt which he owes Henry Burt is but 10s., and this he ingaged 2 bushells of wheate towards it and noe more: and he hath paid Henry Burt in worke so that Henry Burt owes him 8s. for worke." Plaintiff Burt admitted "his owing him 8s. which says he John Henryson was to have a shurt cloth for and John owning it is adjudged to take the shurt cloth." But for the remainder of the balance due Burt, commissioners Elizur Holyoke and John Pynchon ordered specific performance: "for the other 10s., John Henryson is adjudged to pay Henry Burt Two bushells of wheate (7s.) and Three shillings in a day and halfe worke."[22]

The dispositive nature of the bargain is also revealed by those cases in which it could *not* be proved. In September of 1680 joiner John Pope complained "against Leiutenant Thomas Stebbins for Taking him off from a peice of Joinery worke and promising him sattisfaction, which he now refuses: to the Damadge of said Pope 39s." But as magistrate Pynchon's investigations found "noe profe being made either of Damage nor yet of any promise made by Leiutenant Stebbins to make him sattisfaction," he ruled in the defendant's favor.[23]

Courts likewise enforced penalties for exceeding deadlines. In one such case, the commissioners ordered forfeiture payments for a delay of eleven days in the fulfillment of Thomas Mirrick's plowing obligations. On September 14, 1660, "John Lamb complaynes against Thomas Mirack for non-performance of a bargayne of ploughing for him the said John Lamb being bound thereto by Bill under penalty of 2s. per day for every day the land should be unploughed after the tyme prefixt in the Bond: John Lamb pleaded for the forfeiture mentioned in the said Bill or bond for that the Land was not ploughed till 11 dayes after the tyme limitted in the Bill." After considering the case, "The Commissioners apprehendinge the lateness in the yeere that the land was ploughed, and that the penalty mentioned in the bond was not unreasonable they adjudged that Thomas Mirack should pay John Lamb 20s. damage and 3s. 4d. for the entry of the action."[24]

While Mirrick was a plowman, most litigants involved in non-

---

[22] *Ibid.*, pp. 252–253.

[23] *Ibid.*, pp. 294–295.

[24] *Ibid.*, p. 247. It is not clear from the judgment what the court meant by "reasonable" in the *Lamb* case. From the context of the commissioners' other decisions, it is likely that it was a "liquidated damages" provision, not consideration that was questioned. I am grateful to Rayman L. Solomon for this observation.

performance suits were skilled artisans. On April 27, 1674, the carpenter David Morgan complained "against Charls Ferry for not weaving linnen yarne into cloth according to agreement: David affirming That Charls Ingaged to pay him for worke in building Charls a shop: Thirty shillings in weaving cloth, which now Charls refuseth to doe." After weighing the evidence, the court ruled "That Charls Ferry make good the Thirty shillings in weaving or otherwise pay him Thirty shillings, in Current Pay: together with Costs of Court, 3s. 6d."[25]

Although weaver Ferry lost this case, he, like all the town's artisans, depended for his livelihood on the assurance that the court would consistently order compliance.[26] In a similar case in 1680, the joiner John Pope complained against Nicholas Rust "for not paying five shillings etc: Pope declaring the debt to be for worke making tuggs etc. of cedar to serve instead of Cork for a net: which Pope's Servant says he wrought halfe a day about it: besides his Master turning the wood etc: which Pope affirmes to be about 3 quarters of a day." After his deliberations, magistrate Pynchon declared that "I find for the Plantiff five shillings and Costs of Court, only the small Bass fish which Pope had is to be accounted toward the five shillings."[27]

The most compelling evidence of the highly commercialized nature of work in early Springfield was the prominence of manufacturing-productive enterprises. Rather than simply being agriculturalists, over two-thirds of the town's men possessed some kind of manual skill, ranging from such highly demanding crafts as blacksmithing to the relatively accessible trade of the cobbler. The presence of so many skilled artisans in Springfield, of course, was no accident. Conceiving their settlement as a commercial enterprise, both William and John Pynchon actively recruited such men whenever possible. The maturation of the Pynchons' marketing enterprises after midcentury attracted still more skilled workers to the community. Many of these individuals displayed competence in several crafts, although usually only formally apprenticed in one. Most work careers included two or three and sometimes more areas of occupational specialization. Depending on how remunerative was a man's principal skill, or how many acres he held under cultivation, he supplemented his income by working as many days at more pedestrian tasks as was necessary.

Overall, using a base figure of £50 as the minimum annual in-

[25] *Pynchon Court Rec.*, p. 279.
[26] Grant Gilmore, *The Ages of American Law*, New Haven, 1977, pp. 44–48.
[27] *Pynchon Court Rec.*, p. 294.

come necessary to feed a family of seven without recourse to large-scale farming, one-sixth of Springfield's men were able to live by their craft alone, and another one-sixth were able substantially to supplement their income by their craft. If their per diem wages are multiplied by a 180-day work-year, the following craftsmen would have earned £50 or more: millers, blacksmiths, millwrights, tanners, house carpenters, coopers, resin workers, brickmakers, shoemakers, and tailors. Those workers who could have supplemented their income by yearly wages of up to £25 included: stonemasons, canoemen, teamsters, shinglers, sackmakers, cobblers, sowgelders, and slaughterers. Finally, those who earned from between £15 (the average yearly income for day-laborers) to £25 included: plowmen, stubbers, ditchers, reapers, and mill hands. To see these figures in the perspective of an exclusively agricultural economy, the annual income produced by raising twelve acres of wheat (based on optimum yields of twenty-five bushels per acre, and payments of 3 shillings 6 pence per bushel) would have been just over £50. Similar yields from barley or oats (at 2 shillings 4 pence per bushel) would have produced an income of £35.[28]

In Springfield's diversified economy, therefore, the labor involved in food growing was only one—and not always the dominant—form of work. Usually, more days per year were spent on farm formation, manufacturing, or commercial activities. As economic historian William N. Parker points out: "Even without a draft-animal and without wild game supplement, the labor of growing food for a family on a diet of rude abundance in corn meal, hog meat, vegetables, and poultry could not have occupied more than thirty working days a year for a frontier family. The rest of the time was spent in the tasks of farm formation, in hunting and fishing, for the men, and food preparation and preservation, for

[28] An intriguing—and fundamental—question relates to the proportion of a family's income ultimately consumed as food. Presently, as Kenneth J. Arrow points out, "in the poorer less-developed countries, roughly two-thirds of income goes for expenditures on food." The data from the Pynchon account books suggests (in very fragmentary form) that such a breakdown would not be out of line for 17th-century Springfield. The town's socioeconomic structure, likewise, appears to accord with Arrow's assertions that in agricultural societies a family's standard of living is usually shaped by the distribution of wealth, not the availability of food. See "Why People Go Hungry," *The New York Review of Books* (July 15, 1982), pp. 24–26; see also (for the source of Arrow's statistical formulations) T. T. Poleman, "Quantifying the Nutrition Situation in Developing Countries," *Food Research Institute Studies*, 18 (1981), p. 25; and Amartya Sen, *Poverty and Famines: An Essay on Entitlement and Deprivation*, Oxford, 1982.

the frontier women."[29] And in highly commercialized towns like Springfield, he might have added, manufacturing enterprises.

MANUFACTURING WORKERS

Manufacturing workers in seventeenth-century Springfield fell into four categories, each of which will be considered in turn. (1) heavy artisans: millers, millwrights, blacksmiths, tanners, and resin workers; (2) light artisans: shoemakers, tailors, and weavers; (3) building trades: house carpenters, shinglers, brickmakers, and stonemasons; and (4) sea trades: coopers and canoemen.

Heavy Artisans

Millers were the most important artisans in the development of early American communities. Because of the savings in labor offered by mills, their presence in a community could make the difference between success and failure. In the areas of both food preparation and farm formation, water-powered mills could cut labor expenditures as much as tenfold. Although rarely more than a few horsepower, waterwheels supplied the motive power for sawing planks, milling flour and sugar, forging iron, tanning hides, and carding wool. Most important were the gristmills. As we have seen, the destruction of Springfield's gristmill during King Philip's War provoked many inhabitants openly to consider quitting the town. The laborious process of using pestle and mortar to grind corn for a family's daily bread took a minimum of two hours' work, and the final product was often unappetizing. Only slightly less necessary for a community's well-being was the sawmill. Water-powered sawmills provided the uniformly flat planks that allowed settlers expeditiously to frame their houses and install level and durable floors. The presence of mills brought new members to a community and kept old ones from leaving. As a recent study by Louis C. Hunter points out, watermills allowed colonists to shift from subsistence to market-oriented agriculture and "often became the entering wedge of a slowly emerging market economy."[30]

Springfield's most successful miller was Anthony Dorchester. By mastering his craft, and working for John Pynchon, he rose from

[29] Parker, "American Farmer,"p. 183.

[30] Louis C. Hunter, *A History of Industrial Power in the United States, 1780–1930*, Volume 1: *Waterpower in the Century of the Steam Engine*, Charlottesville, Va., 1979, p. 41; Mark Rose, review of *Waterpower*, in "Watermills and the History of American Technology," *Reviews in American History*, 9 (1981), pp. 34–39; William Fox, Bill Brooks, and Jane Tyrwhitt, *The Mill*, Boston, 1976; Account Books, 5, p. 509.

landless laborer to a position of substantial wealth. When he died in 1683, Dorchester left an estate valued at £436, a not uncommon sum for an early American miller.[31] He negotiated the first of his many mill contracts with the Pynchon family in the early 1650s. On February 10, 1653, John Pynchon and his brother-in-law Elizur Holyoke "agreed with Anthony Dorchester for the Tole of the Mill for a yeare . . . He is to allow us Thirteene Pounds for our Share of the Tole of the Mill, the which Thirteene Pounds he is to pay us in such Corne as he grinds: quarterly he is to pay it: he is to maintaine all Coggs and Rounds fit for grinding and to leave the Mill in as good repair as he found it." Because the grain Pynchon intended to export downriver constituted such a large proportion of the total amount ground, Dorchester's contract included a proviso for rating the cost of grinding it: "This thirteen Pound he is to pay us besides in valuation to what Corne the Plantation grinds: what percent corne I may grind into meale to Send out of Towne: he is to allow us half the Tole of that besides, and so Hee [is] to have half the profit of such corne according as I may agree with him for grinding it." The provisions evidently were satisfactory to Dorchester, as he took the initiative in renewing the contract the next year. Pynchon wrote in his account book that "Anthony Dorchester desires we would accept of £13 10s. for our share of the Toll of the Mill for this yeare 1654 which we yeilded to." During the early 1660s, the gristmill rent was raised to £18, where it remained until the destruction of the mill during the 1675 Indian attack. Dorchester also paid twenty-five shillings yearly for the land on which the mill was situated.[32]

The skills of an experienced miller were as considerable as they were varied. He monitored the density of his grinding, and likewise judged the density and content of the grain, which varied according to the wetness of the harvest and the manner in which it was threshed and winnowed. Moreover, Pynchon's requirement that Dorchester "maintaine all Coggs and Rounds fit for grinding" meant that he had to master the complicated mechanisms of the water-powered mill. Like all colonial gristmills, Pynchon's was built next to a small tributary stream and included that traditional nexus of dam, head- and tailrace, wheelpit, shafting, and gearing. The dam was constructed by piling up boulders, stumps, earth, and planks in the streambed. An undershot waterwheel powered the large wooden cranks that rotated the grinding stones. The horizontal shaft of the

[31] HCPC Rec., 2, pp. 17–18.
[32] Account Books, 1, pp. 128–129, 296–297; 3, pp. 105, 252; 5, pp. 132, 352–353.

wheel intersected with a bevel gear inside the mill that transmitted its power to the millstones. Grinding surfaces were of stone, whether the substance to be ground was grain, malt, bark, or flaxseed. Mills in the Connecticut Valley used red sandstone, generally from quarries on Mount Tom (ten miles north of Springfield center). The gears and all other working parts of the mill were lubricated by applications of sheep's tallow. The mill's wooden wheels were protected from ice and the elements by being enclosed in a small one-story building. Operations could be interrupted by flooding, drought, ice, or a collapsed dam, as well as by mechanical malfunction. When things went well, Dorchester could count on producing as many as twenty barrels of flour each week.[33]

Because the peak demand periods for gristmills came in the fall and those on sawmills in the spring, Dorchester also occasionally leased one of John Pynchon's sawmills. He paid £26 in 1673 to hold a gristmill and sawmill simultaneously.[34] The sawmill Dorchester rented was similar in appearance to the gristmill, but it was a good deal more complicated to operate. Seventeenth-century sawmills employed a reciprocating saw, in which the saw blade was fastened to a vertical, sash-like framework. The axle of the undershot waterwheel turned a crank attached to a connecting rod (the "pitman") that moved the saw frame up and down with each revolution. A connecting wheel powered the sliding carriage that pushed the log against the saw. (In more primitive sawmills, this was done by means of a large elastic pole.) In Springfield the races for sawmills and gristmills alike consisted of long trenches dug down from the dammed-up portion of the stream.[35] The tasks of keeping the races clear of debris and the dams in repair kept John Pynchon's day-laborers at work long hours in all kinds of weather. When things went smoothly, experienced tenders like Dorchester could saw five thousand feet of pine boards during an average

[33] Dorothy Hartley, *Lost Country Life*, New York, 1979, pp. 144, 188; Anthony F. C. Wallace, *Rockdale*, New York, 1980, pp. 14, 120, 131; Victor S. Clark, *History of Manufactures in the United States*, New York, 1929, 1, pp. 174–178; Account Books, 1, p. 128; 5, pp. 395, 518–519. When Anthony Dorchester finished grinding the grain into flour, he bagged it up in sacks made by John Barber. At various times in 1670, Pynchon paid Barber for "61 yards ½ yard which you allow in of Sacking at 2s. per yard which you have made into 20 sacks and allow the making into the Baragin [all is] £6 2s." and "By 77 yards of Sacking made into 25 bags [all is] £7 14s." In November 1676 Pynchon paid him 16 shillings 6 pence for "making 40 Baggs." Barber used part of his income from sackmaking to lease "5 acres at Cold Spring Bottom" at an annual rent of 30 shillings. Account Books, 3, p. 295; 5, pp. 43, 292–293.

[34] Account Books, 5, p. 352.

[35] Fox, Brooks, Tyrwitt, *The Mill*, pp. 44–48; Clark, *History of Manufactures*, 1, pp. 175–176; Account Books, 3, pp. 75, 107, 147, 160, 185.

week's work. The toll normally charged each customer was one-twelfth of the boards sawn.[36]

Throughout his association with Pynchon, Dorchester performed a myriad of timber-related activities. Account book entries during the early 1660s credit Dorchester for "your selfe and [son] John [10 days] Sawing . . . sawing for my Cider howse . . . 950 boards at 7s. . . . 400 of Boards." In 1666 he contracted to cart all the timber needed for a new sawmill being built by two of Pynchon's carpenters. The owner "Agreed with Goodman Dorchester . . . to cart the Timber for the Saw Mill; he is to cart al the Timber [that the carpenters] shall need . . . for all which I am to allow him £4 15s." And in January 1677, Pynchon paid Dorchester £7 for "sawing and getting Timber for my grist mill."[37]

The watermills utilized by Anthony Dorchester were constructed by one of the several millwrights periodically employed by John Pynchon. Millwrights were the prototypical mechanicians—those who alone carried and transmitted industrial skills until the separation of design from the manual arts in the mid-nineteenth century. Masters of the hydrologic cycle, they also combined the skills of carpenter, smith, mason, and surveyor.[38] Isaac Gleason was the most frequently utilized of Pynchon's millwrights. On April 2, 1684, Pynchon paid him for "the Running geare for my Mill [at] £10." Three years later, the owner "Agreed with Isack Gleason . . . that he is to Build me a house over my mill 25 foote long and 20 foote wide [for] £11 and some land." Gleason was also called in when the mill broke down. In 1683 Pynchon paid him 26 shillings for "worke at my Mill this Spring . . . mending the water wheele [and] 2 days worke about the Cog wheele." On other occasions, Pynchon credited the millwright for "25 days . . . at my Mill (at 3 shillings 6 pence daily) . . . 8 days at the mill at 4s. 6d." In one year, Gleason earned £9 7s. "for worke about my Saw Mill at Schoaungonick."[39] Another millwright, Zachariah Field of Northampton, was the man who supplied Pynchon with his millstones. After hewing the stones, the craftsman cut the radial flanges with a specially shaped stone adze. For a good pair of grinding stones, he earned between £20 and £25. Early in the 1670s, Pynchon paid Field for "making a pair of Millstones and delivering them at my mill for £21."[40]

After millers and millwrights, blacksmiths were the heavy artisans

[36] Account Books, 5, p. 352.

[37] *Ibid.*, 2, pp. 129–130, 137; 3, p. 85; 5, p. 353; William Pynchon Account Book, pp. 221, 272.

[38] Wallace, *Rockdale*, pp. 232–233.

[39] Account Books, 5, pp. 470–471, 518–519; 6, p. 221.

[40] *Ibid.*, 3, p. 223.

most highly prized in early New England communities. Springfield's first blacksmith, John Stewart, came to the town after he and his fellow Covenanter Scots were captured at the Battle of Dunbar in 1650.[41] The victorious Cromwellians sent the captives to Massachusetts as indentured servants and, as Stewart's contract identified him as a blacksmith, John Pynchon bought it soon thereafter. The two men struck a bargain for Stewart's eventual freedom but he failed to repay the £30 compensation according to schedule. Pynchon then consented to accept repayment in the form of a yearly work allocation: "I agreed with John Stewart to allow me yearly 12s. in smithy worke for three years which is for my staying so long for that £30 which is due to me for payment for releasing him from my service. And he . . . consented and promised to allow me for Three years, Twelve shillings per yeare in mending and making of Iron worke."[42]

No town could do without a blacksmith and, while Stewart may have grieved for the glens and moors of his native land, he found in Springfield a community eager for his services. A virtuoso among craftsmen, the blacksmith combined the talents of metallurgist and artist along with simple brute strength. As a nineteenth-century parents' directory to the professions asserts, "theirs is a laborious business, which chiefly consists in the management of the fire, the hammer, and the file." The blacksmith's tools, as this tripartite division suggests, were separated into three working areas. The first was the hearth, complete with bellows, water trough, shovels, tongs, rake, and poker. Second was the anvil, with its array of sledges, tongs, swages, cutters, hammers, and chisels. Third came the shoeing box, with its horseshoes, files, rasp, and knives.[43] Stewart rented most of his tools from Pynchon, including "1 greate Anvill, 1 great hand hammer . . . 1 left hand hammer . . . an Iron to imbritch guns . . . 3 great Tongs, 3 pair of Tongs, 1 chissell, 7 Punchers . . . a steele drill, one small chest with a good lockey there . . . a spring lock, and 21 pairs of horseshoes."[44] The smith worked with charcoal iron, named after the fuel used in the forging furnace. The quality of the charcoal iron depended upon the quality of the ore and the skillfulness with which the iron was extracted

[41] Maurice Ashley, *The Greatness of Oliver Cromwell*, London, 1962, pp. 246–258; Antonia Fraser, *Royal Charles: Charles II and the Restoration*, New York, 1979, pp. 93–94.

[42] Account Books, 1, p. 230.

[43] Henry J. Kauffman, *Early American Ironware, Cast and Wrought*, New York, 1966, pp. 51–79; quotation is found on p. 53.

[44] Account Books, 2, p. 283.

from the ore. Usually, ore was mined from soft surface deposits of bog iron (from areas adjacent to swamps) by means of pick and shovel. Even with the best ore, the limitations of the refining and rolling processes gave the iron an imperfect, fibrous texture. To compensate for this condition, the blacksmith heated the iron in the forge and then hammered it out on the anvil. This "drawing-out" process would then be repeated, increasing the iron bar's length or width by means of a cross-pein hammer. Additional tasks included upsetting (decreasing the length of a bar and hammering it flat) and punching (for decorative purposes or for joining together pieces of iron). The all-important plow chains were made by a process known as "collaring." This was done by wrapping a heated band of iron around two smaller pieces in order to join them together.[45]

The most common products made by seventeenth-century smiths like Stewart were plows, chains, harrows, horseshoes, pig rings, hearth utensils (andirons, trammels, tongs, cranes, skillets, pots, and skewers), door hinges, latches, and candlestands. One of Stewart's most frequent tasks in Springfield was to ring all swine above three months old in order to prevent them from rooting up crops. This duty involved a twice-weekly excursion through the community during the planting season in order to find any unrung pigs. Likewise, when the town needed "a lock 6s. and bolt 18d. and plate 6d. for the lock for the meeting house and keyes and cotters for the bell . . . hookes and hinges for the Meeting house windows," or "a branding iron" or "irony for the pound," it turned to Stewart.[46] The quality of his work must have pleased his fellow citizens, for in 1659 the town meeting voted that "The Smith's shop [shall be] given to John Stewart as his own forever."[47]

But, in comparison to the volume of work he performed for John Pynchon, Stewart's income for services done for the town remained secondary. Not until the mid-1660s did Stewart fully repay Pynchon the £30 owed for his release from service.[48] From the late 1650s onward, his credits for "smithy work" for the Springfield leader became progressively larger. In April 1654, Pynchon paid him £3 14s. for "Smithery worke and some few days about other worke and by smithery work for the mill." From earlier levels of between £3 and £6 annually (in addition to the work for his

[45] Kauffman, *Early American Ironware*, p. 55; *Springfield Town Recs.*, 2, pp. 347–348.
[46] *Springfield Town Recs.*, 1, pp. 216–217, 252–253, 366, 391, 408, 427.
[47] *Ibid.*, 1, p. 261.
[48] Account Books, 1, pp. 230–231.

freedom dues), Stewart's labor credits increased by 1664 to £11 for "Smithery worke for my mill and other work," and in 1667 Stewart earned £19 for "worke as in his booke." In 1671 he received £8 for smithery work for Pynchon as well as payments of £11 for labor performed for his son John and son-in-law Joseph Whiting. In 1677 Pynchon wrote in his account book that he had "Received by worke, all as in Goodman Stewart's Booke . . . the whole is £20 4s. 1d." Between 1680 and 1682 Stewart performed labor worth £13.[49]

Dependent on each other, Pynchon and Stewart forged patron-client ties that allowed the blacksmith to defer but not prevent forfeiture of his lands and housing. In November 1663 Stewart owed his former master £23 and "for the Payment . . . [Stewart] doth for my security formaly Ingage and make over to me his howse and orchard and lot . . . also a Lot of foure acres over the great River . . . which I am to have in case he pay me not this Sum of £23 2s. 4d. . . . within a yeare or Two."[50] As with other clients, Pynchon allowed Stewart an extension of the default date, but it was to no avail. In February 1670, five years after the original forfeiture date, he took formal possession of Stewart's "howse and all his land in Springfield . . . so I cross [out] his account." He allowed the blacksmith "Liberty to Live in the house till midsumer." Stewart thereupon secured a leasehold from Pynchon, after agreeing to "stub cleare and bring to Mowing about an acre and ½ or 2 acres of land . . . [part of which is] Routy high weeds and stubs, he to cleare it and bring it . . . to be mowing meddow and for so doing, he is to have the use of it 3 yeares now coming . . . and then to leave it."[51] Largely as a result of the volume of smithy work performed for Pynchon, Stewart was able to right himself financially. When he died in 1691, he left an estate valued at £225.[52] In an earlier petition to Governor Sir Edmund Andros seeking compensation for an impressed horse, the then bed-ridden Stewart emphasized that he had "a trade which might afford him a comfortable living." He told the governor that "God [had] bestowed some small estate [on him] . . . whilst he gave him ability to labor."[53]

After blacksmithing, the most recondite and technologically sophisticated of the heavy artisanal crafts was tanning. Making leather out of animal hides was an exceedingly laborious, time-consuming, and often unpredictable process and men experienced in this trade

[49] Ibid., 1, p. 231; 3, p. 137; 5, pp. 91, 407.
[50] Ibid., 2, p. 282.
[51] Ibid., 3, p. 137.
[52] HCPC Rec., 1, p. 273.
[53] Springfield Town Recs., 1, pp. 64–65.

were hard to come by. Communities, accordingly, spared few efforts in trying to attract tanners to settle in their midst, as a Springfield town meeting resolution of 1684 reveals. The inhabitants voted to give Thomas Sweatman a generous land grant "because they would accommodate themselves with such a tradesman as he is (viz. a dresser of leather)." The necessary equipment for tanning consisted of a number of wooden vats or boxes which were countersunk in the ground near a stream, and similar vats above ground for liming. A small lean-to or shed was used for a beam house. Bark was crushed at the rate of half a cord a day, usually by means of alternate wooden and stone wheels drawn around a fifteen-foot circular trough. Connecticut Valley tanners used sumac or the bark of hemlock as the main tanning agent, in contrast to the superior oak bark used in the southern colonies. As the Pynchon account books reveal, most of the leather produced by Springfield tanners was used to make shoes and breeches (the archetypal buckskin breeches of frontier lore).[54]

Springfield's first tanner, Griffith Jones, arrived in the town from his native Wales in the mid-1640s and immediately went to work for William Pynchon as a field hand. Presumably familiar with the tanner's craft from an earlier apprenticeship, he now worked to build up enough capital to establish his own tannery. By the early 1660s, this was accomplished and Jones began operation. The early income he derived from his craft suggests how well a skilled tanner could do in Springfield. In February of 1663 John Pynchon credited Jones £14 16s. for "Tanning 16 ox hides at 14s. and 9 Cow hides at 8s."[55] Needing leather both for local consumption and for export downriver, Pynchon could be counted upon to buy virtually all the hides Jones could tan.[56] The artisan's future appeared secure. The difficult days of field laboring were behind him, the tanning vats and sheds were fully operational, and he had mastered the rudiments of his craft. But Jones had neglected to build an equally important form of self-protection, patron-client ties with Pynchon, and this indiscretion eventually cost him the tannery.

In the early 1660s, Jones's indebtedness to Pynchon stood at £53 and Pynchon demanded immediate payment. The debtor could come up with only £18, and Pynchon refused to allow a further extension of the deadline. On April 8, 1663, he took "the howse and Lot and orchard all togither with the Tanhouse, Tan vats etc.,

[54] *Ibid.*, 2, pp. 263–264; Account Books, 2, p. 173; Clark, *History of Manufactures*, 1, p. 167; Russell, *A Long, Deep Furrow*, p. 175.

[55] Account Books, 2, p. 173; William Pynchon Account Book, pp. 110, 211–212.

[56] Account Books, 2, p. 173; 3, pp. 209, 219½.

that Lot as also a Lot of Three acres in the muxy meddow and also a woodlot of 4 acres and Likewise a Lot in the Plaine of 7 acres and ½. Togither with a yearling calfe I take all at £35 9s." Although he agreed to "promise that if I dispose not of it, I shall [allow Jones] the use of Tan vats if he please," Pynchon sold the house and homelot to Samuel Terry six weeks later, and in November he sold the tannery itself to Reice Bedortha for £15.[57] After the forfeiture of his house, land, and tannery, Jones reverted to his former status as a day-laborer for Pynchon, doing field work, mill work, and stringing wampum. In addition, he managed to purchase an £8 share in one of Pynchon's sawmills. Through these efforts he established a modicum of financial security. When he died in 1676, Jones's estate was valued at £119, and his outstanding debts to Pynchon were calculated at £24.[58]

Strikingly similar in technique to tanning was resin, tar, and turpentine manufacture. During the 1690s, John Pynchon decided to exploit Springfield's abundant supply of pine trees to produce naval stores. For those willing to go about the arduous and tedious processes needed to produce these substances, the work offered considerable profits. Tar kilns consisted of a pile of corded pitch pine knots, built on a clay-bottomed floor. The floor was built on an incline to drain off the tar into wooden barrels sunk into the ground. The pile was covered with either turf or dirt (as in making charcoal). Turpentine would then be distilled from the tar, and usually commanded a price twice as high as the parent material.[59]

The blacks Roco and Sue were among those most actively involved in naval stores production. Both workers came to Springfield as slaves. The date of their arrival in the community remains problematical. There were slaves in the Connecticut Valley as early as 1657, when John Pynchon paid John Leonard seven shillings, sixpence for "bringing up [the river] my Negroes."[60] In 1678 the town meeting paid a ten-shilling bounty for "one wolfe the Major's [Pynchon] black man killed."[61] This presumably was Roco, but subsequent events make it unlikely that he was one of the blacks who had come upriver in 1657. Possibly he was one of the offspring of the first black immigrants, or he may have been a later arrival.

[57] *Ibid.*, 2, pp. 173, 200, 316.

[58] *Ibid.*, 5, p. 45; HCPC Rec., 1, p. 192.

[59] *Ibid.*, 6, pp. 199, 267; Clark, *History of Manufactures*, 1, pp. 137–138, 165. In 1693, one of Pynchon's resin workers described his labors about the "Burning [of] Pine Trees at Rosin Hall . . . [as] such sore worke [that] he would not doe that for 3s. a day in money." Account Books, 6, p. 267.

[60] Account Books, 1, p. 98.

[61] *Springfield Town Recs.*, 1, p. 416.

Roco's initial appearance in the town records was not an auspicious one. Under examination by his master, Roco acknowledged "that he had (upon [Margaret] Riley's tempting him) the carnal knowledge of her body." Miscegenation was not viewed with disproportionate alarm in seventeenth-century Springfield, and Roco received the traditional punishment for convicted fornicators of a choice between fifteen lashes or a £3 fine.[62] The slave's next appearance in the records came on a more positive note. In 1687, he stood before the magistrate and married Sue, another Pynchon slave. Their master entered into the court records that "Roco and Sue, my Negroes [were] Joined in Marriage."[63]

Not long after their marriage, Roco and Sue moved from being slaves to being clients of John Pynchon. Roco secured a freedom contract from Pynchon for both himself and his wife, freedom that was eventually to be paid for in turpentine and tar. The first concrete expression of this agreement came in the town meeting on December 28, 1687. Pynchon rose up to request "a grant from the Town of four or five acres of Land at Skipmuck adjoining to that Land on the brooke which he bought of Charles Ferry, to be added to that where he is settling Roco his Negro."[64] Four years later, the two men signed a formal freedom agreement. Under its terms, Pynchon promised to release Roco and Sue from bondage and to lease them a farm at Skepnuck. The farm included broken-up land, meadow, a house, oxen, a mare, cow, plow, tackling, and "other Implements and household stuff (al which are mine and are to be returned to me when he shal dy or leave my farme)." The landlord also committed himself to build a 30-by-32-foot barn on the property. For rent, Roco was to pay £1 the first year with subsequent increments through the sixth year when the fee would level off at £10. He also agreed to "winter" (shelter and feed) three cattle for Pynchon.[65]

Anxious to pay off his freedom dues as soon as possible, Roco turned to both sawmilling and turpentine production within the next four years. In 1693 Pynchon leased to Roco and Joseph Thomas (a white) his sawmill at Pine Hall. Under the contract's provisions, Pynchon was to receive four hundred out of every thousand logs sawn. And in 1695, with part of the freedom dues still unpaid, Pynchon agreed with Roco "for his and his wife's freedom . . . He is to . . . pay me Twenty Five Barrels of good cleane pure Tur-

---

[62] *Pynchon Court Rec.*, p. 105.
[63] *Ibid.*, p. 105, n.9.
[64] *Springfield Town Recs.*, 2, p. 272.
[65] Account Books, 6, pp. 260–261.

pentine of 40 gallons to a Barrel and Twenty one barrels of Good merchantable Tarr."[66]

Light Artisans

The Pynchons' heavy demand for coats to exchange with the Indians for furs made tailors the most prosperous light artisans in Springfield. Thomas Stebbins, for one, began working for William Pynchon during the mid-1640s. Initially his labor was confined exclusively to agricultural tasks. In May of 1646 Pynchon paid Stebbins £4 for "worke in winter 60 days at 16d." and £3 for forty-four days of summer work. In a later entry for the same year, Stebbins took £6 for an additional eighty-two days of work. But doubtless recognizing the rising demands for coats at the Pynchon general store, he began to concentrate increasingly on tailoring. As with most of the town's artisans, Stebbins purchased the raw materials for his craft from the Pynchons. During the winter of 1647 William Pynchon "delivered to Tho. Stebbins . . . 59 yards ¼ and ½ red cotton," receiving later in payment from the tailor "4 dozen and ½ wastecotes . . . 6 wastecotes and 13 pair stockens . . . 2 dozen and 1 pair blue and white stockens."[67]

Every year Stebbins could be counted upon to supply the Pynchons with between seventy-five and one hundred waistcoats, caps, and pairs of stockings.[68] Four account book entries from January to October 1649 credit the tailor for "12 wastecoats . . . 12 Capps . . . 6 Caps more . . . 19 pair Stockens . . . 1 doz. and ½ of waste-coates . . . 12 Red wastecoates . . . 12 white wastecoates . . . in making stockens, wastecots, Caps, and Taylery worke . . . [2] dozen white wastecotes [19] capps . . . 1 dozen stockens . . . 6 white shag wastecotes."[69] Stebbins, doubtless with considerable help from his wife (and possibly apprentices as well), worked quickly. Between May and August of 1650, with the fur trade booming, he produced

---

[66] *Ibid.*

[67] William Pynchon Account Book, p. 54. Stebbins's tailoring evidently kept him out of his own fields, as in 1648 one of William Pynchon's workmen plowed "Tho. Stebbins's 5 acres and ½ and 2 acres of New ground." Pynchon and Stebbins had arranged beforehand for "the Ploughing done this yeare 1648 which [Stebbins] agreed should be paid halfe in worke . . . [and] halfe in wheate at 3s. 8d." But while Stebbins was too busy to do his own plowing he continued to perform occasional agricultural work for Pynchon. An earlier entry credited him for "Taylery worke, harvest work and carting £4 10s." And later in 1648, Stebbins was paid for "worke . . . for going with the plow . . . 7 days worked at 20d. . . . 9 days worke about hay," "6 days work at dung cast and some plowing," "and 2 days reaping." *Ibid.*, pp. 33, 139, 200.

[68] *Ibid.*, pp. 54, 137–139, 141, 199, 200, 201, 214, 249; Account Books, 1, pp. 91, 253–254.

[69] William Pynchon Account Book, pp. 199, 201, 249.

sixty-five coats of various colors. No less impressive is an account book entry for August 1652 crediting him for 197 coats, 120 caps, and twelve pairs of stockings, as well as three days' work mending harness.[70] During the subsequent ten months he produced an additional 95 coats and 264 caps.[71] In 1654 he again was paid for mending tack as well as tailoring: "[for] 10 days dressing Bever" and some "Taylery worke, mending Saddry." And at the same time, he received credits for 168 coats and 76 caps.[72] In later years, Pynchon simply allowed the tailor to keep his own books. In an account book entry two decades later, he paid for "worke of Serjeant Stebbins and else as in his Booke all from the years 1670, 71, 72, 73, 74, 75, and to this 26 Jan 76."[73]

Such productivity kept Stebbins and any assistants he had at work long hours. Sitting at his workbench next to the window, surrounded on the one side by stacked bolts of uncut cotton cloth, and discarded clippings on the other, the tailor's day had the kind of mechanical, predictable quality characteristic of most of the town's light artisans. These men could ply their craft come rain or shine, and the howling winds of winter demanded only more frequent banking of the fire. Productivity in Springfield did not cease with the onset of winter. Between December and March, when the frozen and often snow-covered landscape reduced outside tasks to gathering wood, carting dung from barn to field, and tending stock, light artisans continued to turn out their quota of coats, hats, shoes, and saddlery. While canoemen waited for the river to thaw and farmers waited for the ground to do the same, Thomas Stebbins continued to wield needle and thread, as well as the pair of "Taylre sheres" he bought from John Pynchon.

Stebbins's productivity as a tailor for the Pynchons made him a natural choice for patron-client ties, and he apparently made the most of it. Again, debt deferrals provide the most convincing evidence. In January 1677, Stebbins's overall debt to Pynchon stood at £57, of which £41 "hath bin due to [me] ever since the 22th of October, 1663."[74] But he lost no lands or housing for his debts, and Pynchon continued to ignore them until the tailor's death two decades after the original loan.[75]

---

[70] *Ibid.*, p. 214; Account Books, 1, p. 91.

[71] Account Books, 1, p. 91.

[72] *Ibid.*, 1, pp. 253–254.

[73] *Ibid.*, 5, p. 97.

[74] *Ibid.*, 5, p. 516.

[75] HCPC Rec., 1, p. 233. As Pynchon's allusions to Stebbins's military rank reveal, the tailor enjoyed the prestige of being an officer in the militia. By 1676 he had risen to the rank of lieutenant, an office that left him subordinate only to Pynchon.

Shoemakers, unlike tailors, worked under direct contract to John Pynchon. He provided the materials and the craftsmen made them into shoes. The contracts usually specified the rate-scale for various types of shoes. In June 1680, he agreed with John Norton "to make my leather into shoes." Pynchon agreed to "pay him for [sizes] 10s 11s and 12s Two shillings a Paire for Plaine shooe: and 2 shillings 6 pence a pair for french heeles." For his compensation, Norton was "to take his Pay out of the shoes and french heeles at 8 shillings 6 pence [a] pair and plain shooes from 10s to 12s at 6 shillings for woman's shoes [from size] 6 to 8 . . . at 6 shilling a pair." An account book entry for 1682 credited him £6 6s. for "shoes mending and etc." and an entry from 1684 allowed £2 17s. for "making 24 pair of shooes." By 1684 Norton no longer labored on a piecework basis, receiving instead weekly wages of seven shillings and sixpence. Weekly wages gave the shoemaker, in effect, the security of having a retainer.[76]

Shoemaking was a highly skilled craft that demanded the traditional five-to-seven-year period of apprenticeship. Unlike cobbling (shoe mending or repair), shoemaking was a well-paying, full-time occupation which could keep the craftsman's family sheltered and fed.[77] Colonial shoemakers worked out of a small kit that contained all the necessary tools: a lap-stone and a hammer, for beating the leather until it was pliable; a leather stirrup to tuck under the craftsman's heel in order to hold the shoe stock firmly in place; an awl for puncturing the leather; and a variety of pincers, scrapers, paring knives, heel knives, and waxed thread. Hammered-out soles were tacked to wooden lasts and then the uppers were sewn on. Upon completion, the shoe was soaked in water for tightening.[78]

High militia posts during the 17th century were invariably accorded to men of substance (in both meanings of that word). Individuals whose names were prefixed by Lieutenant, Major, or Colonel were recognized leaders, men the community could trust with the sometimes grave responsibilities attendant to militia service. The complexities of occupational status in early Springfield, therefore, are suggested by the inhabitants' decision to choose a tailor for such a position. An occupation that throughout the folklore and mythology of western culture has been synonymous with diffidence and humility proved no barrier to positions of social influence in early Springfield. Stereotypical assumptions are further confounded by Stebbins's agreement with the town in 1659 "about the setting up of the Towne pound." And in January 1679, the town meeting voted to allocate "Six pound . . . [to] Leifftenant Stibings for sweeping the meeting house the year 79 & 80." *Springfield Town Recs.*, 1, pp. 263, 422.

[76] Account Books, 5, p. 551; 6, Index, p. 12.

[77] *Ibid.*, 2, p. 157; 3, pp. 151, 161; 5, pp. 105, 267, 291, 551; 6, Index, p. 12.

[78] Alan Dawley, *Class and Community: The Industrial Revolution in Lynn*, Cambridge, Mass., 1976, p. 42; Clark, *History of Manufactures*, 1, pp. 443–445.

Building Trades

In the building trades, house carpenters were the craft aristocrats. With the demand for their services unrelenting throughout the seventeenth century, carpenters and joiners commanded the highest wages paid in early Springfield: from three shillings to five shillings per day. Homes, barns, and outbuildings needed to be built—and rebuilt—throughout the period and woodworkers were needed to do it.[79] As the career of Joseph Leonard shows, these craftsmen rarely experienced real poverty. When, after outliving five wives, he died at the age of seventy-five in 1719, Leonard left an estate valued at £640.[80] Apparently never formally apprenticed as a carpenter, Leonard began his work career in Springfield as an agricultural laborer. In June 1663, with the hay already heavy in the meadows, Pynchon "Agreed with Joseph Leonard well to mow and make and cart and rake . . . 10 acres of grass over Agawam for 6s. per acre."[81] His first woodworking contract came while Leonard was in his mid-twenties. In addition to "Mowing making and carting Hay at Agawam," Leonard received £9 for "shingling my Mill house" and "47 days worke about my Mill dam and hewing the Timber for the dam."[82]

Shingling commonly served as the first formal work for would-be carpenters. While not requiring the finished skills necessary for carpentry or joinery, shingling demanded the ability to lay the lathwork and fasten the yard-long shingles in a watertight fashion. To construct shingles (as well as clapboards, fence poles, or staves), suitable lengths were cut from the boles of straight-grained pine, ash, or oak. A hammer blow on a metal frow would split off a sheet of wood of the required thickness. The shingle would then be finished off with a drawing knife.[83] John Pynchon mandated that siding shingles be three feet in length; roof shingles were to be one and one-half feet.[84] The July 1667 contract for Pynchon's mill house spells out Leonard's obligations in detail. Pynchon "Agreed with Joseph Leanord to shingle my howse at the Mill with 3 foote shingles. I finding the shingles and laying them by the house . . . then Joseph is to lay them well and he is to get and lay all the Lath: he getting the lath which I am to cart . . . for every hundred of

[79] Account Books, 1, pp. 78, 176; 2, pp. 40, 353; 3, pp. 57, 115, 199, 295; 5, pp. 67, 171, 199, 383, 385, 441, 467, 527, 537; 6, p. 81.

[80] HCPC Rec., 4, pp. 14–15.

[81] Account Books, 2, p. 314.

[82] *Ibid.*, 3, pp. 57, 63.

[83] Russell, *A Long, Deep Furrow*, p. 84.

[84] Account Books, 2, pp. 145, 347.

shingle layd I am to allow him 12d. and to saw the lath at my saw mill."[85]

The relatively modest wages garnered for shingling contrast sharply with the payments for finished carpentry work. Seven years after the shingling contract, the now thirty-year-old Leonard signed an agreement to build Pynchon a house in Suffield. According to its provisions, Pynchon "Agreed with Jos. Leonard to Build me a house at Suffield . . . 29 foote long and 20 foote wide 10 foot standing: he to doe all the carpentry worke from falling [trees] to shingle: viz. dore, chimny, Runges, stairs, partition, windows, floares, and etc. all that is to be done by carpentry for closing and smithy all whatsoever." The contractor promised to "allow him the use of my Saw Mill to saw the Bords Into braces and struts." After all was "Compleated well . . . and substantial is all handsome and work-manlike I am to allow him £25 and 2 gallons of rum."[86] In a later contract for a sawmill in Springfield, Pynchon compensated Leonard equally well. For "the Sawmill over the River which is gon to Ruin But his worke he did before it was blown up Reckones to be about £40."[87] As we saw earlier, Sam Gaines earned £75 for building Pynchon's two mills in Suffield.[88] In 1694, for the relatively easy task of "Groundsilling my Barne," Pynchon paid Leonard £5.[89]

Oak and pine provided the primary materials for early New England carpenters like Joseph Leonard. Houseframes and clap-boards were of oak (or sometimes ash), siding was usually of pitch pine. Rough siding, floor planks, and fence rails were constructed by splitting small trees, followed by any necessary dressing with axe or adze. Tools needed for the production of lumber, fencing, or cordwood included the handaxe, adze, saw, and frow (used to split both shingles and clapboards). Lumber was cut by one of two meth-ods: up-and-down whipsaws located in trenches; and, in those towns lucky enough to have them, water-powered sawmills.[90]

The century-long boom in housing construction offered constant and remunerative employment for brickmakers as well as carpen-ters. Colonial communities need the brickmakers in order to free the inhabitants from reliance on either the notoriously combustible mud-and-thatch chimneys or cumbersome stone structures that

[85] *Ibid.*, 3, p. 57.
[86] *Ibid.*, 5, p. 67.
[87] *Ibid.*, 6, p. 63.
[88] *Ibid.*, 6, pp. 271, 273.
[89] *Ibid.*, 6, p. 63.
[90] *Ibid.*, 2, p. 34; 3, p. 57; 5, pp. 89, 459; Russell, *A Long, Deep Furrow*, pp. 83–84.

were the only alternatives to fired brick.[91] As always, John Pynchon was among the artisans' most eager customers. In December 1659, for example, Pynchon paid the brickmaker Francis Hacklington £28 for "a parsell of Bricks we guess in all 32 thousand and so many come to by the agreement." Hacklington also earned an additional five shillings for "making an oven over the River [and] mending my oven," as well as twenty-seven shillings for "200 Pavement at 13s." and "300 of bricks." On the same day, the two men signed a new contract for ten thousand more bricks. Pynchon "Agreed with Francis Hacklington for ... Brickes to be delivered in the middle of May next for which Ten thousand I am to allow or pay him Nine Pounds."[92] In his zeal to fill the order, Hacklington neglected to observe the colony's strictures against work performed on Sunday. On September 24, 1661, he found himself again standing before Pynchon, this time as defendant rather than employee. According to the trial record, "Francis Hacklington beinge presented for breach of the Sabbath in working by carrying of bricks at his Kilne at Northampton on the Sabbath day, to the profaninge that holy tyme: The Corte judged him culpable."[93]

Early American brickmakers like Francis Hacklington performed their work by means of an iron-shod mold. After gathering the clay, molding it, and firing it in his kiln, the artisan stacked the finished products on pallets until an order was filled. A brick kiln, unlike an iron forge, could be kept in operation in subfreezing temperatures, so weather-related curtailments of his working periods were minimal. Accordingly, Hacklington signed his contracts in the fall for delivery the following spring or summer. Once the consignment was filled, the artisan was responsible for carting the finished brick to the customer (although hopefully not on the Sabbath).[94]

Housing construction also demanded the services of stonemasons, the human truckhorses of colonial America. Their task was to dig, cart, and lay the stones used to construct the cellars and foundations for the community's various dwellings. Their work was arguably the most backbreaking of any performed in Springfield. But, for those willing to accept its demands upon body and spirit, stonemasonry could offer substantial rewards. Unlike most forms of unskilled labor that paid the standard twenty pence daily rate, stonemasons earned between two shillings sixpence and four shil-

[91] Account Books, 2, pp. 212–213, 249; 3, pp. 26, 93; 5, p. 171.
[92] Ibid., 2, p. 213.
[93] HCPC Rec., 1, pp. 7–9.
[94] Clark, History of Manufactures, 1, p. 166; Account Books, 2, p. 213.

lings daily. This high level of remuneration resulted not from the skill level of the work, as in carpentry, but rather from its grueling physical demands. For men like Rowland Thomas who were able to meet these demands, stonemasonry offered a route from day-laboring to freeholding. And, as with most work in early Springfield, this route began at the Pynchon general store.[95]

Thomas began and ended his career in Springfield as one of the Pynchons' most valued employees. Soon after his arrival in the community during the early 1640s, he began working as a field laborer, sawyer, teamster, and stonemason. Various entries from William Pynchon's account book credit him for "reaping . . . sawing fetheredged bords . . . bringing up goods . . . 24 loads of stones for my sellre at 20 pence . . . 910 foote boards, abating 10 foote for cracks . . . [caulking] a boate 22 foot and ½ . . . keeping 10 cows . . . fetching 3 load wheat . . . in fetching some stones from the upper falls."[96] During the decade of the 1650s, Thomas increasingly concentrated on stonemasonry and canoe work, being paid for "putting stones under my cobhouse . . . Stones for Griffith Joanes Tanning" and taking twelve shillings for "carrying down 35 bushels of wheat and 6 hogsheads of goods."[97] By the 1660s, Thomas's work for John Pynchon was confined almost exclusively to stone-masonry, sawing, and mill work.[98] A single account book entry in 1660 credits him for "falling Timber for my howse . . . 56 Trees containe 133 foote at 3d. per foote . . . 7 days hewing Timber . . . 3 days ½ raising the howse . . . about underpinning and daubing . . . By getting stones 100 load from the sixteene acres Stone at 12d. per load is £5, By 50 load of Stone from the hither stone place at 15d. per load." Likewise, entries two years later credit Thomas for "falling the Timber for the howse of correction . . . getting chimney stones for the prison howse . . . By 10 load of stone."[99]

Springfield's midcentury population boom offered constant employment for the town's stonemasons. During the late 1660s, Pynchon paid Thomas for "working about stones . . . digging stones" and "By worke at Westfield for my son[-in-law] Whiting 24 days the first about getting stone and 20 days when stonning the celler . . . 63 days worke in all at 65 days for loss in goeing and coming at 2s. 6d. [is] £8 2s. 6d. . . . By 36 load of stone (besides) at 12d.

[95] William Pynchon Account Book, p. 155; Account Books, 3, pp. 35, 197.
[96] William Pynchon Account Book, pp. 124, 155–156, 218.
[97] Account Books, 1, pp. 73–74, 236.
[98] Ibid., 2, pp. 159, 197.
[99] Ibid., 2, p. 159.

... By allowing for your dyet there 10 weeke."[100] Thomas's digging skills could also be applied to less exalted tasks. In November of 1665 Pynchon paid him £5 10s. for "36 days at the Mill Trench [and] 4 days about the Dam." Two and one-half years later, the workman took £2 3s. for "20 days worke at the Mill Breech." In 1671, he earned £3 for "24 days worke at Quabaug Mill Trench ... at 2s. 6d." Advancing age did not keep Thomas from his work, as his employment by Pynchon continued unabated through the decades of the 1670s and 1680s. Entries from the 1670s show "3 weekes at Stony River Saw mill ... By underpinning my litle Room ... By 5 days ½ underpinning Mr. Glover's house."[101] An entry from 1680, with Thomas nearing his sixties, credits him £19 for sixty days gathering stones, getting timber, and mill work.[102]

But despite the constancy of his work for John Pynchon, Rowland Thomas apparently failed to establish patron-client ties with the Springfield leader. Both his wage-rates and indebtedness records point to this conclusion. When Thomas built the foundation for Pynchon's son-in-law, Joseph Whiting in Westfield, he earned daily wages of two shillings sixpence for his efforts.[103] But two other stonemasons, Thomas Bascomb and his son, were also working on Whiting's cellar and the elder Bascomb's compensation was one shilling per day higher than Thomas's. Pynchon paid Bascomb £6 for "worke for Mr. Whiting about stoning his cellar and chimny ... 35 days at 3s. 6d." Likewise, in 1675 Pynchon paid Bascomb £3 17s. for "worke in June ... [getting] stone ... 22 days at 3s. 6d."[104] Additional entries for "8 weekes worke and halfe is 51 days ... 18 days ... 24 days worke ... 44 days worke at [stoning] my mill house" were made at the three shillings sixpence level.[105] On some projects, Pynchon paid Bascomb as much as four shillings per diem. For "worke hewing and Carying stone [for] my kitchin floore, hearth, and etc.," he credited the stonemason for "18 days himself at 4s. per day £4 12s. [and] 12 days his son at 2s. 6d. per day £1 10s."[106] Despite the fact that Thomas was an experienced, adult stonemason, he received the same wages as did Thomas Bascomb's son.

[100] *Ibid.*, 3, pp. 159, 197.
[101] *Ibid.*, 3, p. 159; 5, p. 15.
[102] *Ibid.*, 5, p. 509. In 1682 Thomas earned £5 9s. 6d. for "worke ... about my Mill house and at the Trench."
[103] *Ibid.*, 3, p. 197.
[104] *Ibid.*, 3, p. 35.
[105] *Ibid.*, 2, pp. 148–149; 3, p. 35.
[106] *Ibid.*, 2, p. 149.

Rowland Thomas's pattern of indebtedness likewise indicates that he failed to establish cliency ties with John Pynchon. As with many of the town's residents, he found himself deeply indebted to Pynchon by the mid-1660s. In 1668 the figure stood at £48 and the creditor demanded payment. Thomas was not allowed an extension on the default, as on March 28 of that year Pynchon formally took possession of the debtor's "land at chikkuppy . . . all this land there being about 50 [acres] whereof 5 or 6 acres of meddow and 6 or 7 Plowed acres and house."[107]

While Thomas's judgment in not forming patron-client ties with Pynchon may be open to question, his tenacity is not. Not one to be broken by adversity, he quickly set about the ultimately successful task of reestablishing his freehold. As before, his principal employer was John Pynchon. By the time Thomas died in the 1690s, he had amassed a comfortable estate worth just under £200.[108]

Sea Trades

The Pynchons' extensive export operations usually gave coopers all the work they could handle. Everything William and John shipped out of Springfield, with the exception of grain, needed to be encased in barrels, and coopers were needed to build them. These craftsmen could also pick up additional income by constructing churns, butter tubs, cowls, clapboards, and shingles.[109]

Aware of the demand for their skills, coopers were among the most highly self-conscious craft societies in early America. Edward Johnson's *Wonder-Working Providence* in 1654 alluded to the successful organization of "coopers and shoemakers, who had either of them a corporation granted." Six years earlier, Massachusetts had organized both cooperage and shoemaking into formal craft societies with regulatory authority. The Court also mandated a five-year period of apprenticeship for those who wished to practice the craft. Like all craft societies, the coopers' motive in organizing were twofold: to ensure product quality and to restrict entry into the trade.[110]

Although requiring great skill, the actual process of barrel-making was characterized by "a functional simplicity little changed from Roman times." For their construction materials, coopers used oak plank for the staves and heads and strips of hickory for the hoops.

[107] *Ibid.*, 1, p. 236; 3, p. 159.
[108] HCPC Rec., 3, p. 46.
[109] William Pynchon Account Book, pp. 104–105; Account Books, 3, p. 87; 5, p. 119.
[110] Clark, *History of Manufactures*, 1, p. 162; Morris, *Government and Labor*, p. 141.

Staves had to be shaped according to the engineering principle of the arch. When each stave rested in a correctly listed position, bound at top and bottom by adequate external hoop pressure, the barrel would absorb any blow or external stress equally throughout every unit of material. This impressive functional utility inspires the foremost authority on early American barrels to rhapsodize that "When one considers the form of the chime, the opening in the center of the heading joints, the narrow and satisfactory croze [the small groove in either end of the stave in which the bead of the head fits], the arch construction of the body of the barrel, and the method of holding the whole together, making of it without doubt, the strongest possible container for any product, it makes one marvel at its simplicity and perfection, and any real improvement in its construction would be almost an impossibility."[111]

Tools for seventeenth-century coopers consisted of an axe for felling the necessary oak and hickory timber, a saw for cutting the timber into lengths, a drawing knife for shaping the staves, a "buckler" for fastening the stave, some clamps, and a windlass for closing the stave ends for hooping. Using these instruments, coopers turned out barrels (25 to 40 gallons capacity), kegs (40 to 60 gallons), and casks or hogsheads (60 gallons or more). Depending on the substance to be carried, the barrels were either "tight" or "slack." Tight barrels are used for liquids or liquid-packed meats (in Springfield, cider, rum, pork, beef, turpentine, or resin) and slack barrels carry solids (in Springfield, furs).[112]

John Mathews was Springfield's most highly skilled cooper. He arrived in the community during the mid-1640s and quickly established what would prove to be a thirty-five-year period of association with the Pynchon family. Various entries in William's account books during the period from 1646 to 1649 credit Mathews for "Coopering and other worke . . . Copery worke and 2 days gardening and one reaping . . . copery work, reaping and other worke."[113] In 1658 John Pynchon paid him £5 for "26 barrels for black lead . . . a beere barrell . . . a milking payle . . . 200 Clapbord [and] one hogshead." Later account book entries reveal a similar diversity. They credit Mathews for "heading 3 barels . . . a New Keeler . . . a Cowle . . . Changing a churn . . . Hooping and Packing one hogshead Beaver [30] Barrels . . . 1 Butter Tub . . . 3 great Barells for Cider . . . 9 hoops and burning Barells . . . 33 barells at

111 Franklin E. Coyne, *The Development of the Cooperage Industry in the United States, 1620–1940*, Chicago, 1940, pp. 7–8.
112 *Ibid.*; Account Books, 1, p. 270; 3, p. 87, 5, pp. 119, 487.
113 William Pynchon Account Book, pp. 104–105.

3s. 9d. per Barell," "38 barrells," "4 Beife Barrels," "51 Barrells for Porke [and] 64 barrells for cider and Porke." Pynchon, who leased six acres of meadow to Mathews, took "10 barrels received as rent" each year from 1664 to 1668.[114] Like other woodworkers, Mathews also supplied the Pynchons with shingles. In the late 1640s, William paid him for nineteen hundred shingles, and in 1658 John Pynchon "Agreed with John Mathews to get me Thirteen hundred and halfe good sound Three foote shingles." The following year, for the sum of £11 Mathews contracted to supply the younger Pynchon with twelve thousand shingles.[115]

But despite his considerable woodworking skills, John Mathews was stalked by indebtedness to the Pynchons throughout his stay in Springfield, and ultimately he ended up as a town charge. Before he was through, Mathews lost his house, lands, and child.[116] The explanation for this demise appears to have been a combination of personal irascibility and, rare in early Springfield, sloth.[117]

Mathews's craft skills enabled him to forge patron-client ties with John Pynchon; but the cooper's failure to keep up with Pynchon's production demands eventually severed the bond, and the employer then called in a number of longstanding debts. The process began in October 1656, when Pynchon "Accounted with Goodman Mathews and he owes me £19 12s. 7d."[118] Seven years later the balance stood at £20 17s. 10d. and the cooper promised to pay Pynchon "this winter in wheate."[119] But in February 1665, for debts of £10, Pynchon took two cows from him, observing "I should have had [them] long ago."[120] Mathews thereupon leased the animals. Two years later Pynchon admonished him to pay up or else. In addition to the old debt of £45, there was "besides the Bill of Laurence Bliss [which] is turned to me for John Matthews to pay me that £31 10s." The cooper was to "pay this sum of £45 or else to forfeite his land if he pay it not within 3 yeares." So "he mortgages his howse and land to me for the payment of it." The mortgaged property included virtually everything Mathews owned in Springfield—his house, homelot, orchard, woodlot, and wet meadow.[121] As before, Pynchon ignored the default deadline, but in December

[114] Account Books, 1, p. 270; 2, pp. 312–313; 3, p. 87; 5, pp. 119, 487.
[115] *Ibid.*, 2, p. 99.
[116] *Springfield Town Recs.*, 2, pp. 147–148.
[117] *Pynchon Court Rec.*, pp. 118–119, 243, 249.
[118] Account Books, 1, p. 269.
[119] *Ibid.*, 2, p. 312.
[120] *Ibid.*, 3, p. 86.
[121] *Ibid.*

1676, nine years after the mortgage was signed, he foreclosed.[122] Needing the property in order to live, Mathews immediately rented it back. In the January 1677 lease, Pynchon "Lett out to Rent to John Mathews the Homelot (and orchard) of four acres and better and wet meddow before it of almost two acres and halfe (all which I bought of him) which he is to hold and Injoy for Seven yeares he . . . paying to me . . . yearly the Rent or Sum of Three Pounds and one good thite Barrell for Porke yearly, and also he is [to] yearly repair and take care of the fencing which he is to leave in repair at the end of his time he being also to pay all the Rates on the said Land."[123] Renting from Pynchon did nothing to improve Mathew's financial well-being. By the time of his death, he had compounded his indebtedness problems by paying Pynchon £71 in rent for nineteen acres of meadow and plowland, an orchard, and two cows, in addition to a house and homelot.[124]

Town records suggest that Mathews helped bring on his own fall by poor work habits. His career reveals that the fact that a man's craft *could* provide a comfortable living was no guarantee that it *would* do so. Character was not destiny, but it counted. Highly skilled artisans who were slothful or truculent fared little better than did landless laborers. As we will see later, Mathews was one of a number of Springfield artisans who used the town's reliance on their skills to test the limits of social tolerance. In 1659 the commissioners ordered Francis Hacklington to serve a summons on the cooper. Mathews thereupon behaved with a "contemptuous and high carriage towards him that was sent with the Summons: commanding him off his ground and holding up his sickle at him and usinge other high words and unfitting carriage." The process-server beat a hasty retreat.[125] A year later Mathews was again fined by the court for "being found drunken and bereaved of his understanding which appeared both in his speech and behavior."[126] In 1669 he was brought before the court on the serious accusation of "abusing" the town's minister, Pelatiah Glover. Pynchon confronted Mathews with evidence of his "exceedinge contemptuous behavior" toward the Reverend Glover. After considering the evidence, the magistrate ruled that the cooper's conduct was "very odious and Shamefull . . . much after the custome of the Quakers,"

[122] Deed, John Mathews to John Pynchon, April 22, 1667, Hampden Co. Deeds, Volume A, p. 72.
[123] Account Books, 5, p. 487.
[124] *Ibid.*, 2, pp. 99, 312; 3, pp. 86–87, 283; 5, pp. 118–119, 486–487.
[125] *Pynchon Court Rec.*, p. 243.
[126] *Ibid.*, p. 249.

and sentenced that he be whipped and compelled to post a £10 bond for future good behavior.[127] Moreover, Mathews's neighbors, as well as the minister, were subject to his maledictions. In 1678, he was bound over by the Hampshire County grand jury for "his Scandoulous vile revileing of his Neighbor Jonathan Burt."[128]

John Mathews's wife was killed in the Indian attack on Springfield and he thereafter descended into the final indignity of his years in the town. Mrs. Mathews's death left the cooper with sole responsibility for the care of the family's infant son, a burden that the town meeting quickly decided he was incapable of bearing. On January 6, 1682, it was "Voted and Concluded by the Town that the Select men shall take Care for the setting out or providing for the Maintenance of John Mathews his child according as they shall Judge most fit." A month later, operating under the provisions of a colony law that "the Select men shal take care for and maintaine and dispose of such poor children whose Parents are either dead or so poor that they Cant nurse or provide for and maintaine such their children," the townsmen indentured young Mathews to Samuel Terry until "the said Child shal attaine the age of One and Twenty yeeres."[129]

The town meeting then addressed itself to what it saw as the critical point of issue—Mathews's indolence and lack of responsibility. Determined to make him use his time more productively, the meeting "voted and Agreed [that] the Select men shall take Care of John Mathews and have an inspection over him that hee follow his employment and make improvement of his time: and to setle him in a way that he may doe it."[130] The efforts of his fellow citizens to build a fire under Mathews came to naught and when he died his estate stood at but £8, with encumbrances five times that amount.[131]

After coopers had packed John Pynchon's barrels for export, canoemen such as Samuel Terry carried them down to Enfield falls or Hartford. Canoe-transport was among the easiest work to get in seventeenth-century Springfield. The canoe's most obvious advantage over the oxcart, of course, was speed. Even when their way was not impeded by mud or a deeply runneled roadway, oxcarts moved slower than a man walking, rarely more than three miles

[127] *Ibid.*, pp. 118–119.
[128] Green, *Springfield*, p. 137.
[129] *Springfield Town Recs.*, 2, pp. 147–148, 152–153.
[130] *Ibid.*, 2, pp. 147–148.
[131] HCPC Rec., 2, pp. 30–31.

an hour.[132] Virtually every able-bodied man in the town worked at one time or another as a canoeman. Over two dozen were active canoemen for most of their adult lives. Canoemen were the ones who carried the surplus grain, pork, beef, and naval stores down the river, to be exchanged for ironwares, textiles, medicine, salt, rum, or molasses. Early recognizing the canoe's importance for their commercial survival, the townsmen voted in February 1639 that "it shall be lawfull for any inhabitant to fell any Cannoe trees [growing on the common] and make them for his owne use or for the use of any inhabitant . . . but not to sell or any ways pass away any Cannoe out of the Plantation untill it be five years old." Indeed, the presence of so many canoes in Springfield was the most visible evidence of the town's deep involvement in the market economy.[133]

The experience of Samuel Terry reveals the extent of this market orientation. Beginning as a servant to William Pynchon during the 1640s, he became the most active of John Pynchon's canoemen a decade later. During seasonable weather, Terry took his birchbark canoe on as many as ten voyages monthly.[134] In July 1655 he received £2 for "carying down [to the falls] 84 bushels [of wheat and] . . . 70 bushels and bringing up 2 Tun of [goods]."[135] On a later journey, the canoeman earned a similar amount for "carying downe to the falls 71 bushels ½ of wheat 2 hogshead [and] bringing up 1 Tun ½ goods your halfe [and] 90 bushels, your halfe." In July 1656 he embarked on "six voyages to the Enfield falls." In a 1665 entry, Pynchon paid Terry for "Carying 76 bushels from the foote of the Falls at 2 pence ½ [per] bushel . . . Carying down 23 barrels of meate at 2s. [and] Bringing up 110 bushels of salt at 6d."[136]

The first nip of frost in the fall signaled the peak of the canoeing season when the town's agricultural surplus was shipped and portaged down to Enfield falls or Hartford. Pynchon's standard rate for the longer trips is suggested by an agreement signed with another canoeman "to Carry downe my Corne and Barrells to Hartford next Spring, my Corne he is to Carry for 4d. ½ per bushel and Barrells for 2s. a piece." The canoe trips usually demanded a two-man crew as Pynchon paid most of his canoemen for "your halfe." The companionship presumably made canoeing among the more attractive tasks available in early Springfield. Canoemen could,

[132] Hartley, *Lost Country Life*, p. 82.
[133] *Springfield Town Recs.*, 1, p. 164; Account Books, 1, pp. 147, 197, 291–292, 300, 316; 2, pp. 117, 245, 261, 360–361; 3, pp. 56, 64, 85, 105; 5, pp. 59, 165, 289.
[134] Account Books, 1, pp. 239–240; 3, pp. 144–145.
[135] *Ibid.*, 1, p. 239.
[136] *Ibid.*, 1, p. 240.

within reason, make their own schedules, and their work was not performed under the watchful eye of their employer. But perhaps most important for Terry and his fellow canoemen, the fifteen-mile round trip to the falls at Enfield was far from being unpleasant. While pushing the graceful birchbark canoe through the water, the two occupants were free to converse, joke, exchange gossip about their neighbors, and the like. And it is possible to imagine more onerous tasks than bringing a canoe into the wharves at Springfield as dusk fell on the Connecticut River.[137]

AGRICULTURAL WORKERS

Agricultural labor, like manufacturing, construction, and transportation work, was highly commercialized in early Springfield. The Pynchons' fields always demanded a labor force of between fifteen and forty men, with variations coming according to the rhythms of the crop cycle. For young men without skills or older men without prospects, field work was always available—weather permitting. The process of clearing new planting fields as well as cultivating established ones continued unabated until the Revolution. There were always trees to be felled, stumps to be uprooted, ditches to be dug, rocks to be carted, and meadows to be bogged. Of all the field tasks listed in the Pynchon account books, none

[137] Ibid., 3, p. 207; John McPhee, The Survival of the Bark Canoe, New York, 1975, pp. 55–56. Terry also leased land from John Pynchon, and his career as a tenant began in the same fashion as did John Mathews's—after a forfeiture of land. On August 7, 1662, he lost "14 acres of land at Chikkupy" for debts of £13 10s. On the same day he signed a lease to take back the land in tenancy. Pynchon agreed to "Let out to Samuel Terry the 5 acres and ¼ of broken up land in the 14 acres above said in Chikkupy which I have bought." Less than a year later, Terry placed himself in Pynchon's debt for an additional £26 in order to buy a house, orchard, and lot that Pynchon had taken for debts from Griffith Jones a month earlier. The payment was to be "in wheat at 3s. 6d. per bushel and in merchantable Porke at 3d. per pound." According to the provisions of the contract, Terry was to "pay [Pynchon] £26 in 3 years. That is to say £9 michalstide coming 12 months which will be ano 1664 and £9 in michalstide 1665 and £8 in michalstide 1666." Unfortunately for Terry, the payment schedule was not kept, and he was forced to rent rather than buy the land and housing. In April 1680, after previously leasing "a horse of mine" and "those 2 oxen which I bought of Miles [Morgan]," Terry signed a contract for Pynchon's 80-acre "Tenement farme" across the river. On April 16, 1680, Pynchon "Delivered to Goodman Terry with my farme which he is to make good again when he delivers it up with my farme . . . a good new plow but 2 days agoe fetched from Thomas Dowey and with a good new share costs me now 16s. of John Stewart and coulter, plow chain 7½ feet long, new whipple and chain, draft yoak, clovis and pin, etc." Ultimately, Terry paid Pynchon £64 for his various lifetime rentals of land, housing, livestock, and tools. Account Books, 2, pp. 200–201; 3, pp. 144–145; 5, pp. 72–73, 447.

was more common than those for "stubbing and clearing." Stubbing involved removal by means of a grubhoe or mattock (and sometimes a team of oxen) of all the stumps and roots left in the ground after trees had been felled. The man John Pynchon usually called on first to do his stubbing was Increase Sikes. In a contract signed in July 1668, Pynchon "Agreed with Increase Sikes to Stub, Cleare and Plough up Sixe acres of Ground in my land comonly called Sheepes Pasture . . . for which well Stubbed and cleared and likewise well plowed and broken up I am to allow and pay him the sum of Eleven Pounds and one worsted pair of stockens . . . He is to doe this worke—wholy to finish the Stubbing and Ploughing of it all up by the 25th of Aprill next come 12 Months, and at least halfe of it is to be done and well plowed by the 25 of Aprill next, and all to be very well Plowed." A contract signed the following year is still more explicit regarding payments per acre. On April 22, 1669, Pynchon "Agreed with Increase Sikes to Stub cleare and plow up the rest of my ground at round hill next to that he was to doe by former bargaine. He is to cleare and Plow up all the remainder to the top of the hill where the cart way goes down to the plaine . . . for all which well stubbed and cleared and Plowed up, I am to allow and pay him Three and thirty shillings per acre and one stubbing hoe already delivered . . . he is to doe this worke by the 25th of . . . Aprill next come 12 Months: and 4 acres of it is to be done and well plowed by the 25th of Aprill next Spring." Payment levels were governed by the relative difficulty of the terrain. While the 1669 contract stipulated thirty-three shillings per cleared acre, one signed the following January included payments fourteen shillings per acre higher. The agreement bound "Increase to Stub that Plough Ground by my 3 corner meddow under the hill . . . all being well done by march come 2 yeare if not before [for which work] I am to allow and pay him 47s. per acre and 1 pair of Gloves of 4s. price already delivered him."[138] Regardless of the terrain, stubbing was a slow and painfully laborious process, and the two-year period allocated in 1668 to clear six acres was not atypical.[139]

[138] Account Books, 3, pp. 172–173.

[139] *Ibid.*, 3, pp. 14, 99, 122; 4, p. 87; 5, pp. 29, 123, 165, 185, 189, 287, 421, 547; 6, p. 71. For a recent study of the cycles of field preparation, cultivation, and harvesting, see Nicholas P. Hardeman, *Shucks, Shocks, and Hominy Blocks: Corn as a Way of Life in Pioneer America*, Baton Rouge, 1981, esp. pp. 20–137. Still invaluable are Paul W. Gates, *The Farmer's Age: Agriculture, 1815–1860*, New York, 1960, pp. 156–270; Percy Wells Bidwell and John I. Falconer, *History of Agriculture in the Northern United States, 1620–1860*, Washington, D.C., 1925; and especially Darrett B. Rutman, *Husbandmen of Plymouth: Farms and Villages in the Old Colony, 1620–1692*, Boston, 1967.

Contracts for stubbing were usually drawn up in the late winter or early spring. Work began with the first thaw. Some projects also involved ditching, filling, and leveling as well as stubbing the ground.[140] In a second contract signed in December 1669, Pynchon "Agreed with Increase Sikes that he shall fill in my ditch at the Round hill, all of it from one end to the other which he is to fill up, throwing in all the Bark to make it plaine fit for Plowing, he is also to stub up all the young Trees and stub in the Bank quite from the Ground plowed up . . . to the south side of the ditch and to doe all well fit and secure for plowing, all which he is to doe early in the Spring for which I am to pay him 20s."[141]

After preparing Pynchon's fields for planting in the early spring, with the arrival of June, Sikes turned to mowing his hay. Hay must be cut while it is still nourishing sap, but must be harvested dry to avoid spontaneous combustion.[142] The laborer passed the sultry Connecticut Valley summers amidst the sweet aroma of freshly cut English grasses. In a particularly detailed contract signed in January 1670, Pynchon "Agreed with Increase Sikes to mow and make into Hay next summer all my 10 acres of meddow over Agawam . . . he is to cut it all well and close and make it good hay and Rake it all up and cock it up . . . also to cart it and Rake after the carts and to set it on a Reeke by the River side fit for the Boate to fetch, and to Rake it well, to secure it from the Raine and all this to doe in season that I may have good hay, at least halfe of it to be done before Harvest if not all, for which I am to allow and pay him 5s. 6d. per acre." As this contract reveals, the mower cut the hay into swathes which were laid in lines to dry. He then raked the hay into small dollops, alternately spaced over the field, before cocking them up for cartage; and all this was to be accomplished before the time came to reap cereal grains. The continuities with English seasonal patterns bear emphasis here. The entry for July in Thomas Tusser's sixteenth-century planting calendar reads, "With tossing and raking, and setting on cocks, grass lately in swathes, is hay for an ox: That done, go and cart it, and have it away, the battle is fought, ye have gotten the day."[143]

[140] Account Books, 1, p. 282; 3, pp. 87, 140, 165, 171; 5, pp. 31, 77, 127, 183.
[141] *Ibid.*, 3, p. 173.
[142] Hartley, *Lost Country Life*, p. 153.
[143] *Ibid.*, pp. 151–153; Account Books, 3, pp. 172–173. Sikes also worked for Pynchon as a canoeman and a carpenter. On November 23, 1670, Pynchon "Agreed with Increase Sikes to Carry downe my Corne and Barrells to Hartford next Spring; my Corne he is to Carry for 4d. ½ per bushel and Barrells for 2s. [a] piece; when I have occasion to use but one Boate at a tyme I am to use him But If I have

After stubbing and clearing, ditching was the most common form
of field work to be had at the Pynchon general store. Ditches were
needed to keep hungry livestock out of the planting fields, or to
serve as the races for John Pynchon's various mills. Because Springfield's soil, like that of most of New England, often appeared to be
nine parts of rock for every one part of earth, ditching was an
especially arduous task. Requiring a strong back and perseverance
but little in the way of skills, it was difficult work and it paid poorly.
In Springfield the closest equivalent to the proverbial ditch-digger
was the Scot, William Hunter.[144] In 1666 Hunter received eight
shillings nine pence for "8 Rod ¾ of ditching by the Indian Fort
over the River" and £8 6s. for "scouring 34 Rod of ditching." In
the fall of 1668, Pynchon "Agreed with William Hunter to make
a parsell of ditching . . . for a stone horse of about 5 yeares old . . .
[for which] he is to make 112 Rod of ditch." And "in payment of
what he owes me he is to make 100 Rod of ditching more." The
acquisition of a stonehorse, needless to say, would considerably
facilitate the removal of boulders from the ditchway. In April 1669
Hunter received for "worke and severall things . . . [the sum of]
£12 18s. 6d.," as well as for "your Plowing 5 acres for [Joseph
Whiting] . . . your son, your horse and oxen £1 15s."[145] The following year Pynchon paid Hunter for the 168 rods of ditching
already completed, while admonishing the laborer that "There is
behind 44 Rod as you say your selfe to which I told you you should
not faile to make me this summer."[146]

---

occasion to send more Boates than one at once I am to use who I se meete." On
January 25, 1676, Pynchon contracted with Increase and his brother Victory to
build him a barn with the dimensions of 52-by-24 feet for a fee of £14. Increase,
in addition, rented bottom land and an apple orchard from his employer, paying
Pynchon lifetime rents of £86. But although he had worked for and rented from
Pynchon most of his adult life, Sikes managed to stay out of the landlord's debt;
and while his work record shows that Sikes spent most of his days with his back to
the wheel, he was spared the anxiety of wondering when he and his family might
lose the roof over their heads. Account Books, 3, pp. 172–173, 207; 5, pp. 161,
417–418, 546–547.

    144 William Hunter arrived in Springfield with his family during the winter of
1663. He entered the community under the sponsorship of two other Scots. On
February 23, 1663, "William Hunter was admitted an Inhabitant of this Town and
John Riley and John Henrison doe bynd themselves . . . to the Town Treasurer
and Select men . . . in a bond of Thirty pounds, to secure the Town from the said
William Hunter or any of his family." The Scot community evidently hived together,
as four years later the town granted "Liberty . . . to John Riley to build on his lott
by William Hunter's." *Springfield Town Recs.*, 1, pp. 306, 361.

    145 Account Books, 3, p. 165; Hartley, *Lost Country Life*, pp. 245–251.

    146 Account Books, 5, p. 31. Hunter also rented land from his employer. In March

Digging ditches for others was not the way to get ahead in early Springfield, and when William Hunter was killed during King Philip's War, his estate included a Bible but not much else. His total wealth was valued at £37, including only sixteen acres of land.[147] Unfortunately for his widow, seven of these acres had been mortgaged to John Pynchon for an unpaid debt of £12, and in 1684 the land was forfeited to him.[148] However she may have felt about his seizure of her seven acres, Mrs. Hunter did not sever her family's ties with the creditor. Her daughter Sarah became a domestic servant in the Pynchon household for a brief period in 1679, and in October of 1690 Mrs. Hunter and Pynchon agreed that her son John would live as a servant with the Pynchon family for a yearly salary of £10.[149]

Some field hands boarded in the Pynchon household for virtually their entire adult lives. Francis Pepper, for one, worked for and lived with the Pynchons for over forty years. Without a wife to support or children in need of a patrimony, Pepper lived frugally but comfortably on his modest wages. When he died in 1686, his entire estate was valued at £155, of which £122 consisted of outstanding bills of credit. His debts totaled £3.[150]

1669 he leased broken-up acreage that Pynchon had taken for debts from Richard Sikes. For the rent, Hunter agreed to "allow and pay . . . Thirty Two shillings for the yeare and to repair the fence . . . formerly belonging to the whole 15 acres all the fence whatever in that field which belongs therto." In addition to tenant farming, he was also engaged in livestock husbandry. In November of 1670 he paid his bills at the general store with "119 pounds of Porke." Hunter's combined annual income from ditching and tenant farming rarely exceeded £35, and to raise additional money he put his daughter out to service—although evidently with some reluctance. On July 29, 1671, Hunter and his fourteen-year-old daughter Katherine stood before the magistrate, accused respectively of harboring a fugitive and desertion from service. John Pynchon examined the girl about "Departing from her Master's [Robert Ashley] service unlawfully." The deposition cited Katherine for disappearing "once last Tuesday and then Coming againe on Thursday and yet goeing away againe on Friday Morning to her fathers: and for noe Cause that shee can relate her selfe but only that her dame once only and that some time before gave her a blow or 2 with her hand." After evaluating the testimony, Pynchon ruled that "there being nothing to justify her in her unlawfull departure I ordered her to the howse of correction, there to abide till I discharged her." The magistrate then turned to her father and declared "And William . . . for Harbouring his said daughter and not discharging her and sending her to her aforesaid Master (none Informing) [should be fined] 20s.," which Pynchon "respited . . . till some other tyme." Account Books, 3, p. 165; 5, p. 31; *Pynchon Court Rec.*, p. 275.
[147] HCPC Rec., 1, p. 182.
[148] Account Books, 5, p. 50.
[149] *Ibid.*, 5, p. 31; 6, pp. 240–241.
[150] *Ibid.*, 5, p. 159; HCPC Rec., 1, p. 259.

Throughout his stay in Springfield, Francis Pepper was the Pynchons' most reliable employee. He first began to serve the family in 1645, and the following spring he "Received . . . in wages to the first of April £4 1s." and "more due to him from the first of Aprill to the end of July which is 4 months at 20s. per month: [all] is £4." By 1647 Pepper was a salaried employee earning annual wages of £8 10s. An account book entry that year credits him for "¾ yeare's service," and in 1648 he "Received a yeare's wages . . . [of] £9."[151] In February of 1649, William Pynchon paid him forty-eight shillings for "4 months winter [work] at 12s. per month" and the following year the worker took forty-two shillings for "4 months service in winter." Soon after this time Pepper moved into the Pynchon household, taking his meals with the other servants in the mansion's kitchen. In October 1654, John Pynchon debited Pepper's account for "your dyet 30 weeks at 4s. per weeke" and the next July he made a similar entry for "36 weekes and ½ dyet at 4s. per weeke."[152] In November 1657 Pepper paid for "a yeares dyet at 4s. per weeke for 52 weeks is £10 8s."[153] This annual payment for bed and board remained constant unless unusual circumstances intervened. The year 1675 was such a time. The Indian attacks made normal field work impossibly harrowing. Resorting to what was more than a mild understatement, Pynchon abated Pepper's boarding charges £5, "it having bin a Troublesome yeare."[154]

For his method of compensation, Pepper alternated work as a wage laborer with work performed on a per diem basis. Those contracts that were signed typically fell within a three- to four-month range. In January 1654, Pynchon "Agreed with Francis Pepper to serve [me] to the end of March next for which tyme I am to allow him £2 5s." Soon thereafter, however, Pepper reverted to per diem compensation, receiving payments later that year for "44 days worke at 16d. [per day] [and] 56 days worke at 20d. . . . [and] more than 55 days worke at 16d. . . . 71 days at 20d." The following year he was credited for "100 days work at 20d. per day is £6 6s. 8d. . . . more 77 days work at 16d."[155] Per diem labor posed a risk because of the possibilities of weather-related curtailments on the number of available workdays. Its advantages were greater flexibility in task selection and the opportunity to work for other employers periodically. Weekly wages could offer the best of both

151 William Pynchon Account Book, pp. 29–30.
152 *Ibid.*, pp. 197–198; Account Books, 1, p. 203.
153 Account Books, 1, p. 208.
154 *Ibid.*, 5, p. 159.
155 *Ibid.*, 1, p. 203.

worlds and tended to be favored by Pepper from the late 1650s onward. In 1657 Pynchon paid him £10 for "17 weeks winter worke . . . [and] 7 weeks 4 days Summer worke." In 1659 he received twenty-one shillings for "16 days worke . . . to the 9 December on which day he gave over working by the day."[156] This service contract, however, was short-lived and by 1660 Pepper was again being paid on a weekly basis, receiving credits for "33 weeks ½ worke at 10s. per week" and "6 weekes worke at 8s. . . . [and] 84 days."[157]

Workers like Pepper who labored on a per diem basis were required to be at their task literally from dawn to dusk. The 1563 Statute of Artificers mandated a working day from 5:00 A.M. to 7:00 or 8:00 P.M. from mid-March to mid-September, allowing two and one-half hours off for breakfast, dinner, and drinking. The work day during winter was to extend "from the spring of the day until night." Massachusetts statutes prescribed a ten-hour day for field workers, and a twelve-hour day for craftsmen.[158] A proposed bill in the General Court in 1670 calibrated field workers' wages on the assumption that they would labor "From the end of June to the end of September . . . 10 houres in the day besides repast."

---

[156] *Ibid.*, 1, pp. 208–209.

[157] *Ibid.*, 2, p. 227. As these figures reveal, Pepper's wages by the early 1660s had been raised significantly from their earlier levels. He now received 10 shillings weekly for summer work and 8 shillings for winter work rather than the original levels of between 16 and 20 pence per day. Whether this increment represents a genuine raise or reflects merely a change in the method of calibration is uncertain. In any case, it was not permanent. In the early 1660s, Pynchon compensated Pepper at a rate of 8 shillings weekly for winter work and 10 shillings for summer work; but these payments reverted to their normal levels of 20 pence and 16 pence daily by the middle of the decade. In 1661 Pynchon paid Pepper £2 15s. for "5 week and ½ . . . at 10 shillings per week"; and in 1662 Pepper received £16 5s. for "32 weeks worke and halfe (some days abated) at 10s. per weeke" and "8 weeks want one day at 8s. per week." In 1663, for "29 weekes to the 10 November," he received £14 10s. and another 13s. for "2 weeks almost . . . at 8s. per week." By 1665 Pepper's wages had returned to their earlier level. In January Pynchon paid him for "8 Months worke . . . at 20d. per day comes to £17 10s." And for "64 days work . . . at 16d. per day" he received £4 5s. For one final time, for "20 weekes sumer worke at 10s.," he was paid £10, and another £2 14s. for "7 weeks winter [work]." By 1666 Pepper's daily wages declined to the 18 to 20 pence level and there they remained. In the spring of that year for "worke . . . 6 weeks 2 days at 20d.," he was credited for £3 3s. 4d.; and for "46 days at the Mill at 20d.," he took £3 16s. 8d. And 30s. in pay compensated him for "18 days work this last summer at 20d. per day." In 1667 "44 days worke . . . winter days at 16d. per day" brought Pepper £2 18s. 8d.; for "89 days worke summer at 20d." he received £7 8s. 4d. Account Books, 2, pp. 227–229; 3, pp. 138–139.

[158] Thompson, "Time, Work-Discipline, and Industrial Capitalism," *Past and Present* (1967), p. 61, n. 16; Morris, *Government and Labor*, pp. 58–59, 65.

For "Master Taylors, and Such . . . one daye's worke [would be] 12 hours."[159]

How field workers were intended to spend their time during the day is suggested by a 1636 prescription for an English plowman's duties: " 'the Plowman shall rise before four of the clock in the morning, and after thanks given to God for his rest, and prayer for the success of his labours, he shall go into the stable.' After cleansing the stable, grooming his horses, feeding them, and preparing his tackle, he might breakfast (6–6:30 a.m.), he should plough until 2 p.m. or 3 p.m.; take half an hour for dinner; attend to his horses etc. until 6:30 p.m., when he might come in for supper."[160] While such a description probably tells as much about the author's desires to keep the workers occupied and out of trouble, it suggests the overall configuration of the day for most seventeenth-century laborers. A typical day for Francis Pepper when he was working on a per diem basis probably looked something like this:

4:30 A.M.	rise
4:30–5:00 A.M.	tend livestock
5:00–6:30 A.M.	field work
6:30–7:00 A.M.	breakfast
7:00–11:00 A.M.	field work
11:00–11:30 A.M.	cider or rum break
11:30 A.M.–2:00 P.M.	field work
2:00–3:00 P.M.	dinner
3:00–6:00 P.M.	field work, livestock maintenance, tool repair
6:00–7:00 P.M.	supper
8:30 P.M.	retire

Early American workers, unlike English field laborers, did not take a regular midday nap. They also relied on pork and cider for their dinner instead of the bread, cheese, onion, ale, and meat that were the standard fare of English workers.[161]

The yearly pattern of Pepper's work was governed by the rhythms of an agricultural society. The seventeenth-century calendar year began in late March, and appropriately so. First, fields needed to be drained and broken up by an ox-drawn plow. Plows were constructed out of ash or oak. Plowing techniques varied with the terrain and quality of soil. Typically, the most productive practice was to plow, crossplow, and harrow smooth. This procedure would

[159] Morris, *Government and Labor*, p. 65.
[160] Thompson, "Time, Work-Discipline, and Industrial Capitalism," *Past and Present* (1967), p. 77.
[161] *Ibid.*; Hartley, *Lost Country Life*, p. 152.

be followed by furrowing and crossfurrowing at three-to-four-foot intervals. Planting was then done at the intersections of the furrows. An experienced plowman like Pepper could turn over an acre or more a day of tilled land. Less assiduous husbandmen simply broke up the land—with a mattock if no plow was available—seeded by broadcast, and harrowed.[162] Plowing, even of soft bottom lands, was arduous work. Seventeenth-century plows, as Dorothy Hartley points out, needed to be "yanked out at the end of straight furrows, turned with a wide sweep, and started back again in a parallel line. Early ploughs could only work in one direction, and turn the furrow to one side. (The turn or 'wrest' plough, in which the ploughshare could be turned over to reverse the cut, was not invented till 1700.)" In addition to avoiding rocks and keeping the share and colter clean, the plowman had to monitor carefully the exertions of the draft animals. Again, from Hartley, "where oxen are used, a hundred and twenty feet is a fair length for a straight pull. The oxherd should always let his oxen stop and rest at the end of every furrow, so they go the whole length in the hope of this expected pause."[163] In addition to plowing Pynchon's fields, Pepper also broke up those of some of the family's tenants as well as those of other townsmen without plows. After the fields had been seeded, there was a two-month lull until haymaking season began, usually in late May. In Springfield the freshly cut hay from the rich bottom lands adjacent to the Agawam River was piled into ten-foot high ricks until it could be transferred to barns for storage until winter. The second crop of hay and the winter wheat were usually cut in early August. Harvesting of spring wheat, barley, oats, and peas (as well as any root crops) began in mid-September. As with the optimal times for sowing and cultivating, oral traditions provided guidance for reapers: "When barley hangs its head, and the oats begin to shed, and wheat stands stiff and begins to open." When these signs appeared, the time for the greatest labor requirements was at hand.[164]

Harvest time, more than any other period, revealed the importance of patron-client ties for Pynchon. He needed both laborers and labor discipline. A large and reliable force of reapers was essential if his extensive stands of grain were to be cut in time.

---

[162] James A. Henretta, *The Evolution of American Society, 1700–1815*, Lexington, Mass., 1973, pp. 18, 31–33; Russell, *A Long, Deep Furrow*, pp. 43, 81–84, 135, 176; William Pynchon Account Book, pp. 40, 72, 119, 192, 212; Account Books, 1, p. 328; 2, p. 63; 3, p. 97; 5, pp. 77, 115, 175, 345, 349.

[163] Hartley, *Lost Country Life*, pp. 78, 81–82.

[164] *Ibid.*, p. 174; William Pynchon Account Book, pp. 30, 136, 212, 216; Account Books, 1, p. 85; 2, pp. 171, 221, 314; 3, pp. 55, 171, 285; 5, p. 121; 6, p. 91.

Wheat and barley cannot be allowed to stand in the fields for more than two weeks after maturity, or the head breaks and the grain is lost; oats become moldy if not cut promptly. Working with a hand sickle, reapers could cut no more than one-half to three-quarters of an acre daily. As a result, John Pynchon could not have harvested his extensive fields without the assistance of Francis Pepper—and between twenty-five and forty of the other village men as well. Unwilling or unavailable laborers could have ruined him.

Once again, the employer's methods of securing adequate labor illustrate the conflation of capitalist and precapitalist relationships, as well as the role of the patron-client bond in mediating between the two and ensuring the dominance of the former. For non-clients, such as Jonathan Taylor, Pynchon guaranteed labor discipline by contractual means. As we saw earlier, Taylor's steer lease included a proviso that "he Ingages and promises me to reape and shock 2 acres of wheate and to cut one acre of pease when I call for it to be done next harvest and to doe it upon 2 days [notice]."[165] But a less cumbersome and equally reliable surety was the sense of personal obligation growing out of clientage. Come harvest time, Pynchon needed to know on whom he could count, and therefore he cultivated his clients in order that they would do the same to his fields.[166]

Once the crops were in, the remaining days of seasonable weather were devoted to sowing rye and winter wheat, gathering and processing fruit, and slaughtering animals. Because of John Pynchon's extensive pork exports, pigs made up the majority of animals slaughtered in early Springfield. Hog slaughtering always came in late fall and was followed by another month's to six weeks' work dressing carcasses, scraping hides, rendering lard, and salting and smoking hams, bacon slabs, and sides. Fall was also the time to cart apples to the cider-mill and dung to the planting fields.[167]

When winter's chill moved work indoors, Pepper began the time-consuming task of threshing and winnowing the grains he had helped plant and harvest. Each morning, his work day began with a trek to one of Pynchon's barns. As with most early American barns, Pynchon's were presumably built facing the wind to ensure a draft across the threshing floor sufficient for winnowing with

[165] Account Books, 1, p. 314.

[166] *Ibid.*, 2, p. 314; 3, pp. 104–105, 285; 5, p. 121; 6, p. 91; Henretta, *Evolution of American Society*, pp. 18, 22; Hartley, *Lost Country Life*, p. 174.

[167] William Pynchon Account Book, pp. 23, 26, 28, 302; Account Books, 1, pp. 78, 266; 2, pp. 227, 229; 3, pp. 241, 247; 5, pp. 81, 89, 423; Parker, "American Farmer," p. 183.

fans. There, working with a leather-and-wood flail, Pepper cleaned and sacked wheat, oats, barley, and peas. Wheat threshing earned Pepper five to six pence per bushel, oates and peas two and one-half pence. In the winter of 1660 Pynchon paid the workman for "threshing and cleaning 180 bushels of wheat at 5d. per bushel . . . threshing and cleaning bushels Pease . . . By 56 bushels ½ of oates and cleaning them at 2d. ½ per bushel." Later that winter, Pepper earned £4 for "threshing and cleaning 126 bushels of winter wheate at 6d. per bushel and 55 bushels of Summer wheate" and another thirty-three shillings for "threshing and cleaning oates and Pease." The following year, for "threshing and cleaning 50 bushels and ½ wheate at 5d. per bushel and 140 bushels of oates and Pease at 2d. ½" he was credited for £2 10s. 2d. With mechanical regularity, Pepper's winter days were consumed by the routine of flailing, separating, and bagging the various grains. He earned £5 in 1662 for "Threshing and cleaning 139 bushels of wheat at 5d. . . . By Threshing and cleaning 69 bushels of Pease, 110 bushels oates, 20 Barley . . . at 2d. ½ bushel." In January of 1665 Pynchon made an accounting and found that "I owe Frances for threshing and cleaning 229 bushels of wheat at 5d. per bushel £4 14s. [and] Threshing and cleaning oates and Pease 17 bushels oats at 2d. ½ per bushel £1 18s."[168] When not threshing, Pepper spent his winter days, like other men, making tools, shaving shingles, and mending tack.

Somewhat remarkably, given the multitude of his other tasks, Pepper also served as a shepherd for John Pynchon's flock of sheep. On October 6, 1656, Pynchon paid Pepper £5 2s. 6d. for "his keeping my Sheepe the yeare 1656," a figure that rose to £5 10s. the following year and by 1661 stood at £7 10s. Most shepherds, in the New World as in the Old, remained unmarried and, as we have seen, Pepper was no exception. Tending sheep meant staying with them twenty-four hours a day, and this left little time for normal familial obligations. Unlike in England and continental Europe, large-scale migratory sheep raising was not practiced in the colonies. Flocks typically remained within the environs of their owner's community, unless overgrazing or inadequate rainfall made brief periods of transhumance necessary. In a second departure from English practices, Springfield did not pasture its sheep in a common flock under the supervision of a town-supported shepherd. The privately hired shepherds such as Pepper stayed with the flocks in the outpastures, rather than returning to the town center to fold them for the night. Springfield likewise made no use

[168] Account Books, 2, pp. 227, 229.

of "stinting"—the practice of assigning the number of each kind of beast entitled to common pasturage under open field farming. Pepper's task was to keep the sheep away from the sown planting fields from March to November, usually by making resort to uncultivated outlying land grants. The early spring movement away from the town center signaled the beginning of an unchanging annual cycle for sheep cultivators.[169] Shearing time came in May, followed in Springfield by the sale of the wool at the Pynchon general store. June and July were devoted to cheese making, although this food was never the staple in American diets that it was in Europe. November brought a return to the planting fields as well as any slaughtering that there was to be done. Lambing time came in midwinter, often around Christmas, and with the onset of warm weather in March the whole process began anew.[170]

FEMALE LABOR

Francis Pepper may have been tempted to take a wife from the continuous stream of female domestics who passed a term of service in the Pynchon household, although by the young women's preference or his, he remained single.[171] In early Springfield the Pynchon mansion was the most available place of employment for young females, and over thirty girls worked in the household for a year or more.[172] In 1684 the mother of twelve-year-old Hannah Jefferys asked John Pynchon to take her daughter as a servant for six years. He entered in his account book that "Goodwife Jefferys being here and proffering her daughter Hanah to come to us: I

[169] *Ibid.*, 1, p. 208; 2, p. 227; *Springfield Town Recs.*, 1, p. 61; Russell, *A Long, Deep Furrow*, pp. 154–158. For a comparison with European practices, see Emmanuel Le Roy Ladurie, *Montaillou: The Promised Land of Error*, New York, 1978, pp. 69–119; Hartley, *Lost Country Life*, pp. 129–141.

[170] Account Books, 1, p. 282; 2, pp. 23, 61, 109, 273, 305; 3, p. 95; 5, pp. 127, 413; Le Roy Ladurie, *Montaillou*, pp. 69–119. Despite his sheep-tending and generally heavy reliance on employment by Pynchon for his subsistence, Pepper may have at least briefly aspired to be a freehold farmer. In February 1667 Pynchon "Sold to Francis Pepper That Alotment which I bought of William Brooks [for debts] in Chikkupy Plaine (a few days ago) being about 32 acres . . . for which Francis allows me £18." Pepper's motives for this land purchase remain conjectural. Perhaps he wanted to strike out on his own; or possibly be bought it for purely speculative purposes. In either case, the transaction availed him nothing, as the tract eventually reverted to Pynchon. Account Books, 3, p. 138.

[171] HCPC Rec., 1, p. 259.

[172] Account Books, 1, p. 224; 2, p. 243; 3, pp. 55, 69, 81; 5, pp. 4–5, 19, 25, 31, 61, 75, 183, 218–219, 249, 298, 461, 489, 512–513, 543; 6, pp. 22–23, 208–209, 248–249, 250.

treated with her and shee yielded to our having her (whom she says is 12 years old and since August last) till shee be 18 yeares old." After listening to Mrs. Jefferys's proposal, Pynchon consented to take the girl. He agreed to provide "her cloathes which shee now needs to wear" and to give her a pair of shoes. Both he and Mrs. Jefferys set their hand to the contract that "shee is to live with us till shee be 18 yeares of age, and [Pynchon] cloathing her and providing well for her." As his offer immediately to provide wearing apparel for Hannah suggests, the Jefferys were in difficult financial straits. For this reason, they had also put out a second daughter (apparently older) to service in the Pynchon household. In June of the preceding year, Pynchon "agreed with Goodman Jeffery for his daughter Sarah to live with us a yeare." Presumably because of his eroding economic fortunes, Jefferys was unusually adamant about the wages Sarah would receive. Pynchon "propounded her wage to be £5 10s. but he said it must be £6." To this demand, the magistrate consented, and "Shee came to us on Thursday afternoon 5th day of July 1683."[173] Abigail Dibble received the same wages as did Sarah Jefferys. Pynchon wrote in his account book that "Abigail Dibble came to us the 1st day of October 1678 and we are to give her £6 for a yeare service."[174] Likewise Hannah Morgan, whose father Miles in 1673 agreed with Pynchon "for his Daughter Hannah . . . [to] Live with us a yeare to begin [the] 1st of May which day shee is to come to us [for] £6 for the yeare."[175] These rates remained constant throughout the seventeenth century, as in 1691 we find that Susannah Ponder "Received by 2 yeares Service at £6 is £12."[176] And Hannah Holeman in 1692 came to the Pynchon household, "as a Servant faithfully and dilligently ought to doe," for annual wages of £6.[177] Finally, in 1699 Alice Beamont joined the Pynchon household at annual wages of £6.[178] The only exception to the £6 wage level, possibly because she was unusually skilled, was Priscilla Warner. On September 7, 1695, Pynchon wrote that "Priscilla Warner came to dwel with us for a yeare and for her yeares service I am to allow her £7 10s. in pay [goods or services] or £5 in money [specie]."[179]

The domestic's typical work-day of baking, brewing, cleaning,

---

[173] *Ibid.*, 5, p. 461.
[174] *Ibid.*, 5, p. 398.
[175] *Ibid.*, 5, pp. 4–5.
[176] *Ibid.*, 5, p. 219.
[177] *Ibid.*, 6, pp. 248–249.
[178] *Ibid.*, 6, p. 250.
[179] *Ibid.*, 6, p. 23.

and milking is suggested by John Pynchon's confrontation with his insouciant (and misnamed) maid, Mindwell Old. Wearied over her penchant for disappearing from the household for extended periods, thereby leaving his wife Amy to scramble to find hired substitutes, Pynchon upbraided Old and eventually docked a portion of her salary. In a revealing account book entry (one that divertingly illuminates the limits of a patron's power, even in towns like Springfield), he observed that, "Mindwel Old besides her many vagarys and often being gone part of a day into Towne, absented her selfe one whole Night and part of a day in June: again about the End of June shee went away and told the folk she would be home; however, we Saw her not next day, at least she did nothing, and often went out in an hour and neglect Milking [so] that my wife was forced to get others to Milk. On July first, or thereabouts, she went away with her Cloaths to Goody Parsons, though [she] Came again; [she also] neglected Brewing one day . . . But went to and fro, sometimes to Morgan's, sometimes to Lamb's, sometimes to [Gilbert's?] [and so often to] Cousin Holyoke that he complained of her being there. [On] July 3d, [she] did something, but only part of the day. [On] July 4th In the Morning she went out and came not neere Milking so that my wife got others, though we . . . saw her [going] to and fro yet came not to my house. In truth shee went from us in June before the end of it though shee was to and fro here to vex us til July 4th." Having had enough of this vexation, Pynchon decided that it was time pointedly to remind Old of her domestic responsibilities. "[A]bout noon, I lit out and told her shee should act like a Maid and right up things and Bake and Brew and [only then] take her liberty." His admonitions, however, had little effect, as "she went away the same day and came all and went out the house and then went unknon to us. She would be so many times gone for a whole Month and more that my wife was often forced to hire others to do the worke."[180]

A woman's contribution to her family's income was not, of course, limited to her wages as a servant. Mindwell Old notwithstanding, all women in early Springfield—unmarried and married alike—worked as long and as hard as did the men, and without constant female labor few households could have escaped privation.

In Springfield, as in all preindustrial societies, the domestic system of production rested on an explicit division of labor according to gender. Men looked after the fields, woods, and flocks. Women were responsible for preparing meals, housekeeping, making and

[180] *Ibid.*, 6, Index, p. 19.

repairing clothes, gardening, putting up preserves, making soap, milking cows, churning butter, pressing cheese, and making candles. The weekly round of a woman's work was as unrelenting as it was necessary. While men might daddle about the barn during winter months or after the first hay cutting, women confronted a year-round regimen of seemingly endless spinning, washing, mending, churning, cleaning, and baking. Moreover, come autumn, women also lent a hand with harvest, as the frequent allusions to "work of your wife's" in the Pynchon account books attest. And of course, women were charged with the task of bearing, nursing, and educating the children.

Emphasizing the potential sense of drudgery brought by such a routine, Mary Beth Norton notes that "The sameness was the quality that differentiated farm women's work from that performed by their husbands. No less physically demanding or difficult, men's tasks varied considerably from day to day and month to month. At most—during planting or harvest time, for example—men would spend two or three weeks at one job. But then they would move on to another. For a farmer, in other words, the basic cycle was yearly; for his wife, it was daily and weekly, with additional obligations superimposed seasonally. Moreover, men were able to break their work routine by making frequent trips to town or the local mill on business, or by going hunting or fishing, whereas their wives, especially if they had small children, were tied to the home."[181]

Because of the wide array of jobs assigned to her, a girl needed to start her domestic education early. Beginning around her seventh birthday, a female would be given instruction from her mother and older sisters on the variety of skills she would need. At age twelve, if the opportunity was available, she would be hired out as a domestic servant. In so doing she would continue her education in household economics and, not incidentally, bring in badly needed income for the family. Typically, as we have seen, a year's service as a domestic was worth £6.

Once married, the only way a woman could usually earn additional money for the household was by spinning wool into yarn. Few households were without a spinning wheel, and in Springfield both flax and wool were used as fibers. Because the labor of flax preparation was particularly long and tedious, the presence of so many sheep in the community helped ease the women's work load. Experienced spinners produced four skeins daily when working

[181] Mary Beth Norton, *Liberty's Daughters: The Revolutionary Experience of American Women, 1750–1800*, Boston, 1980, pp. 3–39.

alone, six if an assistant carded the wool.[182] As with their male counterparts, women workers usually found John Pynchon to be the one most eager for their services. In 1678 he wrote that "Goodwife Parsons had cotton made for my wife to Spin and brought hom the yarne this July . . . which I weighed and it was 8 pounds of yarne; for the spinning whereoff I paid her 10 pounds of cotton woole." The next month he "delivered her more cotton woole to spin for us . . . 16 pounds." And in January of the following year, he paid Mrs. Parsons nineteen shillings eight pence for "Spinning yarne for us 15 pounds at 20d. per pound." After men such as Samuel Marshfield sheared the fleece, it was given to women workers who dexterously pulled out, rolled, and bundled the fleece. After women like Mrs. Parsons had spun the wool into yarn, they returned it to male weavers such as Charles Ferry. When the weaving was finished, women again entered the productive process to "full" the cloth under water and stretch it out on "tents" to dry.[183]

Literate women were also able to earn income as private tutors. In November 1653, Pentecost Mathews (wife of the cooper) was credited by John Pynchon for "worke schooling my child . . . as in John Mathews booke [the sum of] £8 2s. 9d."[184] Again, on October 12, 1656, Pynchon wrote that "John Mathews came to me to set things straite about the schooling of my children and he ordered and agreed that I should allow him 40s. for all that is due to him."[185] Three years later, Pynchon credited "John Mathews Wife . . . By schooling Elizur [Holyoke] 2 yeers and Hannah till this November 1659 in all 35s." In addition to her schoolteaching, Mrs. Mathews received payment for "keeping of Marriage Bans."[186]

CHILD LABOR

Children were likewise vital to the labor force, especially for those families without sufficient resources to hire day-laborers. As Mikiso Hane has pointed out, "Farmers must have children. Three children are not enough. There must be at least five. If a farmer has too few children, the world will close in on him. If he has too many, he will have trouble supporting them, but there must be at least

[182] *Ibid.*, p. 17.
[183] Account Books, 5, p. 347; Hartley, *Lost Country Life*, pp. 133–138; Russell, *A Long, Deep Furrow*, pp. 139–141.
[184] Account Books, 1, p. 127.
[185] *Ibid.*, 1, p. 269.
[186] *Ibid.*, 2, p. 99.

five working hands in the family."[187] Accordingly, children's duties began at a tender age. Boys as young as five gathered wood, took pork and cider to field workers, and chased crows out of the newly sown planting grounds. They also began the ten- to fifteen-year-long process of learning how to farm by following their father and elder brothers about their respective rounds of chores. In communities such as Springfield where pork export was important, preteenage boys acted as swineherds, rounding up pigs with the aid of a dog and driving them out to grub for roots and acorns in order to fatten them for the winter slaughter. Young girls worked over the hearth or out in the garden, and as dairymaids they also helped to care for the town's large herds of livestock. Dairymaids, in addition to milking, skimming, and churning, looked after suckling calves and saw to it that after a sow farrowed, the piglets were cosseted, warmed, and fed on milk. Girls and boys together shared the onerous task of weeding, work that occupied much of the spring months. To quote again from Thomas Tusser's farming calendar: "In May get a weed-hook, a crotch and a glove and weed out such weeds, as the corn do not love. For weeding of winter corn, now it is best: but June is the better for weeding the rest."[188]

Work in seventeenth-century Springfield was a family—not a community—affair. Among the most striking omissions from the tasks listed in the local records are any references to communal labor projects: barn raisings, log rollings, fence buildings, or corn huskings. As the Pynchon account books plainly show, large projects in Springfield were accomplished by private contract, not public cooperation. Working to get ahead left little time for working for others, and the result was a settlement where conflict, not communalism, was the rule.

[187] *Peasants, Rebels, and Outcasts: The Underside of Modern Japan*, New York, 1982, p. 81. Hane is here quoting from a 20th-century Japanese informant, described as an "old farm woman." This citation was brought to my attention by E. J. Hobsbawm, "The Lowest Depths," *The New York Review of Books* (April 15, 1982), pp. 15–16.
[188] Hartley, *Lost Country Life*, pp. 103–104, 125.

· *Chapter 5* ·

Community

"Man is incapable of self-completion, and therefore never wholly predictable: a fallible, a complex combination of opposites, some reconcilable, others incapable of being resolved or harmonized; unable to cease from his search for truth, happiness, novelty, freedom, but with no guarantee, theological or logical or scientific of being able to attain them: a free, imperfect being, capable of determining his own destiny in circumstances favorable to the development of his reason and his gifts."
Sir Isaiah Berlin, *Four Essays on Liberty*
(New York 1969), p. 205

IN SEVENTEENTH-CENTURY SPRINGFIELD communal obligations were subordinated to individual needs. The town's inhabitants, far from reifying the concept of community, accepted the primacy of the individual family household as their dominant public value. The residents would cooperate with their neighbors when they had to, work in concert when it was necessary, or band together against outsiders when attacks came, but otherwise they concentrated on securing exclusively individual goals. These goals were, first, to earn their daily bread and, second, to provide a patrimony for their children. And in both of these pursuits they relied not on corporate solidarity, but on the maintenance of successful personal ties with the town's patron, John Pynchon. Non-familial relationships within the community tended to be vertical, between patron and client, rather than horizontal, among neighbors of equal status. When someone needed work, land, credit, or adjudication of a conflict, he turned to Pynchon, not the town meeting.

Rather than being an end in itself, community was the means to another end—personal advancement. Although the inhabitants publicly embraced the doctrine of the covenant, their central goals were rooted in the private acquisition of wealth. The "Articles of

Agreement" founding the town in 1636 reflect these priorities. The
settlers began by professing their fealty to God and to each other:
"We whose names are underwritten, being by God's providence
engaged together to make a plantation at and over against Agawam
upon Connecticut, do mutually agree to certain articles and orders
to be observed and kept by us and by our successors." Their first
resolution was that "We Intend by God's grace, as soon as we can,
with all convenient speed, to procure some Godly and faithful
minister with whom we purpose to join in church covenant to walk
in all the ways of Christ." But the remaining fifteen resolutions of
the articles pertain not to the moral ordering of a godly community,
but rather to sundry formulae for allocating homelots, upland, and
pasture. The second resolution asserted that "We intend that our
town shall be composed of forty families, or, if we think meet
after[ward] to alter our purpose, yet not to exceed the number of
fifty families, rich and poor." The expectation that the town would
be composed of both "rich and poor," as we have seen, was prophetic. The remaining resolutions divided up the shares of the
town center (for homelots), the "cow pasture," the "Hassokey Marsh,"
as well as the various planting fields on the periphery of the center.[1]

As the pragmatic nature of its founding articles suggests, early
Springfield bore little resemblance to the subsistence-oriented covenanted communities. It was not a "peasant utopia" or a "Christian
Utopian Closed Corporate Community." Nor was it a "peaceable
kingdom," a "one-class society," a "homogeneous communal unit"
or a "nucleated, open-field village."[2] The inhabitants of early
Springfield would have looked with wonder on such characteri-
zations of their society. Their community was founded not as a
peasant utopia, but as a fur-trading post. Although comprised of
believing Christians, Springfield failed to make rigorous efforts to
distinguish the unregenerate from the Visible Saints.[3] Significantly,
the townsmen built a house of correction, as well as a church, to
help promote an always precarious domestic tranquility. The community's inequitable land distribution patterns made tenancy and

[1] "Articles of Agreement, Springfield, Massachusetts," in John Demos, ed., *Remarkable Providences, 1600–1760*, New York, 1972, pp. 53–56.
[2] Lockridge, *A New England Town*, pp. 13, 16–17, 20, 167; Zuckerman, *Peaceable
Kingdoms*, pp. 54, 143.
[3] The town's early church records have not survived, but the high rate of antisocial
behavior among freemen (those during the first charter period who were fully
admitted church members) suggests that the requirements for church membership
were not excessively rigid. For an examination of religious discord in the Connecticut
Valley generally, see Paul R. Lucas, *Valley of Discord: Church and Society along the
Connecticut River, 1636–1725*, Hanover, N. H., 1976.

day-laboring commonplace. And no sooner had Springfield been founded than it began to fragment into four separate communities.

Nucleated settlement patterns, we have been told, were one of the principal reasons for widespread social conformity. These concentrated settlements engendered an atmosphere of continuous "neighborly scrutiny" of each other's actions. As Kai Erikson puts it in his influential study of deviance in early New England: "The towns were small and compact, the congregations watchful; every person was tuned in to the movements of his neighbor."[4] It has become axiomatic that the subsequent fragmentation of these nucleated communities signified a falling away from the first settlers' high ideals. Springfield, however, was almost from the beginning a dispersed settlement. Because of the Indians' refusal to decamp, the early inhabitants built their town on the east bank of the Connecticut River but established their planting fields on the considerably more promising west side. Some of the town's residents quickly wearied of the tiresome and dangerous trek across the river to tend their fields and, despite the Indians' protestations, built homes on the west bank. Others moved to more propitious locations north and south of the town center for the same reasons. By the late 1640s, three separate communities had emerged, and the town meeting appointed individual fence viewers for each section.[5]

By the mid-1660s, four discrete villages existed within Springfield, separated by either the Connecticut River or a minimum of three miles of forest. [See Springfield map.] These included: the town center on the east side of the river; Long Meadow, four miles south of the center; the west bank settlement (including Chicopee plain); and Skepnuck, three miles northeast of the center. In several letters to Boston, John Pynchon provided detailed presentations of this diffused settlement pattern. Writing to Governor John Leverett to dramatize Springfield's vulnerability to Indian attack, Pynchon asserted that "our People of this Towne [are] extremely scattered."[6] In 1688, while seeking increased military aid from the governor's council, he stated that "this Towne . . . consists much of out farms and a few houses together . . . above half our people are abroad and at a distance from the Towne 3 or 4 miles each way."[7] Shortly thereafter, Pynchon presented a still more specific

[4] Kai Erikson, *Wayward Puritans: A Study in the Sociology of Deviance*, New York, 1970, p. 170.

[5] *Springfield Town Recs.*, 1, p. 195.

[6] John Pynchon to John Leverett, August 4, 1675, Rare Book Room, Boston Public Library, typescript copy, CVHM.

[7] John Pynchon to the Governor's Council, August 21, 1688, London, C.O. 1/65 51, typescript copy, CVHM.

description of the town's settlement pattern: "Springfield [contains] about 120 [households] But much scattered, and the men are in 4 parts, remote one from the other like so many smale villages." He then proceeded to give his reader a breakdown of the population distribution of the four settlements: "at the Long meddow about 4 miles Southward from the Towne 20 men, on the west side of the great River 28, at Skeepmuck ful 4 Miles North 12 other farms . . . in the Towne [center] about 60 men."[8]

Sectional rivalries developed in the town meeting within a generation of settlement. Initially these conflicts involved relatively inconsequential matters, but eventually the issues separating one community from another assumed greater import. In 1667 the inhabitants on the west side of the river received abatement of one day's work on the county road on the east side in order to "make and repair their own highwayes."[9] Five years later the "Neighbors on the West side of the great River" received fifty acres from the town meeting on which to construct their own sawmill.[10] The west siders' request for a boat for crossing the river sparked a particularly nettlesome controversy, one that eventually required outside arbitration. In May of 1674 the west siders petitioned the town meeting "that a Boate might be made at the charge of the whole Towne" by reason of "their great trouble in getting over the river to come to the Publique worship of God and for other publique Meetings." The east siders resisted this proposal and "after Some Arguing about the matter," the meeting voted that "the question shalbe comitted to be decided and determined by three indifferent men that are not of this Town."[11] Despite the inhabitants' agreement to seek and abide by outside arbitrators, the boat problem remained unresolved. Five years later, the town again considered "an old Question," as to "whether or no the making a boat for the conveighance of the Inhabitants on the West side of the River over to the publike worship of God, and to other publike meetings" was not "rationally Chargable to the whole Town." Still deadlocked, the townsmen voted to refer the matter to mediators from Northampton and Hadley yet another time.[12] Labor conscriptions for road maintenance fared no better. In 1672 "Diverse persons that dwell on the East side of the great River haveing land . . . on the West side of the great River" publicly complained that they were "op-

---

[8] Mass. Archives, 36, p. 56.
[9] *Springfield Town Recs.*, 1, p. 360.
[10] *Ibid.*, 1, pp. 402–403.
[11] *Ibid.*, 2, p. 122.
[12] *Ibid.*, 2, p. 141.

pressed" because they made "little or noe use of that way [which] they should be called to repair." Those dwelling in the settlements north and south of the town made similar refusals.[13]

After 1670 the town's judicial and civil institutions routinely differentiated among the four communities in their deliberations. A discovery jury convened in 1674 to find out how Abel Wright's four-year-old son died, selected "but 6 persons" instead of the customary twelve "in regard of the remoteness of the Place from the Towne, over at Skepnuck."[14] When the grammar school opened in the town center in 1679, children living in Long Meadow, Skepnuck, and the west side were excused from compulsory attendance. Their remoteness from the center often deprived the outlying communities of important information relating to town affairs. In 1688 both Skepnuck and Long Meadow complained that fines levied on them for non-performance of highway work were unjust because they were "not warned" of these obligations.[15]

Neighborly cooperation within, as well as among, the four villages was often at a premium. As each of the four communities elevated autonomy over corporate obligations, so did individual inhabitants often scorn cooperation within the hamlet itself. The critical problem of fence maintenance is a case in point. With hungry livestock always eager to feast in the planting fields and vegetable gardens, secure fences were essential in order to protect the community's food supply. Both the common fences around the planting fields and the individually maintained homelot fences needed to be kept "hog tight and horse high." Because the common fences were only as secure as their weakest section, all stood to suffer by any one person's negligence. Violations of the community's fence ordinances were especially common in the southern half of the town center. On September 23, 1645, the town meeting recorded that "divers neighbors between Francis Ball his lott and Benjamin Cooly's lott have complayned that some of that Neighbor hood refuse to Joyne with them in makinge a fence to save theyr neighbors harmless." The meeting thereupon reiterated the mandate that "all the sayd Inhabitants shal Joyne together in a sufficient generall fence, every man brakinge a proportionable share accordinge to each man's quantity of acres." The meeting likewise reaffirmed the need to build and keep homelot fences in good repair, even at the price of coercion: "if any neighbor from Francis Ball's lott to Goodman Cooly's shall desire to Inclose his yard with a garden or an

[13] *Ibid.*, 1, p. 398.
[14] *Pynchon Court Rec.*, p. 282.
[15] *Springfield Town Recs.*, 2, p. 197.

orchard, If his next neighbor refuse to Joyne for the one halfe of the said fence, he may compell his neighbors on each side of his lott to beare the one halfe of his fence, provided he compell them not to Joyne for above 20 rodds in length."[16] The same story was true in Long Meadow. In April 1649 the town meeting observed that "there is notice taken of a disagreement amongst severall of the neighbours who have lands lyinge in the longe meddowe." The landowners there had originally agreed to complete all fencing by the fifteenth of April, but it soon became evident that this goal was unattainable. Livestock roamed and foraged through the unfenced lots "to the aparent damage of many in the said field." Therefore, "for the better settlinge of this difference" and "for avoydinge of all contentions that may arise about the settling or proportioninge of the said fence," the town adopted yet another maintenance scheme. In 1669 when "Severall persons" complained that "they cant get theire Neighbours, where theire fences is in particular, to make up theire fence sufficient," the selectmen attempted to give fence viewers new enforcement powers. Where "there are Complaints against Neighbours, that any one of them doth not make good fence . . . where either Neighbour desires," the viewers were to demand on-the-spot rectification.[17]

The reluctance of Springfield's inhabitants to behave in a "neighborly" and confraternal fashion is likewise reflected in both criminal proceedings and civil litigation. The incidence of physical assaults, slander, family feuds, fraud, and witchcraft accusations suggests that Springfield did not enjoy the strong communitarianism of Dedham and Andover. Social conflict, of course, is not itself a sign of communal ill-health. The function of conflict in a community could often be ameliorative. Verbal and physical assaults and similar confrontations provided outlets for pent-up aggressive feelings that might otherwise have worked in more insidious ways to undermine social harmony.[18] Likewise, as David T. Konig convincingly argues, we must be careful in equating rates of litigation with levels of conflict. The courts could, and did, play an integrative role in seventeenth-century Massachusetts. Yet these considerations notwithstanding, court records offer the best available portrayal of the prevailing system of values. The dramaturgical or symbolic function of court proceedings publicly established the boundaries of acceptable behavior. Court records suggest what kinds of antisocial activities were common in the community as well as the bounds

[16] *Ibid.*, 1, pp. 181–182.
[17] *Ibid.*, 1, pp. 197, 379–380.
[18] Stanley Coser, *The Function of Social Conflict*, London, 1956, Chapter 1.

beyond which certain actions could not be sanctioned. Because the official court records for seventeenth-century Springfield are incomplete, accurate per capita statistics for various crimes and civil offenses cannot be compiled. But even when used only as literary evidence, the community's judicial records can be illuminating. Using a tip-of-the-iceberg approach to crime and civil wrongs—the assumption that resort to court bespoke deeper-seated animosities not accommodable to informal or ecclesiastical resolution—court proceedings can tell much about the broader substream of social relations.[19]

These records suggest that contentious and generally non-Puritan behavior was common in early Springfield. If a resident found himself enraged at a fellow villager, he was not constrained from expressing this antipathy by an overriding need to maintain communal harmony. Self-assertion, not self-abnegation, was the rule. The town always contained a number of contumacious and mercurial inhabitants, and their actions call into question quietistic images of early Massachusetts.

Most troublesome were the artisans. Their skills, not their personal rectitude, brought them to the community and they often displayed a marked unwillingness to abide by Puritan ethical norms. Moreover, Springfield's tendency to judge men by standards of utility rather than godliness allowed some of the more highly skilled craftsmen to flout social mores with relative impunity. Their economic value to the town in general—and Pynchon in particular— allowed artisans more latitude in personal behavior than farmers and the unskilled enjoyed. The experiences of shoemaker John Norton, shingler Philip Matoone, blacksmith John Stewart, brickmaker Francis Hacklington, and canoeman Samuel Terry all point to this conclusion.[20]

John Norton originally came to Springfield as a soldier during King Philip's War and decided to remain in the community, possibly at the urging of militia leader John Pynchon.[21] Pynchon always kept a sharp eye out for skilled craftsmen, and in a frontier setting shoemakers were especially prized. But no sooner had Norton settled down than he began to run afoul of the law. He was convicted at various times of philandering, drunkenness, and aggravated as-

---

[19] Konig, *Law and Society*, pp. 88, 158–191; Nelson, *Dispute and Conflict Resolution*. For an argument that the 16th century witnessed the "surfacing of the litigious spirit" generally in Western society, see Richard L. Kagan, *Lawsuits and Litigants in Castile, 1500–1700*, Chapel Hill, 1981, pp. 3–162.

[20] *Pynchon Court Rec.*, pp. 247, 263, 289, 315; HCPC Rec., 1, pp. 7–9.

[21] Account Books, 5, p. 551.

sault. In June 1678 he was "Complained of by Mary Crowfoote and Hanah Morgan for offering abuse to them especially to Mary Crowfoote taking up her Coates and offering baseness to her, etc." Norton pleaded intoxication as a defense, "he professing his not knowing what he did And it appearing by the Testymonys and otherwise that he was Drunk." For "his· Drunkenness" as well as "his wicked and Lacivious cariage," the shoemaker received a £2 fine.[22] Again in 1686 drunkenness brought Norton before the bench. Springfield's tavernkeeper, Samuel Ely, entered an action of battery in that "Norton strake, abused, and drew Blood from the said Ely, cutting a great Gash Just above his eye and sorely bruising his forehead." The court learned that the altercation was sparked by Ely's denial of additional cider to Norton on the grounds that he had "had enough." Livid, Norton "rose up from the Table's end . . . and said By God I wil make you fetch me cider, and Coming to [Ely] struck me in the forehead with his hand or Fist with something (I suppose a shilling which before I saw in his hand) which Cut a great Gash."[23]

The shingler Philip Matoone behaved in an even more egregiously non-Puritan fashion. One of John Pynchon's most active woodworkers, Matoone, during the construction boom following King Philip's War, was paid for "6 days worke shaving shingles . . . By worke shingling over my ox house . . . By sawing 5600 shingles . . . By covering my share of the Mill" as well as "6 days worke about the mill floore." On March 1, 1679, Matoone agreed to shingle Pynchon's 51-by-24-foot barn in Round Hill for £6 10s. and "all the left over shingles."[24] He also periodically worked in one of Pynchon's sawmills, receiving £2 in 1687 for "sawing 4000 of Bords."[25] Matoone was a valuable and versatile member of the pool of woodworkers needed to forge a town out of a wilderness. And their skills allowed these craftsmen continually to test the limits of acceptable behavior.

Shortly after his arrival in Springfield during the mid-1670s, Matoone began to show signs that he could not always be counted upon to act in an upright and brotherly fashion. Within the space of little more than a year, he was called before the magistrate to answer charges of breaking and entering, cardplaying, defecating in another man's cellar, and aggravated assault. In March of 1678 the selectmen of the neighboring town of Hatfield informed mag-

[22] Pynchon Court Rec., p. 290.
[23] Ibid., p. 315.
[24] Account Books, 5, p. 537.
[25] Ibid., 6, p. 199.

istrate Pynchon "of severall persons unseasonably Playing at Cards in their Towne, and other Misdemeanors: one of whom they say Lived in this Towne, viz: Philip Mattoone." Pynchon thereupon "sent for him the said Philip Mattoone and examining him, thereabouts: He very readly and Ingeniously owned That Sometime in February last, being at Hatfield he did at an unseasonable tyme of the Night at William King's Cellar, being there till about 10 or 11 of the clock at Night Play at Cards." The cardplayers' offense was compounded by the fact that they also "layd their Tailes on King's Beame and Loome, etc. [defecation]." For "being at so Nasty a busyness," Matoone received a fifteen-shilling fine.[26] A year later, Matoone was again brought before the magistrate, this time on a charge of assault and battery against the joiner John Pope. On July 18, 1679, Pope complained "against Philip Matoone for abusing him by word, and striking him on the head yesterday, etc." Moreover, the joiner declared that "he goes in feare of [his] life for that Philip formerly abused him 2 severall tymes and now came secretly behind him and strooke him on the head and . . . displacing of his Jawbone, disabling him from speech . . . and afterward profferring his Hatchet towards him." John Pynchon, both as employer and magistrate, wanted construction workers using their hatchets on buildings, not each other, and he bound Matoone in the "sum of Ten Pounds" to ensure his good behavior. Millwright Isaac Gleason and smith John Stewart, like Matoone both from Scotland, posted the "Suertys in five Pounds a peice." The relative mildness of his punishments—Matoone was not whipped for any of these offenses and Pynchon released him from the bond within three months— suggests that he may have had established patron-client ties with the magistrate. Such a possibility might also account for the fact that he was not warned out of town.[27]

The blacksmith John Stewart likewise took advantage of the fact that Springfield was a commercial enterprise, not a peasant utopia. In the late 1670s he engaged in a heated quarrel with John Bliss and ended up assaulting his adversary with a knife.[28] After a brief jail term, he received his freedom, but was soon brought back before the magistrate for "unseasonable night meetings" and to answer charges that "he Commonly suffered the [illegal game of cards] to be played at his house."[29] The blacksmith also may have drunk too much. Account book entries from July 12 to August 20,

[26] *Pynchon Court Rec.*, pp. 289–290, 292.
[27] *Ibid.*, pp. 292–293.
[28] *Ibid.*, p. 112.
[29] *Ibid.*, p. 263.

1677, debit him for "1 Gallon Rum . . . ½ pint Rum sugard [and] 1 quart Rum."[30]

The brickmaker Francis Hacklington, as we saw earlier, was once fined for hauling bricks on the Sabbath. But he also violated other ordinances, as well as the sensibilities of his fellow villagers. On July 13, 1660, Hacklington complained against Mary Ely for "Slander for sayinge that he was seen at an unseasonable tyme of the night with Hester Bliss and that there were unseemely passages between them."[31] In September 1661 he entered suit against Alexander Edwards for "defamation in Saying that he runne away with his mare." On the same day, Hacklington likewise sought no less than £20 in damages from Henry Cunliffe in "an action of defamation, in Sayinge he is a man of noe good report."[32]

Samuel Terry was John Pynchon's most active canoeman, and this may have helped make amends for his various sexually related offenses.[33] These transgressions began in Terry's youth and continued on throughout adulthood.[34] On July 28, 1650, two witnesses told magistrate William Pynchon that "they saw Samuell Terry standing with his face to the meeting house . . . next the street chafing his yard to provoak lust [masturbating]." Terry's offense was compounded by the fact that it occurred on "the Sabbath day," even "in sermon tyme." Because the two witnesses assured the magistrate that "they had kept it private," Terry received "private Correction with a rod on his bare back, 6 lashes well set on."[35] Fornication was Terry's next offense, as on September 24, 1661, "Samuel Terry and his wife beinge presented for that they beinge marryed on the 3d of January last, they had a Son born [on] the 10th of the 5th month, beinge about 12 weekes short of the ordinary tyme of women's goinge with child." The court concluded "it manifest that they did abuse one another before marriage" and offered the Terrys the option of a £4 fine or a public whipping of "10 Lashes appiece."[36] In February 1673 Terry and eight other men stood before magistrate John Pynchon "concerning an uncivill play acted." After characterizing the play as "Immodest and beastly," the court levied fines ranging from five to twenty shillings on each of the participants.[37]

---

[30] Account Books, 5, p. 91.
[31] Pynchon Court Rec., p. 247.
[32] Ibid., pp. 250, 254.
[33] Account Books, 1, pp. 239–240; 2, p. 201; 3, pp. 144–145.
[34] Pynchon Court Rec., pp. 224, 276–277; HCPC Rec., 1, pp. 7–9.
[35] Pynchon Court Rec., p. 224.
[36] Ibid., p. 255.
[37] Ibid., pp. 276–277.

Avarice, as well as concupiscence, got Terry into hot water with the local authorities. In August 1681 he was accused by the selectmen of malfeasance while holding the office of constable. During a meeting "for Calling former Constables to an account for overpluss money . . . Samuel Terry Senr . . . did agree to pay six bushells of indean Corn (being overplus mony in his Country Rates when hee was Constable) to the town."[38]

These various transgressions did not make Terry an alienated outcast. As the court records make plain, this kind of behavior was not unusual in early Springfield, and the inhabitants were accustomed to taking it in stride—particularly from hardworking or highly skilled craftsmen. No one chose to ostracize Terry. He had been selected to wield the considerable power of the community's constable; and less than six months after his conviction for official malfeasance, the selectmen gave Terry custody of John Mathews's infant son.[39]

Artisans were not the only ones in Springfield to violate Puritan norms, as several instances of physical assault reveal vividly. Like humble people in most preindustrial societies, Springfield's residents protected their dignity with their fists when necessary, acting first and weighing the consequences later.[40] In one such encounter, an exchange of hot words between Daniel Beamon and Thomas Sweatman soon led to a hair-pulling, rib-kicking brawl in the dust. Testimony given before the magistrate the following day cited Beamon for "his abusing said Sweatman yesterday by Reprochful words, calling him Rogue and Theife: Threatning his life, and by striking him and breaking the Peace." Sweatman told the court that Beamon "gave him many Blows with his fist and kickt him when he was downe, Tore the haire off his head and tore his jacket."[41] Likewise, an argument between William Morgan and John Earle led one of the disputants to grab a wooden kitchen bowl and use it to pummel the other. In filing complaint against Earle, Morgan offered his mangled face as evidence. He asked damages from Earle "for stringe him . . . with a bowle uppon his face and nose." The attack "broke his nose, which also was evident, his nose beinge much bruised and bloody."[42] In July 1679 some of James Sexton's hogs escaped from their pen and were attempting to do violence to a neighbor's vegetable garden. Following accustomed procedure, John

[38] *Springfield Town Recs.*, 1, pp. 436–437.
[39] *Ibid.*, 2, pp. 152–153.
[40] Richard Critchfield, *Villages*, New York, 1981, p. 115; William B. Taylor, *Drinking, Homicide, and Rebellion in Colonial Mexican Villages*, Stanford, 1979.
[41] *Pynchon Court Rec.*, p. 323.
[42] *Ibid.*, p. 247.

Sackett's adolescent son attempted to put the errant swine into the town pound. Enraged, Sexton accosted the boy and "gave him 3 blows with his fist and tooke him by the Throat and hindered the putting the rest of the hogs into the Pound."[43]

Small things, such as the theft of a watermelon, could bring men to blows in early Springfield. On September 20, 1680, the millwright Isaac Gleason complained against Isaac Morgan, a field worker and tenant of John Pynchon, "for that Isack Morgan Beate his servant Josias Miller at Chikuppy last Friday, and tooke away his Gun and knife." Magistrate Pynchon thereupon "sent for him the said Isack Morgan who putts the beating of him on profe and saith that he tooke his gun and knife from him that he might doe him noe hurt, he accounting him a distracted fellow." Possibly moved by clientage ties with Morgan, Pynchon fined both defendant and complainant equally, citing Miller's provocation: "what [Morgan] did was because Josias Miller tooke away and was eating his water Million. I adjudge the said Isack Morgan for taking a Gun: and beating him to pay but five shillings because of his taking his water Million to the said Josias Miller, and also a fine of five shillings to the County for quarrelling and disturbing of Peace."[44]

But the most common kind of assault in seventeenth-century Springfield was verbal, not physical. Henry Gregory's resentment over a fine he received in 1640 for "Cheating" John Woodcock out of a pig suggests the frequency of slander in early Springfield. He told the court that "I marvill with what consi[derations] the Jury can give such damages: Seeinge in the case of John Searles I had of him but Twenty shillinges for three slanders."[45] At a court session three months earlier, "John Leonard complaines in an action of the Case against Henry Gregory for taking more recompense for driving home of certaine stray sowes than his share comes to," and "William Warrener complaines against Henry Gregory in an action of the case for layenge false imputations of money dealinge in taking of those pompions that Richard Everit gave to both of them." Four days after Gregory's protest over the slander fine, "John Woodcoke [came to William Pynchon] for a warrant to warne Henry Gregory to answer him in 2 actions of slander."[46]

Springfield's tendency to judge a man's contribution by economic instead of godly standards produced a more tolerant attitude toward sexual misconduct—and hence more opportunities for sex-

[43] *Ibid.*, p. 291.
[44] *Ibid.*, p. 294.
[45] *Ibid.*, p. 207.
[46] *Ibid.*, pp. 206–207.

ually related accusations of slander.[47] A telling example of the town's willingness to overlook sexual misdeeds to retain a productive worker is the relationship between Arthur Dudley and the widow Anna Petty. When her husband John, who had been renting thirty-five acres of town land in Chicopee, died in 1681, Mrs. Petty "covenant[ed] and promise[d] to and with the present Select men, that she wil fulfill the Conditions [of the lease] to the abovesaid terme of years." The widow Petty's confidence that she could fulfill the conditions of the lease rested on the knowledge that, despite her husband's death, she would have help with the farm work. Arthur Dudley was already living with her, a fact that came to the selectmen's attention three months later. On July 25, 1681, they "Agreed upon that a stranger that for some tyme hath had his Residence at the Widdow Petty's [is given] notice . . . to depart the Town." But Dudley did some fast talking (presumably both to Mrs. Petty and the selectmen), as four days later the town fathers retreated from their earlier order: "Whereas . . . at the former Meeting, Arthur Dudly was according to order warned out of the Town and now making his application to the Townsmen, they give him a month's liberty to answer his ingagement to the Widdow Petty."[48]

Springfield's tolerance of premarital sexual offenses apparently inspired Thomas Stebbins, Junior, to author a satiric poem on the suspect virtue of the town's maids. In 1671 magistrate John Pynchon examined Stebbins about "Publishing a mariage intended betweene Richard Barnard and Sarah Clarke" (already pregnant out of wedlock by Barnard) "which was set up on the Post in greate letters without order or knowledge of the partys or Parents." Moreover, the sign was "underwrit in smaler Letters with a foolish and reprochful Rime casting reproch upon the Towne and the Maides in [the] Towne."[49] Springfield's women did not always wait for the magistrate to protect their reputations. When Joseph Brown made sexual advances toward Lydia Morgan, she turned on him with "abusive carriage and Language towards him" using "reprochfull and Scandalous speeches . . . as calling him base Baudy Rouge and saying of him he was so mad he was ready to gore out her Gutts."[50] But more typically, it was the husband who brought suit to protect his wife's reputation. In 1686 Benjamin Knowlton accused Charles Ferry of "defaming the wife of [Knowlton] By false reports and aspersing her as being the Raiser of scandalous reports on Miriam

[47] *Ibid.*, pp. 209, 236, 272–273, 292.
[48] *Springfield Town Recs.*, 1, pp. 415, 436.
[49] *Pynchon Court Rec.*, p. 273.
[50] *Ibid.*, p. 287.

Mirrick, deceased."[51] John Stiles of Windsor complained against Springfield's John Bennet for "defaminge his wife, in saying shee was a light woman and that he could have a leape on her when he pleased."[52]

Springfield also experienced the most extreme form of slander—witchcraft accusations. During the late 1640s and early 1650s Goody Marshfield, Hugh Parsons, and Mary Parsons were all brought before the magistrate to answer charges of malefic witchcraft.[53] In May of 1649 William Pynchon ordered Mrs. Parsons to suffer twenty lashes or pay a fine of £3 for criminal defamation of Goody Marshfield. Mrs. Marshfield had "Complained against Mary . . . for reporting her to be suspected for a witch." The cooper John Mathews testified that Mary Parsons had told him that when Mrs. Marshfield lived in Windsor, "she was suspected to be a witch . . . and that it was publikely knowen that the divill followed her house." Mrs. Parsons also informed Mathews's wife Pentecost that "there were divers stronge lightes seene of late in the meddow that were never seene before the widdow Marshfield came to Towne, and that [Mrs. Marshfield] did grudge at other women that had Children because her daughter had none, and about that tyme (namely of her grudging) the child died and the cow died."[54] But while the witchcraft allegations against Mrs. Marshfield merely earned the accuser a public whipping, the charges against Mary Parsons herself and her husband Hugh brought a public inquisition.

The Parsons witchcraft controversy symbolized three of the most prominent themes in early Springfield—acquisitiveness, individu-

---

[51] *Ibid.*, pp. 311–312.

[52] *Ibid.*, p. 236.

[53] *Ibid.*, pp. 219–220; Samuel Drake, *Annals of Witchcraft in New England*, Boston, 1869, pp. 249–250. For studies of early New England witchcraft, see Boyer and Nissenbaum, *Salem Possessed*; John Demos, *Entertaining Satan: Witchcraft and the Culture of Early New England*, New York, 1982; and "Underlying Themes in the Witchcraft of Seventeenth-Century New England," in Stanley N. Katz, ed., *Colonial America*, Boston, 1976, pp. 99–118; for a discussion of the relationship between social alienation and witchcraft, see Demos, "John Godfrey and His Neighbors: Witchcraft and the Social Web in Colonial Massachusetts," *WMQ*, 33 (1976), pp. 242–265; Konig, *Law and Society*, pp. 158–185, examines the relationship between witchcraft and attitudes toward the courts. For a comparative perspective on witchcraft in various cultural settings, see Max Marwick, ed., *Witchcraft and Sorcery*, Baltimore, 1970; H. C. Erik Midelfort, *Witch Hunting in Southwestern Germany, 1562–1684*, Stanford, 1972, esp. pp. 164–192; E. E. Evans-Pritchard, *Witchcraft, Oracles and Magic among the Azande*, Oxford, 1976; Clyde Kluckhohn, *Navajo Witchcraft*, Boston, 1962; Michael T. Taussig, *The Devil and Commodity Fetishism in South America*, Chapel Hill, 1980.

[54] *Pynchon Court Rec.*, pp. 219–220.

alism, and tolerance of social deviance. The nature of the accusations against Hugh and Mary Parsons tells us as much about the
community as about the defendants. Several years before the witchcraft controversy began, there had been indications that the Parsons
would not conform to conventional norms of social behavior, even
by Springfield's tolerant standards. In 1645, while still married to
"one Lewis a papist," Mary fell into what William Pynchon characterized as "a league of amity" with brickmaker Hugh Parsons.
Confessing that she had not cohabited with her lawful husband
"above 7 years," Mrs. Lewis asked Pynchon to secure permission
from the General Court to marry Parsons.[55]

Four years later Mrs. Parsons began to accuse fellow inhabitants
of the crime of witchcraft, first Goody Marshfield and then her
own husband.[56] While the town rallied around Mrs. Marshfield,
they decided that Mary's suspicions about Hugh were well-founded.
Although she became her husband's "principal accuser," thirty-five
additional town members came forth to testify against the suspected
witch. The Springfield tax list of 1646 contained the names of only
thirty-nine householders, so Parsons apparently had managed to
alienate most of his fellow villagers.[57]

The most striking revelation from the witchcraft testimony is that
Hugh Parsons was a virtual parody of Springfield's self-image:
acquisitiveness become greed, individualism become vengefulness,
deviance become diabolical. Whether the accusers were simply pro-
jecting their own guilt for the town's generally non-Puritan ways
must remain conjectural, but the witness examinations invite such
a supposition. Moreover, they underscore the general relationship
between commercial opportunity and witchcraft throughout early
New England. All the major instances of seventeenth-century witchcraft occurred in highly commercialized communities: Windsor,
Salem, and Springfield. The parallels between the Parsons case and
Salem seem particularly revealing. Hugh Parsons embodied the
extreme economic individualism that was, in fact, tempting everyone else. And, as in Salem where Boyer and Nissenbaum found
that the most obvious targets of witchcraft accusations were *not*
directly charged (because of their political or psychological power
over the accusers), so in Springfield people may have deflected
their dissatisfactions with William Pynchon onto Parsons: the accusers couldn't really go after the magistrate, so they sought a

[55] William Pynchon to John Winthrop, September 15, 1645, *Winthrop Papers*, 5,
pp. 45–46.
[56] Drake, *Annals of Witchcraft*, pp. 224–240.
[57] *Ibid.*, pp. 219–256; *Springfield Town Recs.*, 1, pp. 190–191.

symbolic victim. The array of charges brought against Parsons lends credence to such an interpretation.[58]

One of the principal charges leveled at Parsons by his wife was that he was "egar after the World."[59] This greed led him to both abuse his wife for not doing enough field work and endanger the life of his ailing infant. Mary Parsons told the magistrate that "though my Child be so ill, and I have much to do with it, yet my Husband keepes adoe at me to help him about his Corne."[60] Because her husband "expected help from her, and . . . her Tyme was taken up about her Child," she "suspected that he was a Meanes to make an End of his Child quickly that she might be at Liberty to help him."[61] Anthony Dorchester, who with his wife resided in the Parsons household, told the examiner that Hugh "never feared eather to greeve or displease his Wife any Tyme." He declared that "I saw Nothing [Parsons] did to comfort his Wife, but he did often blame her that she did not throw in the Corne from the Dore." When Parsons denied mistreating Mary, Dorchester retorted that "he never knew him [to] blame her for doinge too much Worke, except (saith he) that she helped my Wife at any Tyme, which Worke did not bring in any profitt to him."[62]

Similar accusations of greed arose from Parsons's dealings as a brickmaker. He argued and threatened over prices and attempted to back out of unsatisfactory contracts. Blanche Bedortha told the examiner that she had earlier clashed with Parsons "about some Brickes." When she "spake Somethinge about the said Bricks that did much displease Hugh Parsons," he replied "Gammer, you neded not have said Anythinge. I spake not to you, but I shall remember you when you little think on it." Soon thereafter, in the latter stages of pregnancy, Mrs. Bedortha awoke from her sleep with "a Sorenesse about her Hart," which "increased more and more in three Places . . . the Paine was so tedious, that it was like the pricking of Knifes, so that I durst not lie downe, but was faint to be shored up with a Bagg of Cotton Wool, and with other Thinges." The mysterious pain persisted for three days and then abated as quickly as it began. Whereupon, Mrs. Bedortha informed the magistrate, "my Thoughtes were, that this Evill might come uppon me from

[58] Erikson, *Wayward Puritans*, pp. 185–205; Boyer and Nissenbaum, *Salem Possessed*; Demos, "John Godfrey," *WMQ* (1976).

[59] Drake, *Annals of Witchcraft*, p. 241.

[60] *Ibid.*, p. 236.

[61] *Ibid.*, p. 241.

[62] *Ibid.*, p. 237.

the said threatning Speech of Hugh Parsons."[63] In a similar dispute, Parsons unsuccessfully attempted to void a contract with no less an eminence than the town's minister, George Moxon. The Reverend Moxon apparently threatened suit for non-performance, provoking Parsons to confide to his wife that "if Mr. Moxon do force me to make Brickes according to Bargaine, I will be even with him." Soon thereafter, the minister's two young children developed epileptic seizures of considerable severity. Their sickness brought speculation that Hugh Parsons "be the Cause of all the Evill that is befallen to Mr. Moxon's Childerne."[64] The threat that material goals, the tendency to be "eager after the World," would be carried too far always posed a danger to highly commercialized towns like Springfield. And perhaps it was with a shudder of self-recognition that the townsmen decided that Hugh Parsons had done exactly that.

For the same reasons, Parsons's vows to seek vengeance on his fellows showed the threat posed by unrestrained individualism. Towns such as Springfield, where the binding powers of the church and town meeting were problematical, were especially susceptible to destructive forms of egotism such as vengeance vows.[65] Accordingly, as the case of Hugh Parsons shows, such behavior was often an invitation to witchcraft accusations. Of all the charges directed against the brickmaker, none was more common than accusations of promised vengeance. John Lumbard testified that "I have often herd [Parsons] say, when he hath been displeased with any Body, that he would be even with them for it." William Branch likewise asserted that "he hath often herd Hugh Parsons say when he is displeased with Anybody, I do not question but I shall be even with him at one Tyme or [an]other." The widow Marshfield told the examiner that when she had refused to abate twenty shillings of a judgment of slander against Parsons, he had replied "well, if you will not, it had bin as good you had—it will be but as wild Fier in your House, and as a Moth in your Garment, and it will doe you no Good, Ile warrent it."[66] When Parsons entered the Pynchon general store to purchase "as much Whitleather as to make a Cappe for a Flayle," William Pynchon's servant Symon Beamon "would not let him have any." Irate, Parsons returned home promising revenge. He told his wife that Beamon "shall get Nothing by it. I will be even with him." She asked him "Husband why do you threaten

[63] Ibid., pp. 224–226.
[64] Ibid., pp. 227–228.
[65] Boyer and Nissenbaum, Salem Possessed, pp. 108–109.
[66] Drake, Annals of Witchcraft, pp. 249–251, 254.

the fellow so, it is like[ly] he was busy." But Parsons brushed aside such explanations, asserting that the real reason behind the clerk's actions was personal animus: "he answered againe, if Goodman Cooly or any One else that he had liked had come he should have had it. But Ile remember him."[67]

Springfield's relative tolerance of social deviance, likewise, could be pushed into destructive realms, as the town's reaction to Parsons's mistreatment of his wife reveals. Deviance of abnormal proportions imperiled the town's always somewhat fragile social bonds, and Hugh's sadistic treatment of his wife posed just such a threat. On some occasions he would return home late at night in a melancholic and surly frame of mind to subject her to all manner of humiliations. Mary testified that her husband "used to be out a[t] Nights till Midnight" and "he used to come Home in a distempered Frame, so that I could not tell how to please him." She related that "sometymes he hath puld off the Bed Clothes and left me naked a Bed, and hath quenched the Fier; sometymes he hath thrown Pease about the howse and made me pick them up."[68] Equally objectionable was Parsons's failure to display remorse when, as Mary predicted, their infant son died. He abandoned his wife and child during the height of the illness and, after the child expired, affected a light, even jovial manner. Magistrate Pynchon queried the brickmaker "why he did not show more Respect to his Wife and Child, but went into the long Meddow and lay there all Night when his child lay at the Point of Death," and when "he herd of the Death of it the next Morning never showed any Sorrow for it." While lying in the meadow that night, he encountered George Colton, who later told the examiner that "Hugh Parsons came into the long Meddow when his Child lay at the Point of Death; and that having Word of the Death of it the next Morning, by Jonathan Burt, he was not affected with it, but he came, after a light Manner, rushing into my Howse, and said, I here my Child is dead; but I will cutt a Pipe of Tobacco first before I goe Home: and after he was gone my Wife and myself did much wonder at the lightness of his Carriage, because he showed no Affection of Sorrow for the death of his Child." This casual demeanor continued through the child's funeral and burial. Benjamin Cooley testified that when he spoke to Parsons at the internment, "he cannot remember any Sorrow that he showed, for he came to him taking a Pipe of Tobacco." By 1652 Springfield's residents had concluded that Par-

---

[67] *Ibid.*, p. 254.
[68] *Ibid.*, p. 240.

sons's failure to grieve for his deceased child, like his mistreatment of Mary, reflected not mere inhumanity, but diabolism.[69]

While less serious than witchcraft accusations, a series of vitriolic family feuds was also symptomatic of the weakness of communalism in seventeenth-century Springfield. Particularly disruptive were the Hunter-Petty and Brooks-Bedortha conflicts. By the early 1670s, the Hunters and Pettys had been engaged in a prolonged verbal war, but now fists and sticks were used as well as words. On October 24, 1673, William Hunter complained against John Petty "for abusing him by striking him etc.: as also against James the son of John Petty for that the youth called him names and gave him bad and Ill language." In response, Petty "owned the full and acknowledged that he being in a rage for Hunter's striking his Boy a Box under the Eare, that he Run to him with a stick he tooke up and struk him a Blow, which Blow having Lamed his arme at present and being scarse well now 2 or 3 days after." The magistrate accordingly ordered Petty "to pay Ten shillings to said William Hunter in way of sattisfaction and five shillings as fine to the County." But Hunter's "sattisfaction" presumably was diminished by the disposition of a second suit filed that day, this time against his termagant wife Priscilla. John Petty had brought suit "against Goodwife Hunter for offering to mischeife his wife and giving her Ill Language." This ill language involved "Railing, Scolding and other exorbitancys of the Toung." Several neighbors came before the court to testify to "her continuall Trade upon every occasion to be exorbitant with her Toung." Magistrate Pynchon held for the plaintiff and sentenced Mrs. Hunter "to be Gagged or else set in a ducking stoole and dipped in water as Law provides: Shee to choose which of them shee pleases within this halfe houre." After the half-hour interval had passed and "She not choosing either," Pynchon ordered her to be "Gagged and so to stand halfe an hour in the open street, which was done accordingly."[70]

William Brooks spent most of his life in Springfield battling his neighbors, as well as indebtedness to the Pynchons. Brooks was accused at various times of fraud, willful assault, and battery. He

---

[69] *Ibid.*, pp. 236–238. Hugh Parsons was indicted by a grand jury at the Court of Assistants in May 1652 and convicted in the subsequent jury trial, but the assistants did not consent to the jury verdict and called for the cause to come before the General Court. On May 31, 1652, this body judged the defendant not legally guilty of witchcraft. Parsons never returned to Springfield. Mary Parsons, after being convicted of murdering her child, apparently died in a Boston jail. *Pynchon Court Rec.*, pp. 22–23.

[70] *Pynchon Court Rec.*, pp. 277–278.

also informed on the illegal activities of his neighbors. His first conviction came in November 1653 for "defrauding sundry persons in witholding from them, and converting to his owne use the goods of severall persons." The defendant "was adjudged to make sattisfaction to the Sum of £18."[71] In September 1670 Brooks and his wife were accused of hurling both curses and sticks at young Joseph Bedortha. Reice Bedortha, the boy's father, made "Complaint against William Brookes and Mary his wife for theire abusing of his son Joseph Bedortha by Bad language, flinging a stick at him and using Reproachfull words, Threatening expreshons and Taunting speeches." The court thereupon ordered Brooks to pay a fine of twenty shillings to the county and twelve pence apiece to seven witnesses.[72]

Some family feuds were conducted internally, as was the case with Obadiah and Joanna Miller. As we saw earlier, over a period of three decades the Millers progressively lost all their land and housing to John Pynchon for debts, and this dolorous plight may have undermined domestic tranquility. In March of 1656, Obadiah complained against his wife "for abusing him with reproachfull tearmes or names as calling him foole, toad, and vermine and threatninge him." Joanna was one to make good on her threats as "yesterday shee fell uppon him indeavoringe to beat him at which tyme shee scratched his face and hands." John Lamb told the court that "he heard her say shee would knock him on the head: and that shee did often call him foole and other reproachfull tearmes." Obadiah's brother Thomas "testifyed that when . . . Obadiah and his wife lived with him, she did comonly call him foole and vermine: and he doth not remember he ever heard her call him husband: and that she said shee did not love him but hated him: yea shee here said shee did never love him and shee should never love him." For her "vile misbehaviour towards her husband," the court ordered Mrs. Miller whipped unless she would promise to mend her ways and treat Obadiah with the respect due him.[73] These efforts evidently came to naught, as in August of 1665 the Millers were again bound over to the county justices for "haveing had Sad bickering and Strife between themselves."[74] In other families, feuds were between generations, as with the relationship between John Stebbins and his apparently enfeebled father. In May of 1655 the commissioners took notice of young Stebbins "for misbehavinge

[71] Ibid., p. 229.
[72] Ibid., p. 270.
[73] Ibid., pp. 235–236.
[74] Ibid., p. 114.

himself towards his aged Father calling him Old foole and uttering other unseemely words towards him." Stebbins was forced to post a bond "in the summe of Forty pounds" for his appearance to answer the charges, but luckily for him, "there was not found full proofe of such evill carriage" and he was discharged from the bond. Similarly, Samuel Ball was ordered to be flogged for using abusive language toward his father-in-law, Benjamin Mun, asserting that he respected him "no more than an old Indian," and exclaiming, "A father! There's a father indeed!"[75]

Social harmony in Springfield was also endangered by ethnic antagonisms—particularly against the Scots. Although the number of Scots in the town never exceeded a dozen men, their impact on the community was considerable. Several, such as the blacksmith John Stewart, were highly skilled and valued artisans; and Edward Foster, Hugh Dudley, William Hunter, and John Riley were all important to the Pynchons either as tenants or field workers. But many of the Scots, unlike the Welshmen, Miles Morgan, Thomas Mirrick, and Alexander Edwards, had come to the community involuntarily—usually as war captives.[76] Hence their personal commitment to Puritan norms was minimal. Most of the Scots appear in the court records as worldly, contentious individuals, who were suffered to remain in the community because of their contributions to the local economy. All of them appeared before the magistrate at one time or another, on charges varying from assault and attempted murder to drunkenness, cardplaying, and slander.[77] The Scots tested the limits of social tolerance in early Springfield, and sometimes the equanimity of their fellow villagers as well. While court records fail to specify if ethnic antagonisms drove John Stewart to take a knife to John Bliss, such animosity clearly sparked a dispute between Thomas Miller and John Henryson in 1659. On November 30, Henryson, a Scot, complained "against Thomas Miller for detayning a cart from him which he sayth he had right unto." Miller compounded his offense by "using reproachfull speeches," one of which included a reference to Henryson as a "Scottish dogg." In his defense, Miller retorted that Henryson had "threatned [him] in Saying that eyther he or Thomas Miller should dy before he should have the cart." The court decided to fine both men ten shillings for "one of them strikinge and the other threatninge Slaughter."[78]

[75] *Ibid.*, p. 234; Green, *Springfield*, p. 142.
[76] *Pynchon Court Rec.*, pp. 224–227; *Springfield Town Recs.*, 1, p. 306.
[77] *Pynchon Court Rec.*, pp. 112, 216, 243, 254, 316–317, 320–321.
[78] *Ibid.*, p. 243.

144 • Chapter 5

While Miller and Henryson disputed over the custody of the oxcart, they shared a common fondness for the illegal game of cardplaying, an accusation often brought against the Scots. Henryson and his wife Martha flouted local ordinances by hosting card games on a regular basis and, despite his threats of mayhem three years earlier, Thomas Miller was among those invited to one such gathering in 1662. On March 20, William Brooks testified before the commissioners that "one Night at John Henryson's house he saw Edward Foster, Thomas Miller, John Bag, and John Scot all foure of them playing at Cards: and I staying in the house neere an houre they continued theire play at Cards all the while." In the subsequent testimony, the novices tried to separate themselves from the more committed players. Foster told the court that "It is true I did then Play, but I am but a beginner to play at cards." Defendants Scot, Bagg, and Miller made similar protestations. But Henryson was forced to admit that he and his wife habitually played the illegal game, although his justification for the practice was somewhat unusual. He explained his actions by declaring that "I did not so well know the Law against it and I was willing to have recreation for my wife to drive away melancholy." Mrs. Henryson's emotional well-being became a central element in her husband's defense. Apparently a manic-depressive, her more melancholic periods drove John nearly to distraction. During his trial, Henryson readily acknowledged "Playing at Cards severall tymes at his howse," but said "he was willing to [do] any thing when his wife was Ill to make her merry." Unmoved by Henryson's husbandly solicitude, the court fined him twenty shillings.[79]

While their ethnicity and penchant for cardplaying may have set the Scots off from their fellow villagers, their violence and litigiousness did not, as the careers of John Woodcock and Thomas Mirrick attest. Neither man was a Scot; Woodcock was English, Mirrick Welsh. Their disputatious and strife-ridden careers symbolize the casual frequency of social conflict in early Springfield.[80]

Unusually godly and other-directed images for the first generation of Puritan New Englanders fail to comprehend someone like John Woodcock. Throughout his stay in Springfield, he engaged in one confrontation after another with his fellow citizens. Not love and forbearance, but disdain and hostility characterized his social attitudes. He took people to court at the drop of a hat and showed respect for no one, including the town's minister. Dissatisfied with

[79] *Ibid.*, pp. 257–258.
[80] *Ibid.*, pp. 204, 205, 206, 207–208, 209–210, 230, 231–232, 246–247, 256–257, 317.

some carpentry work performed on his house by John Cable, in November 1639 he sued Cable in an action on the case "for certaine worke he did to a house that was built on Agawam." One month later Woodcock again stood before the magistrate, this time to answer an accusation of slander against the Reverend George Moxon. Apparently finding Moxon's exhortations from the pulpit less than uplifting, he was charged with "laughinge in Sermon tyme" as well as "his misdemenor [of] idlenesse." The minister sought damages of £9 19s. but the jury awarded him only £6 13s.—which was still an unusually high sum for slander. Uncowed, Woodcock replied that "he owed Mr. Moxon no money nor none he would pay him," and compounded this defiance by the assertion that "he had showed Mr. Moxon more respect and reverence than ever he would againe."[81]

Despite the jury's judgment against Woodcock, his truculent behavior continued unabated. On September 10, 1640, he complained against Henry Gregory for "Cheatinge [him out of a] Pigg" to the amount of £4 14s. Woodcock's litigation was initially unsuccessful, but magistrate William Pynchon allowed the plaintiff a new trial on a writ of error and eventually ruled in his behalf. Civil actions in early Massachusetts, unlike criminal proceedings, were usually tried before a jury, and they ruled that Woodcock's claims for damages were exorbitant and awarded him but twenty-four shillings.[82] Later that week, he returned before the magistrate to accuse Gregory of "2 actions of slander." Pynchon used this opportunity to query the plaintiff regarding the £6 13s. damages still owed to the Reverend Moxon. Informed by Woodcock that he had no intention of paying, Pynchon thereupon ordered the constable to "attach the body of John Woodcoke [and see that you] kepe his body in prison or irons untill he shall take some course to satisfie the said George Moxon." If incarceration failed to achieve this end, the constable was to "put him out to service and labor till he make satisfaction."[83] Out of jail four months later, Woodcock was sued by Robert Ashley for non-delivery of a gun Ashley had bought from him. Ashley demanded compensation for "a gunn that he bought of him and paid him 22s. 6d. for it, yet the said John Woodcoke did not deliver it to him accordinge to bargaine." Woodcock denied the charges and attempted to impeach the plaintiff's credibility. Ashley, he said, "was a pratinge fellow" for "he had set off his gunn and now he did not owe him past 7 or 8s." Woodcock

[81] *Ibid.*, pp. 204–205.
[82] *Ibid.*, pp. 206–207.
[83] *Ibid.*, pp. 207–208.

then attacked one of the plaintiff's witnesses, accusing Judith Gregory of slander for "swearing before God I would break her head."[84]

Thomas Mirrick, like John Woodcock, spent much of his time in litigation with his fellow inhabitants. During the period from 1639 to 1661, he appeared before the bench a total of sixteen times.[85] On November 14, 1639, William Pynchon complained against Mirrick "for not delivering back the Boards he lent him."[86] A month later, Mirrick had more problems with unreturned lumber. He entered suit against his neighbor Thomas Horton "for 3 boards that the said Thomas Mirrick wants."[87] Going to court over such seemingly inconsequential provocations was not unusual in seventeenth-century Springfield, and Horton accordingly retaliated in kind. He charged Mirrick with "not doinge a sufficient daye's worke for the wages of a day," "taking away certaine planks or boards," "felling of two trees in the lot of Thomas Horton," and "changing of 4 bushells of corne after it was delivered." That same day, Mirrick complained against John Woodcock in an action of debt for two shillings sixpence as well as for the unpaid price of four bushels of corn.[88] In January 1642 Richard Hull brought suit against Mirrick for purloining "a Rugg [and] certaine tooles."[89] On December 21, 1643, Mirrick disputed with another neighbor, Robert Ashley, over "keepinge a pig which Mr. Thomas Mericke saith is his."[90] And, as we have seen, Mirrick was also fined at least twice for non-performance of contractual obligations.

Thomas Mirrick's inability to live harmoniously with his neighbors persisted for the next two decades, sometimes taking an uglier tone. In 1648 he broke up a fist fight between his son and young Samuel Edwards, with apparently something less than total impartiality. Samuel's father Alexander, like Mirrick a Welshman, brought Mirrick to court "for abusing his child named Samuell Edwards, being about 5 or 6 years ould the 14 of Aprill last." The court judged Mirrick guilty of "3 batteries besides vilifieing words, as hang him better kill him than he kill my child." The actions of his daughter Hannah likewise brought Mirrick into conflict with his neighbors. In 1673 she successfully accused Jonathan Morgan

[84] *Ibid.*, pp. 209–210.
[85] *Ibid.*, pp. 204, 205–206, 209, 211, 214, 215, 216, 230, 231–232, 246–247, 256–257, 317.
[86] *Ibid.*, p. 204.
[87] *Ibid.*, pp. 204–205.
[88] *Ibid.*, pp. 205–206.
[89] *Ibid.*, p. 211.
[90] *Ibid.*, p. 214.

of the paternity of her child, securing a court order that he pay
two shillings sixpence weekly in child-support for four years.[91] Finally, in October 1686 "Deacon Jonathan Burt [was] plaintiff against
Thomas Mirick Senior for saying of Deacon Burt that he lyed basely
and was a Lying man."[92] All these confrontations with his neighbors, however, did not make Thomas Mirrick a social pariah. He
served as sergeant of the militia, a post of some distinction, as well
as town constable. Moreover, he was a fully admitted member of
the church, who was described in the General Court's 1665 certif-
icate of freemanship as a "settled inhabitant . . . orthodox in religion
of pious and laudable conversation." The Court, therefore, "allowes
and approves of him to be a freeman of this jurisdiction."[93] Mirrick
was not an outcast because, as we have seen, in early Springfield
confrontational behavior was not unusual.

The General Court's formulary description of Thomas Mirrick
raises the pivotal question of the church's role in Springfield—a
question rendered especially difficult by the loss of all seventeenth-
century church records. What evidence does exist points to the
fragile and problematical nature of the minister's position and authority in the town, analogous in many ways to the role the Reverend Samuel Parris played in Boyer and Nissenbaum's study of
Salem. Springfielders lived without a meetinghouse for the settlement's first decade, and without a minister during most of the
1650s. The two ministers who spent prolonged periods in the town,
George Moxon and Pelatiah Glover, engaged in a variety of heated
confrontations with their parishioners, including slander suits, salary disputes, and appeals to the General Court over ownership of
ministerial lands. Moxon, as we have seen, saw his two children
"bewitched," was slandered and treated contemptuously by the day-
laborer John Woodcock, and cheated by the brickmason Hugh
Parsons. Possibly such remembrances contributed to his decision
to return to England with William Pynchon in 1652. The community's two succeeding ministers made similar decisions within
months, not years, of their arrival. The town recorder laconically
observed in March of 1656 that the Reverend Mr. Thompson had
"deserted this Plantation." Glover, in residence from 1661 until his
death in 1692, threatened in 1669 to quit Springfield because he
believed his salary inadequate. And from 1676 until his death, he
bitterly contested the town's decision to retract ownership of his
house and lands, a dispute not resolved by a General Court decision

[91] *Ibid.*, pp. 216–217; Green, *Springfield*, p. 140.
[92] *Pynchon Court Rec.*, p. 317.
[93] *Mass. Recs.*, 4, Part 2, p. 285.

in the minister's favor in 1681. Not until January 1696 did the town meeting vote to compensate Glover's son for the loss of his inheritance: "It was voted to give mr. Pelatiah Glover [Jr.] a deed to Secure to him the Land that the Town did give him in way of Compensation for the ministry Land." Somewhat belatedly, the inhabitants also "voted that the Town Treasurer should see to the getting the arrears of the rates payable to the Reverend mr. Glover, his father." As the elder Glover had doubtless discovered a good deal earlier, the trials of the faithful shepherd in communities as contentious as Springfield were many and the rewards few.[94]

That such contentiousness was acceptable, as well as common, is shown by the town's relatively low level of out-migration. While, as with all New England communities, the settler generation was characterized by an exceedingly high level of population movement, by 1660 most inhabitants had ended their peregrinations. Of the seventy-two inhabitants entered on the tax list of 1664, fifty-five, or 76.4 percent, would die in Springfield. In 1672, seventy-six male inhabitants lived in the town. Sixty-one, or 80.3 percent, of these men remained permanently in the community. Even during the troublesome and dangerous decades of the Indian wars after 1675, Springfield's population continued relatively stable. Of the 120 male inhabitants on the tax list of 1685, seventy-six, or 63.3 percent, remained in the town until they died.[95] We cannot automatically assume that those who stayed in Springfield did so willingly; those men inextricably indebted to John Pynchon were not free simply to pull up stakes and move on. Those who tried it rarely escaped eventual property attachments.[96] But it is likely that most of the town's inhabitants remained in Springfield on their own volition. Economic peril there was, but there was opportunity as well—the reason most of them had come in the first place. If they had been seeking quietude, corporate security, and communal harmony—and had been sufficiently well-to-do—Dedham or Andover would have been a more logical choice. Even in the parochial world of seventeenth-century New England, towns doubtless quickly developed reputations for certain modes of behavior and public ethos. Migrants resting by the wayside exchanged intelligence regarding what various settlements "were like." Men traveling without family and without capital assets, like many of Springfield's earliest arrivals, learned where to expect a welcome and where to expect a

[94] *Springfield Town Recs.*, 2, p. 341; Green, *Springfield*, pp. 128, 180–181.
[95] *Springfield Town Recs.*, 1, pp. 159–161, 171, 175, 190–191, 220–221; 2, pp. 77, 115–117; 1685 Tax List.
[96] "Records of Execution," CVHM.

warning-out. They found out which towns were looking for skilled artisans and which were looking for Visible Saints. What these first settlers needed most was work, short-term credit, and an eventual chance to become a husbandman or even a yeoman. These were prospects that the Pynchons could offer. Developmental towns, therefore, grew out of the decisions made by workers as well as merchant-entrepreneurs.[97]

Springfield's settlers were a motley lot, and the community they built reflected this diversity. What bound them together was a kind of primitive Christianity and the desire to work. They were united by opportunity, not affection, and accordingly behaved as individuals, not as a community. They were tolerant of everything except laziness, as John Mathews learned to his grief. This was not fertile ground for generating and nourishing a common and coherent system of values, and much of what did emerge was the rough agrarian justice timeless in the English countryside. Ronald Blythe's description of Victorian villages could well apply to Springfield: "They were leisure-less communities for most of their inhabitants, full of cruelty and injustice, greed and pride—and full of imagination and satisfactions and goodness."[98] There is no need to see the town's inhabitants as either better or worse than they were. They were not the antiacquisitive communalists memorialized by Rousseau, nor were they Maxim Gorky's "half-savage [men], stupid, heavy, . . . lazily, carelessly, incapably slumped" across the land. Most of Springfield's residents emerge as decent, hard-working, reliable, if somewhat prickly, individuals. The town also included its share of less attractive people—malicious, dishonest, apathetic, and mean-spirited. Whatever their character, however, the motivation of these inhabitants—although preindustrial—was probably not remarkably different from our own.[99] What kept the settlers of early Springfield going were the small joys, gratifications, and reveries that make life meaningful or bearable in any place or time. Bone-weary, weatherbeaten men and women surely found respite and solace—perhaps even a small epiphany—from the quotidian: luminous stars, flowering orchards, awakening songbirds, or the lapidary joy of fine craftsmanship. But among these pleasures and

[97] For emphasizing this point (and many others) to me, I am indebted to Fred V. Carstensen.

[98] Ronald Blythe, "The Way We Lived Then," *The New York Review of Books* (June 25, 1981), p. 37.

[99] Jonathan Lieberson, "The Silent Majority," *The New York Review of Books* (October 22, 1981), p. 36.

satisfactions, forming strong affective ties with one's neighbor was not prominent.

The ties that mattered most in Springfield were not with one's neighbor, but one's patron—a point doubtless appreciated by Thomas Mirrick, one of John Pynchon's most active canoemen. And because of the strength and scope of patron-client ties in seventeenth-century Springfield, the townsmen challenged one another instead of their social betters—even during the most tumultuous period in the colony's history.

Chapter 6

Decline of the Gentry, 1684–1703

"They lied when they told me I was everything."
William Shakespeare, *King Lear*

THE GLORIOUS REVOLUTION was the greatest test of John Pynchon's authority in Springfield. The wave of antiauthoritarianism unleashed by the overthrow of the Dominion of New England brought rocketing factionalism and conflict to virtually every community in Massachusetts, of which the hysteria at Salem was only the most spectacular example. But in Springfield, tranquility reigned. While selectmen, representatives, and militia officers who had served the Dominion were summarily removed from office elsewhere, in Springfield the old guard remained secure. This docility was largely the result of Pynchon's financial hold over so many of the town's inhabitants. With the livelihood of over half the community's citizens resting in his hands, Pynchon's political authority remained unimperiled. But the same was not true *elsewhere* in the Connecticut Valley. Despite his activities as plantation founder and his ownership of extensive acreage in every settlement, Pynchon relied on deference, not dependence, to implement his will in the valley. And while dependence did not decline as a consequence of the Dominion, deference did. Nothing better illustrates the dichotomy between financial dependence and personal deference than the events of the decade after 1689.

The Dominion of New England is the central divide in the history of colonial Massachusetts. Within five years, it swept away the conditions by which men like John Pynchon asserted such remarkable dominance over their communities. The two prerequisites for this ascendancy had been their status as mediators and the fealty of the general population. Its results had been land grants and economic power. The Dominion, however, deprived the gentry of both their mediator's role and the inhabitants' fealty. During the second charter period (1691–1774), the Pynchons of Springfield, the Otises of Barnstable, and the Willards of the Merrimack Valley would have to share their power with competing elites. And they would have to earn, not assume by right, the loyalties of the general populace.

This decline was a direct result of the gentry's identification with the authoritarian Dominion government. The Dominion of New England (1686–1689) grew out of the Stuart Kings' determination to curb smuggling and reassert royal control in the northern colonies. By the early 1680s, the Crown's investigator, Edward Randolph, persuaded the Lords of Trade to issue a writ of *quo warranto* against Massachusetts.[1] The writ served notice on Massachusetts to show cause why its disregard of the Navigation Acts should not result in abrogation of the 1629 charter. The colonists' protestations of innocence were of no avail, and in 1684 the Crown suspended the first Massachusetts charter. Soon thereafter, Massachusetts, Plymouth, and New Hampshire were consolidated into a unified Dominion of New England, later to be joined by Connecticut, Rhode Island, New York, and the Jerseys.[2]

Centralization of authority—political, judicial, and military—became the byword of the Dominion. A royally appointed governor and council replaced the popularly elected governor, House of Deputies, and council. Justices of the peace, appointed by the governor, replaced magistrates as custodians of the county courts. Militia officers were likewise appointed by the governor alone. Together, the governor and council held exclusive power to legislate, tax, regulate trade, and enforce a system of quitrents. Church membership ceased to be the basis of political participation; and county courts were replaced by Courts of Quarter Sessions and Courts of Common Pleas—both staffed by justices of the peace. All writs were to run in the name of the King. Finally, town meetings were to be limited to one a year. Authority now emanated from Boston instead of being shared among local and provincial leaders working in

[1] For an examination of Randolph's role in the suspension of the 1629 charter, see Michael Garibaldi Hall, *Edward Randolph and the American Colonies, 1676–1703*, New York, 1969, pp. 79–97.

[2] The best recent case study of the local impact of the Dominion period is found in Konig, *Law and Society*, pp. 158–185. For the overall impact of the Dominion throughout New England, see Richard R. Johnson, *Adjustment to Empire: The New England Colonies, 1675–1715*, New Brunswick, N. J., 1981, pp. 71–305. Although dated in some of its interpretations, Viola Barnes, *The Dominion of New England*, New Haven, 1923, remains indispensable. See also T. H. Breen, *The Character of the Good Ruler: Puritan Political Ideas in New England, 1630–1730*, New Haven, 1970, pp. 134–202; Breen, "War, Taxes, and Political Brokers: The Ordeal of Massachusetts Bay, 1675–1692," in Breen, *Puritans and Adventurers: Change and Persistence in Early America*, New York, 1980, pp. 81–105; and Kenneth A. Lockridge, *Settlement and Unsettlement in Early America: The Crisis of Political Legitimacy Before the Revolution*, Cambridge, Eng., 1981, pp. 31–36.

concert. Because the governor, councilors, justices, and militia officers were now all appointed by the imperial authorities, local influence over these officials sharply declined.

But while the Dominion centralized authority in Boston, it factionalized it in the countryside. For mediators like John Pynchon, the replacement of a single assistant in a locality by several justices of the peace ended the exclusivity of access to provincial authorities that the old gentry had previously enjoyed. In the Connecticut Valley, rather than having to deal only through Pynchon, men could now solicit any one of the near dozen justices that served the region.[3]

The suspension of the first charter in 1684 transfixed Pynchon on an insoluble dilemma. The preservation of his dominant position depended on support for and by the colonial leaders in Boston. His role as mediator, by definition, demanded that he retain links with both the valley residents and the provincial government. The erosion of one position threatened the vitality of the other. If Pynchon alienated valley inhabitants, or alternatively, estranged himself from the provincial leaders in Boston, he risked losing his mediator's role. And because it was through this role that Pynchon had achieved preeminence, he could not lightly countenance its destruction.

After some hesitation, Pynchon chose to cast his lot with the rulers of the new regime, despite the likelihood that their authoritarian designs would deeply antagonize most New Englanders. In September 1685 Edward Randolph submitted Pynchon's name to the Committee of Trade and Foreign Plantations as a person "well disposed and fit" for membership in the reorganized government. Randolph's confidence that Pynchon would be a loyal servant of the Dominion proved well placed. The former Springfield magistrate accepted appointment as councilor immediately after the arrival of interim president, Joseph Dudley.[4] During the hiatus of authority, he acted as an intermediary between the incoming and outgoing governments. He and William Stoughton were "sent to the Magistrates to acquaint them with the King's Commands being

---

[3] John M. Murrin traces the impact of the judicial reorganization under the Dominion and second charter period in "The Legal Transformation: The Bench and Bar of Eighteenth-Century Massachusetts," in Katz, ed., *Colonial America*, 1971 ed., pp. 415–448; see also Murrin, "Review Essay," *History and Theory*, 2 (1972), pp. 226–275; Murrin, "Colonial Political Development," in *Oxford Conference in American Colonial History*, New York, 1983; Richard S. Dunn, *Puritans and Yankees: The Winthrop Dynasty of New England, 1630–1717*, New York, 1971, pp. 225–227.

[4] *Pynchon Court Rec.*, p. 49.

come." At Dudley's initial meeting with the old rulers on May 17, the order of entrance into the General Court was "Major Dudley the President, Major Pynchon" followed by the remaining members of the council.[5] In the succeeding days Pynchon accepted a variety of positions within the new government, including membership on the committee assigned to audit the previous treasurer's accounts, the committee formed to recommend more efficient procedures for collecting duties on wines and liquors (a position not likely to endear Pynchon to his fellow merchants), and the committee responsible for overseeing the proprietors of Narragansett County.

These services, however, were subordinate to Pynchon's more critical charge of using his influence to gain general acceptance of the Dominion government. Repeatedly Dudley called on him to lobby reluctant New England leaders into supporting the new government. In addition, both Dudley and his imperious successor, Governor Sir Edmund Andros, asked Pynchon to identify potential appointees who would look favorably on the new regime. The identification of potential officers for the militia was particularly critical. On June 1, 1686, Dudley informed the Committee of Trade and Foreign Plantations that "Our next case was to Intrust the Militia in the hands of persons well affected to his Majesty, the Chiefest whereof being Members of the council."[6]

Pynchon also helped Dudley and Randolph effect the submission of Connecticut, perhaps the most pressing objective of the new government. In July 1686 Randolph arrived in Springfield to confer with Pynchon about strategies for achieving this end. Shortly thereafter the Dudley council decided that Pynchon and Wait Winthrop would be dispatched as emissaries to the recalcitrant colony. The president mandated that "a letter . . . be sent unto Governor Treat of Connecticut, and Major Pinchon and Wait Winthrop Esquire desired to undertake a visit to so many of the Councill of said colony as can be conveyned at Hartford by the 3d day of August next."[7] In December 1686, in a related letter to Pynchon, Randolph revealed both his contempt of those New Englanders who opposed the Dominion and his expectation of support from the Springfield leader. In reference to the leaders of Connecticut, Randolph observed: "I hear the little Quacks there are endeavouring to divert their coming under one government, but his Excellency [Andros] has his Majesty's commands to accept of

[5] M. Halsey Thomas, ed., *The Diary of Samuel Sewall*, New York, 1973, 1, pp. 112–113.

[6] "Dudley Records," *Proc. Mass. Hist. Soc.*, 2nd Ser., 13 (1899–1900), p. 240.

[7] *Ibid.*, p. 259.

their surrender, which they cannot avoid." Randolph urged Pynchon to haste and assured him of the governor's esteem: "Now I intreat you . . . to come as soon as you can . . . I am to tell you his Excellency has a great kindness for you." He also informed Pynchon of a forthcoming letter "in which is an order of the Governor in Council to be communicated through your whole county." Randolph assured the Springfield leader that "We have Road Island already, and I fear not Connecticutt." He closed with a final contemptuous reference to Connecticut's civic leaders: "A dutifull submission will well become them . . . His Excellency will propose greater advantages for their ease and happiness than their weak phancy's can project."[8]

The arrival of Governor Andros in December 1686 further solidified Pynchon's position in the government. The two men were not strangers to each other. In October 1680, as we have seen, the Springfield leader had received a commission from the Massachusetts General Court to travel to Fort Albany and seek the "advice and consent" of Andros (then governor of New York) in negotiations with the Mohawks.[9] In addition, Pynchon had also come into contact with Andros through his trading connections with Robert Livingston. Accordingly, Pynchon's appointments multiplied under the new governor. He was renominated to the council and received a commission as a justice of the peace for Hampshire County. He was also chosen to sit on the Quarterly Court of Sessions, the Inferior Court of Common Pleas, and the Prerogative Court of Hampshire. In recognition of his former fur-trading activities, Pynchon was appointed to a committee with Gershom Bulkeley and Jonathan Tyng "for setting and ordering the methods of the beaver trade with the Indians."[10] And last, he accepted commissions as lieutenant colonel and eventually colonel of the Hampshire County militia.

Andros then reaffirmed the importance of Randolph's goal of using Pynchon's influence to secure the capitulation of Connecticut. In late October 1687, the governor, accompanied by a cavalcade of seventy-six men, traveled to Hartford to gain the colony's formal recognition of his government's sovereignty. Seven councilors, including Pynchon, made the five-day journey.[11] Pynchon's task was

[8] "Pincheon Papers," *Coll. Mass. Hist. Soc.*, 2nd Ser., 8 (1819), pp. 237–238.
[9] *Pynchon Court Rec.*, pp. 44, 51.
[10] "Andros Records," *Proceedings of the American Antiquarian Society*, New Series, 13 (1899–1900), pp 237–268.
[11] Albert C. Bates, "Expedition of Sir Edmund Andros to Connecticut in 1687," *Proc. Amer. Antiquarian Soc.*, N.S., 48 (1938), pp. 279–280.

doubtless eased by the enthusiastic cooperation of his two powerful
relatives, John Allyn and Samuel Willys. Earlier, Allyn had written
Fitz John Winthrop, another Andros adherent, asking for sugges-
tions for overcoming the opposition of his fellow leaders in the
colony; and Willys, according to Richard S. Dunn, was "one of
Andros' warmest admirers."[12] A year later, Governor Andros again
traveled to the Connecticut Valley. This time his objective was to
insure the support of all "principal officers and magistrates," and
to conduct inquiries into any real or potential opposition to his
government. The governor began his eyre at Hartford by consulting with Allyn and other Connecticut leaders. His next stop was
Springfield, where he conferred with Pynchon. After similar visits
to Hadley and Brookfield, he returned to Boston via Worcester
and Marlborough. Andros's obvious attempt to intimidate his op-
ponents by these draconian inquests only cast the Dominion deeper
into public odium. And in the Connecticut Valley, as elsewhere,
those supporting Andros came into increased disrepute.

Within a year of its creation, the Dominion utterly alienated most
New Englanders. The very presence of Andros, the first royally
appointed governor of Massachusetts, galled inhabitants long accustomed to running their affairs untrammeled by imperial controls. Moreover, his reforms hit at the very core of New England
life. He increased taxes, undermined all existing land titles, reduced
local control over judicial institutions, enforced the Navigation Acts,
and actively fostered the Anglican Church, still repugnant to many
New Englanders. And the governor's inability to check Indian attacks on outlying settlements earned him the wrath of all who lived
in frontier communities.

The Massachusetts version of the Glorious Revolution in April
1689 drove Governor Andros from office and ended the Dominion's transitory and strife-filled existence. Not surprisingly, the governor's fall from power occasioned great rejoicing throughout New
England. Those celebrating, however, did not include many of the
long-standing colonial leaders, most of whom had served Andros
and now saw their status imperiled by his political demise. And, as
subsequent events revealed, they had good reason for these fears.

The Glorious Revolution in Massachusetts resulted in the most
complete repudiation of the colony's leaders since its founding. At
both the local and provincial levels, those who had served the Dominion were summarily removed from positions of authority. In
Dedham the "hatred of the 'foreign' regime was so great . . . that

[12] Dunn, *Puritans and Yankees*, pp. 242–243.

the townsmen followed up Andros' fall by repudiating every selectman who had served during the years of his rule." Eight men
with cumulative service exceeding fifty years held office between
1687 and 1689. Only one of these was ever elected again.[13] Plymouth colony experienced a similar overthrow of the old order.[14]
In Barnstable on Cape Cod the period after the Glorious Revolution "witnessed the unseating of the old order on the one hand"
and on the other "a period of dynamic experimentation and social
mobility that brought with it the advent of a political and economic
nouveau riche."[15] At the provincial level, this repudiation of leadership was no less dramatic. These disruptions, according to John
M. Murrin, resulted in "sweeping political changes." He observes
that "Remarkably few members of the colonial House of Deputies
ever got into the new House of Representatives in the 1690s."
Excepting Plymouth colony towns, "only one out of eight representatives had seen legislative service under the old Charter." He
concludes that the "real problem of the decade appears to have
been a lack of acceptable leadership at all levels. The old gods had
fallen, and nobody was convincing enough to proclaim their successors."[16] Still another historian describes Massachusetts as "utterly
bereft of first-class leadership."[17]

This wholesale repudiation of leadership, in turn, initiated a
period of protracted chaos and factionalism. The rejection of the
old rulers left Massachusetts rudderless, for the first time without
a coherent sense of hierarchy. From the beginning a patriarchal
society where men expected their leaders to "order them" and exact
"due obedience," New Englanders now floundered about in efforts
to erect new political structures. With their former officers in disrepute, the colony's inhabitants looked in vain for someone to in-
terpret their vision. The result, in the words of an unsympathetic
English observer, was a "Labyrinth of Miserys," and a search for
scapegoats.[18] The most dramatic manifestation of this collective loss
of moral authority was the witchcraft controversy at Salem, which

---

[13] Lockridge, *A New England Town*, p. 88.

[14] George Langdon, Jr., *Pilgrim Colony*, New Haven, 1967, p. 234.

[15] John J. Waters, Jr., *The Otis Family in Provincial and Revolutionary Massachusetts*,
Chapel Hill, 1968, pp. 50–51; Richard R. Johnson denies that the Glorious Revolution dramatically affected patterns of officeholding at the town level; *Adjustment
to Empire*, p. 114. But much of his own carefully gathered data suggests otherwise;
see especially pp. 71, 102–103, 116.

[16] Murrin, "Review Essay," *History and Theory* (1972), pp. 259–260.

[17] Dunn, *Puritans and Yankees*, p. 192.

[18] Professor T. H. Breen offers a convincing interpretation of the changes effected
during and after the Andros regime; see *Character of the Good Ruler*, pp. 134–239.

grew out of a clash between two factions within the town.[19] And in the Connecticut Valley, John Pynchon, the dominant figure in western Massachusetts for over forty years, now found himself rebuffed and traduced by those who had always offered him deference and obedience.

At first it appeared that Pynchon would ride out the storm. After the Glorious Revolution he gradually but surely recaptured his former official positions. Although his support for Andros led to exclusion from the Council for the Safety of the People and Conservation of the Peace (created as an interim government after the fall of the Dominion), Pynchon did not long remain out of power. In September 1689 he was reconfirmed as an Associate for the County Court of Hampshire. He reverted to the rank of major in the militia but remained the highest officer in the Hampshire County regiment. In 1693 he was again elected to the council and retained this position until his death a decade later. Pynchon soon discovered, however, that the authority that these positions had once conferred had diminished sharply.

Part of the reason for this decline was structural. The second Massachusetts charter of 1691 retained many of the political and judicial changes instituted under the Dominion. In particular, the centralizing features of the earlier reorganization remained virtually intact, thus depriving Pynchon of his former status as a mediator. Under the second charter, the governor nominated and appointed judges, commissioners of oyer and terminer, justices of the peace, and other lower judicial officials, although he now needed consent from the council. Councilors were not directly appointed by the governor as under the Dominion, but neither were they popularly elected as under the first charter. Under the second charter, assistants were elected by members of the two houses immediately after the May elections for the House of Representatives.[20] Accordingly, Pynchon failed to reclaim his "gatekeeping" function between the locality and the province. The post-Dominion centralization and proliferation of justices, again, denied him exclusivity of access between local and provincial spheres.

Equally important as the structural curtailment of his mediator's role was John Pynchon's loss of moral authority within the valley. By associating himself with the odious Dominion government, he lost the fealty of the general populace. And without this deference, his effectiveness as an instrument of General Court policy was

[19] Boyer and Nissenbaum, *Salem Possessed.*
[20] Dunn, *Puritans and Yankees*, p. 238.

markedly diminished. Under the first charter, Pynchon received land grants, fur-trading monopolies, and other emoluments because he successfully implemented General Court directives in the Connecticut Valley. His mediating functions rested on a delicate equipoise between deference in the valley and influence in Boston. Whether it was town founding (or governing), adjudication of boundary disputes, maintenance of social order, or oversight of the county militia, Pynchon's word had been law in the first charter period. After the Glorious Revolution, however, this was no longer true—particularly regarding the militia. His inability properly to "order" the militiamen was the most palpable sign of his fall from grace among valley residents. And the trouble began within three months of the Glorious Revolution.

In July 1689 the Springfield leader informed the authorities in Boston of the rise of a "discontented party" within Hampshire County. The militiamen in Northampton had mutinied against the officers who had led them during the Dominion period. With what seemed to Pynchon astonishing boldness, the malcontents demanded the overthrow of the existing militia leadership. One Sergeant James King had taken it upon himself to lead a rebellion against the old officers, and his efforts had been enthusiastically supported by the militia's rank-and-file. As Pynchon described the situation to the council: "there is a Party at Northampton who fal in with Serjeant King, or rather that are stirred up by him, who doe so blow up discontents against their former officers as make it difficult [to restore order]."[21] In open defiance of Pynchon, King and his cohorts decided that they could now choose their own officers without the General Court's prior approval. The rebels "account they have now Liberty to do what they Please without Consulting." King, moreover, was not confining his activities to Northampton. "For that an order hath lately been Improved in some of the Townes (By Serjeant King) for a new choise where were officers standing and under most sufficient settlement who had their Comissions from the former Government." To Pynchon's chagrin, King's rabble-rousing was having its desired effect. It had "disquieted some others that were quiet before."[22]

Unlike a riot in Hadley in 1675 in which Pynchon swiftly and forcefully disciplined the malcontents (without seeking or expecting help from Boston), he now stood by helpless. In an uncharacteristically pusillanimous fashion, he confessed to the colonial

[21] Mass. Archives, 107, p. 239.
[22] *Ibid.*, 107, p. 178.

leadership that his authority was insufficient to pacify the "disorderly faction." Replying to the governor's injunction that he take more forceful measures to reimpose authority, Pynchon confessed the futility of his previous efforts in this regard: "Concerning the Disorders and Irregularitys of the Soldiers in this County which you mention, I have not been wanting to allay the same." In this contest between Pynchon and an obscure militia sergeant from Northampton, James King emerged triumphant.[23]

Sergeant King succeeded in his efforts to turn out the militia officers who had served under the Dominion and replace them with democratically elected leaders. And King's methods in achieving these ends repudiated time-honored notions of order, hierarchy, and authority. Rather than appealing for support for those "able men" whom the community recognized as its natural leaders, King forged his alliance with a naked appeal for political support from his friends and relatives. Power politics and personal ambition replaced diffidence and popular passivity. Commenting on King's self-aggrandizing tactics, Pynchon observed "I understand it was carried on in designe by himself that he might be Captaine, and it hath so far prevailed that he is Nominated for Lieutenant." Pynchon ascribed this success to King's extensive kinship ties. He attributed King's election as lieutenant to his "having so many Relations as I am Informed about 32 in that Towne by Marriage and Blood who have halpen it on and are the Faction in that Busyness." According to the Springfield leader, others likewise cast their support to Sergeant King in order to achieve political ascendancy themselves. Medad Pomery "join[ed] with them and being of them (which also helpt him to the place of Deputy)." Most distressing to Pynchon was the success of this self-serving and rebellious faction rather than the "most sober and considerate" men who were "otherwise disposed and would rest in and with their former officers who were Commissioned before May 1686." Largely as a result of the agitators' efforts, people were "questioning everything."[24]

Two weeks later Sergeant King's defiance of John Pynchon passed beyond repudiation of duly appointed militia officers into open refusal to obey military orders. In early August of 1689, the Springfield leader attempted to organize an expedition aimed at protecting the most northerly valley towns from impending Indian attack. Pynchon successfully filled Springfield's complement of volunteers, but when he sought a similar levy from Northampton, he ran into a roadblock. He wrote the governor's council that he "sent

[23] *Pynchon Court Rec.*, pp. 284–286; Mass. Archives, 107, p. 239.
[24] Mass. Archives, 107, p. 239.

away 15 men from Springfield who readyly attended." But the directive that the "upper Townes [contribute] for more to make up 50 at Northampton" fell on deaf ears. He told the council that "Serjeant King cavilled about my Power, hindered the Comittee of Militia, etc. told them Springfield men would not obey me (tho it proved otherwise)." Continuing, Pynchon related an affront from King that would have been unthinkable a decade earlier. Without mincing words, the sergeant described Pynchon as nothing less than a political nullity. King asserted that "I had noe Power and they mattered me [not at all]." And to add insult to injury, King declared that he "would not give 3 skips of a louse" for Pynchon's authority. He concluded his tirade with the observation that Pynchon was effectively a eunuch because "the [General] Court could act nothing." As Pynchon later summarized the unhappy situation for the council, "[King] and Pomrey bid defiance to the old Commission officers, such a height of Pride are matters come to [at Northampton] that nothing would or could be done by or from my orders and directions. But they said they would If any came from Springfield goe as volunteers."[25]

Faced with such brazen contempt for his authority, Pynchon capitulated. Under the first charter, outright defiance of his will invariably brought the offender under the lash. Now, however, Pynchon did nothing. Like Sergeant King, he recognized that in the post-Dominion political climate, he needed the direct and open support of both the General Court and the local populace. One without the other was not enough. King's taunt that the "Court could act nothing" doubtless rankled the more because it was true.

The militia rebellion soon engulfed the entire upper valley. In every town except Springfield soldiers defied their superiors and repudiated John Pynchon's officer appointments. In direct violation of the 1668 General Court law banning local trainband elections, the rank-and-file of every militia unit followed King's example and argued that they themselves and not their colonel or governor should choose company-level officers. Pynchon informed the council in May 1690 that the importunate militiamen had refused to serve under any officers but those of their own choosing. "Our Soldiers I know wil much desire and Insist upon it, to have Commission officers of their owne (I meane such as they know)."[26] Pynchon continued to emphasize in his correspondence to the council

[25] *Ibid.*, 107, p. 258.
[26] Mass. Archives, 36, p. 56. For an examination of the changing pattern of militia elections in the seventeenth century, see T. H. Breen, "English Origins and New World Development: The Case of the Covenanted Militia in Seventeenth-Century Massachusetts," *Past and Present*, 57 (1972), pp. 74–96.

that any officers selected would have to be acceptable to the soldiery. Now he routinely asked the troops beforehand if a candidate would be satisfactory to them. Regarding one such case, he told the council that "Our Soldiers also were something Trobled they had not a Commission officer of their owne: But I pacified them and apointed them a Sergeant."[27] In February 1692 the Springfield leader appointed Jonathan Wells lieutenant of the Deerfield militia company. Pynchon assured Governor Simon Bradstreet that Wells was both "the fittest to take charge" and, more important, he was "to their owne Sattisfaction."[28]

In the critical area of military strategy, the militia companies likewise demanded local autonomy. The transparent need for a coordinated policy against the Indians failed to inspire the companies to heed John Pynchon's commands. Beside himself with frustration, in February 1690 he told Samuel Willys and John Allyn: "we are extreme naked and open and cant agree upon fortification, some being for one way and some another So that I feare we shall ly to the mercy of the enemy."[29] In December 1694 he wrote Secretary Isaac Addington, again underscoring the grave peril created by the militia companies' unwillingness to abide by his directives. Most alarming to Pynchon was the failure adequately to fortify the various valley settlements. "I did hint something to you about Fortifications in these towns. We are not in any good posture: both Hatfield, Hadley etc. as wel as this Towne and al Rest are too open." He directly ascribed the shoddy efforts at fortification to the antiauthoritarianism occasioned by the Glorious Revolution. The "Fortifications [are] gone to decay [because] for repairing or making new [fortifications] the People a litle wilful, inclined to do what and how they please or not at all." In concluding his letter, Pynchon sounded a theme that appeared with increasing regularity in his correspondence after 1689—the need for direct intervention from Boston. He told Addington that "an order from authority is necessary to enforce to what is meete and will strengthen the hands of those here [who have tried to] have something done but find obstructions to their discouragmt and laying it aside."[30]

The most vivid manifestation of the new antiauthoritarianism was the collapse of the Hampshire County Horse Troop. John

[27] Mass. Archives, 35, p. 102.

[28] Ibid., 37, p. 306A.

[29] John Pynchon to Samuel Willys and John Allyn, February 24, 1690, Edes Ms., Mass. Hist. Soc.

[30] John Pynchon to Isaac Addington, December 3, 1694, Pocumtuck Valley Memorial Association, Deerfield, Mass., typescript copy, CVHM.

Pynchon, as commander of the cavalry troop, watched in dismay as the unit, once the pride of the valley, disintegrated. Disgruntled over the loss of some of their perquisites under a military reorganization bill in 1691, and caught up in the general malaise of the period, the horse troopers effectively disbanded. Many of the cavalrymen declared that the only unit they would join was the less financially demanding foot regiment. The substantial eligibility requirements for membership in the horse troop, ownership of £100 in estate, a horse, saddle, bridle, holster, pistol, and sword, perforce limited its recruitment pool to the "better sort." The majority of citizens simply did not possess the resources necessary for service in the cavalry. Accordingly, because of their class origins, when the horse regiment mutinied their actions were an especially serious blow to social order.[31] In July 1690 Pynchon wrote to Major General Wait Winthrop to "lay the state of the Troope in this County before your judicious Consideration." So dispirited was the troop, he lamented, that the question now was "Whether it be meete wholy to give it up or to Continue and settle it, or a Troope here or noe: For we are almost Come to Noe Troope now." He described the precipitous decline of the unit. "I think some few yeares ago This for a Countrey Troope was in as good a Posture, and the Troopers suitably spirited for service, wel equipped and Generally as compleate in Armes, as most Troopers or Troops were." However, "of late some discouragemt have made some decline the service, and let their armes and furniture goe to Ruine."[32]

The obvious need for a combat-ready cavalry force in the face of the ever-present threat of Indian attack failed to prevent wholesale defections. Recognizing the troop's strategic importance, Pynchon spared no effort to keep it intact. But his exhortations, admonitions, and outright threats of legal reprisal failed to stem the tide. The defection to the foot regiment of the officers and most experienced veterans was particularly galling to the Springfield leader. Some men had even thrown away their weapons and equipment. He informed Winthrop that "many and Generally the best of the Troopers here have [en]listed in the Foote, dispose[d] of their armes and Furniture, some out of the Country: and have left the Troope: And besides the officers of the Troop are taken off . . . and Indeed it is a Question whether now the Troope hath any Commission officers or any others almost." As their actions implied,

[31] Jack S. Radabaugh, "The Militia of Colonial Massachusetts," *Military Affairs*, 18 (1954), pp. 3–4; Morrison Sharp, "Leadership and Democracy in the Early New England System of Defense," *American Historical Review*, 50 (1945), pp. 244–260.

[32] John Pynchon to Major General Wait Winthrop, July 17, 1690, Winthrop Mss.

the soldiers were "much disgusted" and irascible and in no mood to cooperate with anyone—least of all Pynchon. "[T]hus you se," he concluded, "how broke the Troope is."[33]

The disintegration of the Hampshire Horse Troop placed serious and occasionally insurmountable restrictions on John Pynchon's options as commander. Deprived of the tactical flexibility offered by the cavalry, he abandoned his former strategy of search-and-destroy. He ordered the upper valley towns garrisoned, but without the troopers he could not pursue attacking Indians into their forest encampments. He described these constraints on his actions in a letter to General Winthrop. "In June last I had thoughts to have called the Troope together which they have not been never since the [Glorious] Revolution [but] . . . we apprehended it might be meete to forbeare til I had writ to you and given you an account of matters." Increasingly, he was forced to place exclusive reliance on foot soldiers. But they too soon rebelled against his authority.[34]

Desertion from the foot, as with the cavalry, was the most troublesome problem. After 1689 its ranks were progressively depleted as more and more men simply laid down their arms and refused to serve. Pynchon, of course, was responsible for prosecuting and disciplining deserters. But, again, his efforts to punish offenders usually came to nothing. Men continued to leave the militia with impunity, to the consternation of those who remained. In December 1689 he described the overall loss of morale because of the rising rate of desertion. Most destructive was the example set by those who fled from military service and remained unpunished. "One man after he was Impressed and particularly ordered to be ready ran away, to the great discontent of some and to the Embolding of others So that some of the Soldiers told me If he were let escape (for what he did was with a high hand) they would also run away."[35]

John Pynchon's inability to reimpose order in the Connecticut Valley led him to turn increasingly to Boston for assistance. He urged Secretary Addington "for the settlement and strengthing the hands of any in Authority in this county, To send orders and Commissions to them."[36] He informed the council of his impotence in the absence of this outside help. "I recken I must cease unless you give further orders to approve of what I have done." He emphasized that this support was necessary "that I may not be ob-

---

[33] *Ibid.*
[34] *Ibid.*
[35] Mass. Archives, 35, p. 102.
[36] *Ibid.*

noxious (as the Comission officers at Northampton are) to the Derision of Mr. King and Mr. Pomrey and such others as Joine with them." He consoled himself by reflecting on the sufferings of Christ. "Al Peckt at the Captain of our Salvation who Indured the Contridiction of sinners."[37]

Petitions for assistance from the authorities in Boston reflected Pynchon's loss of local autonomy. Under the first charter, Pynchon, as magistrate, colonel of the militia regiment, and county court judge, had been accustomed to acting on his own to resolve local issues. During the period from 1655 to 1685, he rarely sought advice or assistance from the governor or General Court. Indeed, the Massachusetts Archives, the repository of all official correspondence between magistrates and the General Court, contains no request for guidance from Pynchon before 1684. When rioters took to the streets in Hadley, militia deployments were needed, or additional provisions required, he acted unilaterally and on his own authority. When he did communicate with Boston, it was to inform the Court of actions he *already* had taken. After the Glorious Revolution, however, this situation changed dramatically. Now Pynchon began increasingly to seek support and counsel from Boston before acting. In January 1692 he told Governor Bradstreet that "we are thoughtful for our own security and desire to be set in the right way thereunto," and "[I] have always thought it a difficult concerne and not meete for me to act without application to your Honors" that "accordingly we may Receive meete directions and orders."[38]

With the legitimacy of his authority openly questioned in the Connecticut Valley, Pynchon was reluctant to take any action without explicit orders from Boston for fear of local recriminations. In 1694, with the militia garrisons at Deerfield and Brookfield undermanned and underprovisioned, Pynchon faced the decision either to abandon the settlements or reinforce their defenders. After a dangerous period of vacillation, he wrote Secretary Addington to complain that his repeated requests for guidance had gone unanswered. "Very desirous I have been to have advice about continueing or quitting the Garrison at Dearefeild and Brookfeild and therefore have several times writ for directions thereabouts, both to his excellency before he went off, and (If I mistake not) to yourself also, But have not Received one line, nor heard any thing in the least concerning the same." The Springfield leader closed

---

[37] Mass. Archives, 107, p. 258.
[38] Mass. Archives, 37, pp. 223–224B.

his letter with the comment that "[I] am loath upon my owne head to discharge them, least If any thing fal out not well, I should deservedly be Blamed."[39] Eight months later, Pynchon informed Lieutenant Governor William Stoughton that he had contemplated raising militia quotas but "yet I am necessitated to leave off, partly upon the account of it being too much for me to undertake upon my owne head without orders," especially "If it should not succeed as I hope for."[40] The following month he reiterated to Stoughton that the "disquiets and exercises . . . proves hard for me to doe what belongs to me . . . [and] I shal be glad of any good directions from your Honor."[41]

The nature of John Pynchon's power, accordingly, was transformed from that of mediator to that of communicator. No longer able to act on his own authority throughout much of Hampshire County, Pynchon became instead a conduit for implementing the policies of the governor and council. This function, of course, had always been an important part of his influence. But this power had always been *discretionary*: the General Court delegated authority to Pynchon to use as he saw fit. The Court had originally granted Pynchon this mandate because it recognized that his power in the valley was unchallenged. After the Glorious Revolution, however, with his authority openly disputed and his institutional autonomy eroded by the recent centralization, John Pynchon sought his legitimacy not as a local gentry leader, but as a commissioned royal official.[42]

The loss of his local autonomy meant that persuasion replaced coercion as the method used to bring offenders in line. In December 1690, a year and a half after the outbreak of the Northampton mutiny, Pynchon wrote to the ringleaders and admonished them to mend their ways. He cited the need for their cooperation in the face of both impending Indian attacks and the continuing threat of civil disorder. "Considering the state and condition of your Company and the unsettledness thereof . . . I have thoughts of moveing you to be in a due use of meanes for your ful Settlement and Establishment as to Military or Commission officers . . . this time of Commotion and danger cals for a meete and due Settlement without delay." Pynchon also explicitly stated that he now saw his

---

[39] John Pynchon to Isaac Addington, December 3, 1694, Pocumtuck Valley Memorial Association, typescript copy CVHM.

[40] Mass. Archives, 30, p. 368B.

[41] Mass. Archives, 51, p. 48.

[42] John M. Murrin explores the wider ramifications of the "royalization" of provincial Massachusetts in "Anglicizing an American Colony."

role as exclusively advisory. No longer did he threaten retribution or invoke the authority of the state. "I thinke it my duty to stir you up thereunto, and doe advise you to cal your Company together, and to propose to them (to whom If you please you may Impart these lines) the Supply and setling of a Captain So far as in them lyes, by Nomination of the most fit persons among you for that End." As suggested by his choice of words in communicating these views to the militiamen—"please," "advise," and "propose"—Pynchon was reduced to cajoling low-ranking militia officials in Northampton, at one point simply to transmit his views to their fellow company members.[43]

In his admonition to the Northampton militia to select the "most fit persons," John Pynchon sounded a theme he would repeat endlessly for the next five years—the hazards of repudiating society's "natural" rulers. He believed that the rejection of the former officers represented a turning away from men of "sober," "moderate," and "sound judgment." Those who supplanted these leaders, in Pynchon's view, were factious, hotheaded, and misguided. They elevated personal advancement above the public good. Accordingly, he urged the Northampton malcontents to "lay . . . aside al headyness, prejudice, commotion of spirit or single respects and misguided affections" and "act Judiciously with respect to the Publike good and advantage." He counseled them to "lay aside al animositys, disatisfaction upon personal and frivolous accounts, and . . . consider the good of the whole." In an attempt to show the rebels the folly of laying the blame for the "troblus times" exclusively at the feet of their former leaders, he resorted to historical allusion. "[A]s once in Padua, when much discontent was and Intentions of election of New Persons to office, one advised them . . . before they rejected the old ones to consider wel where they might find better, which advice allayed the hot spirits so that al the former were continued." He concluded by reiterating the need for social order and a due submission to legitimate authority. He urged the company to "Consider the best and fittest persons upon al accounts, and make noe alteration but what may be safe and beneficial to the Company and Publike good." The paramount necessity for an orderly transition of power was heightened by the "unquiet some of your people have been (upon what good Grounds or Reasons I know not, and they would doe wel to Consider)."[44]

John Pynchon's hopes for a restoration of public order rested

---

[43] Mass. Archives, 36, p. 242.
[44] *Ibid.*

on the receipt of a more authoritarian royal charter. Increasingly he believed that only new and more draconian directives from the Crown would quell the discontented spirits in the valley. He applauded when Secretary Addington received the first such communication. He expressed confidence that things would begin to get better "Now that you have new orders and directions from England which wilbe more available and effectual than former orders." In December 1689 he informed the council of "The Great Incouragement we have, that we spedyly may have our charter." With an uncharacteristic lapse into sarcasm, Pynchon declared that a charter would "quiet and settle al moderate and well disposed spirits" and as "for others, might they goe off . . . for I persuade my selfe the Country could well Spare them."[45] In May 1692, again bewailing the chaotic conditions, he expressed hope that the newly appointed governor, Sir William Phips, would bring about a "tendency to a hopeful good Settlement" of what Pynchon later refered to as this "Pore low Country."[46] Five days later, Pynchon wrote that he trusted that "God wil Incline the king to send good Governors to us."[47] Deprived since 1689 of his mediating functions, the Springfield leader still hoped for a restoration of his old authority—but now under the mantle of royal legitimacy. However, as his subsequent treatment at the hands of the General Court revealed, a return to the old days was impossible.

A corollary to John Pynchon's declining authority in the Connecticut Valley was his decreasing influence in Boston. As he had achieved dominance largely because of the reciprocal nature of local and provincial power, the erosion of one threatened the credibility of the other. By the early 1690s, largely dependent on support from the governor and council for his influence, Pynchon no longer commanded automatic diffidence in Boston. Under the first charter, the General Court handsomely rewarded him for his services because it could count on him to deliver. But with his post-Revolution impotence in valley affairs (Springfield, of course, excepted), Pynchon's petitions for remuneration for his services usually elicited only a token payment.

The most dramatic evidence of John Pynchon's fall from political grace was the result of one such petition presented to the General Court in late 1696. In an elaborately detailed rendition of his many services as militia commander since 1692, he importuned the Court to make restitution for his time and expenditures. In requesting

---

[45] Mass. Archives, 35, p. 102.
[46] Mass. Archives, 51, p. 1.
[47] *Ibid.*, 51, p. 6.

compensation for his "Imploy as Commander of the Regiment of Militia" he told the court that "[your petitioner] Hath according to his ability unwearedly Served the Countrey Foure yeares and Halfe, ever since the arrival of Sir William Phips: In which service he hath laid out himselfe more than a litle for the Publike: This end of the Province Having in this time of War been Infested with the enymys several attempts upon our Townes, which hath occasioned your Petitioner to spend a greate part of his time every yeare in attending the Duty of his Place and Command, Besides much experience otherwise therein: For all which He never had any least Consideration or allowance for the same." These services included "Impress[ing] and sending out men, Besides the Inspecting of the Garrisons at Dearefeild and Brookfeild." He also underscored his fidelity of service and burden of command. "The Care and ordering of al, Having wholy layne upon your Petitioner . . . [a] ready attending his duty therein upon al occasions," but "especially in times of greatest Exigency for the Publike advantage." The scope of these services "Imboldens your Petitioner, From these Premises, to aske your Honors' meete grattification and ordering him such a due allowance as your Honorable selves, [as] This general Assembly Shal judge a meete compensation for his Past and already chearful service." And the Springfield leader openly implied that his future availability for assistance to the Court would hinge on a satisfactory response to the petition. Adequate compensation, he observed, "wil be an obligation upon him to persist in whatever further Service he is Capable of."[48]

Although Pynchon submitted his request to the Court in November 1696, it was not answered until almost a year later, an unprecedented delay by the standards of the first charter period. On October 15, 1697, the document was read aloud in the House of Representatives. Without debate, the legislators proceeded to a vote. The result of the balloting was to pay the man, who a decade earlier had received eight square miles of land for a similar request, "for his Extraordinary Service and charges, the Sum of . . . Ten pounds, no more."[49]

The eclipse of John Pynchon's mediator status, did not, of course, signal the loss of authority within Springfield itself. Although no longer able to exercise the traditional prerogatives of a gentry leader at the county or provincial levels, Pynchon's hold over his own community remained secure. He continued his role as the patron

[48] Mass. Archives, 70, p. 309.
[49] *Ibid.*

of a town that had been since its founding the virtual fiefdom of his family. With the new royalization of Massachusetts, however, the days of their dominance were numbered. The conditions that had brought the family to power were eliminated by the Glorious Revolution, and the next generation would have to adjust to a very different political world. They would do, not command, the bidding of others. Although John Pynchon left no record of his thoughts during these declining years, one of his sharpest disappointments doubtless was the personal and financial ineptitude of his only surviving son, John. When his father breathed his last in January 1703, the younger Pynchon inherited the family's wealth and business enterprises; but the days of the titans were over. Even if he had been a more able and charismatic figure, he was powerless to prevent the emergence of new competing elites, men who—unlike his father and grandfather—served their King rather than their community.

Springfield, John Pynchon, and New England Society

THE SALIENT CHARACTERISTICS of seventeenth-century Springfield chronicled herein—developmentalism, diversification, acquisitiveness, individualism, contentiousness, and stratification—were not unique to the Connecticut Valley settlement. All existing studies of coastal ports such as Boston and Salem have revealed similar societies. Paul Boyer and Stephen Nissenbaum, in particular, found the same combination of factiousness, market-orientation, and witchcraft in late seventeenth-century Salem. Several recent examinations of Plymouth show the tenuousness of communalism in that colony; and a study of Windsor, Connecticut finds a markedly high level of tolerance for socially deviant behavior. David T. Konig's *Law and Society in Puritan Massachusetts: Essex County, 1629–1692* reveals litigiousness, social conflict, and heterogeneity from the mid-seventeenth century onward throughout northeastern Massachusetts. Paul R. Lucas entitles his study of church and society in the Connecticut Valley from 1636 to 1725, *Valley of Discord*. David Grayson Allen's, *In English Ways*, published in 1981, speaks of the "remarkable" diversity of land usage and custom in early New England and ascribes it to the variety of regional differences in the mother country. Social diversity in seventeenth-century Massachusetts is—or should be—an established fact.[1]

What we don't know is the respective population breakdown for the developmental, coastal, and corporate communities. Only such information will provide a means to measure whether Dedham or Springfield more nearly typified the experience of most New Englanders. Given the disproportionate size of Boston and Salem (Boston's population in 1700 was 6,700, Salem's in 1683 was 2,489,

---

[1] Rutman, *Winthrop's Boston*; Boyer and Nissenbaum, *Salem Possessed*; Richard P. Gildrie, *Salem, Massachusetts, 1626–1683: A Covenant Community*, Charlottesville, Va., 1975; Young, *From 'Good Order' to Glorious Revolution*; Demos, *A Little Commonwealth*; Langdon, *Pilgrim Colony*; Linda A. Bissell, "Family, Friends, and Neighbors: Social Interaction in Seventeenth-Century Windsor, Connecticut," Ph.D. dissertation, Brandeis University, 1973.

while in 1710 some 980 souls lived in Dedham), and Springfield's example from western Massachusetts, continued exclusive reliance on the Dedham model seems untenable.[2] It appears that many, if not most, seventeenth-century New Englanders lived in acquisitive, market-oriented societies. But the verdict is still out. We need more comparative data on patterns of work, land tenure, bankruptcy, and economic dependency generally in a much wider cross section of communities. To do this, historians of early America must turn away from primary reliance on church and town records, and exploit more fully available account books, probate inventories, and court records. Only then can the gap between prescription and performance be measured. Only then will we be able to bring the mosaic of images that we now have for Puritan New England into sharper focus. Despite calls for a moratorium—not a mandate—regarding new research on colonial Massachusetts, much work remains to be done.[3]

Even at the current vantage point, some of the wider implications of the Springfield experience seem clear. First is the developmental role of the merchant-entrepreneurs in the settlement of early New England. There was something exceptional about this New World gentry. They were able to control land, command commercial enterprises (unlike the English gentry studied by Lawrence Stone and Hugh Trevor-Roper), and to implement a new form of informal but effective social control without any of the official marks of the old aristocracy. The principal reason for their success, it seems, was their role in capitalizing and directing the development of New World settlement. In contrast to Old World gentry who, as Joyce Appleby observes, "spent rather than invested their income," the landed rich in early Massachusetts constantly rechanneled their profits into new enterprises.[4] While the function of English landlords was essentially preservative—to protect the integrity of an estate ultimately to be bequeathed in tail to the eldest son—New World landlords were risk-taking entrepreneurs who supplied the capital and leadership needed to turn a wilderness into a settlement. Their acquisitive values found expression in a legal system geared toward growth, not stasis. As strict enforcement of contractual obligations between employer and employee promoted predictability

[2] Cook, *Fathers of the Towns*, pp. 194–195.

[3] Bruce C. Daniels, *The Connecticut Town: Growth and Development, 1635–1790*, Middletown, Conn., 1979.

[4] "Ideology and Theory," *American Historical Review* (1976), p. 500. I am obliged to Olivier Zunz and Edward L. Ayers for helping me to reformulate these observations. Professor Ayers also suggested the book's title.

and efficiency in the labor market, so too developmental leases guaranteed improvement of the landlord's acreage.

This entrepreneurial role was played by some two dozen men in seventeenth-century New England, of whom John Pynchon is but one example. Examinations of the Willard family in the Merrimack Valley, the Winthrops of Boston and elsewhere, and the Otises in Barnstable all underscore the importance of merchant-entrepreneurs in financing and orchestrating settlement throughout early New England. Without these men, colonial America would have remained resource rich but capital poor. Through trade, investments, credit, work, developmental leases, manufacturing enterprises, and the like, the merchant-entrepreneur opened up new regions for settlement and served as a magnet for additional migrants thereafter. The modest initial endowments of many of the first settlers and their willingness to work made it sensible to accept what the merchant-entrepreneur had to offer—even at the price of personal dependency.

The parallel between the merchant-entrepreneur careers of Simon Willard and John Pynchon, both fur traders who became land magnates, seems particularly striking. Willard founded, exclusively as fur-trading posts, Concord (1636) and Chelmsford (1655) before moving on to Lancaster to compete for furs with its founder, John Prescott. There, and later at Groton, he reaped the benefits of being a mediator, including large land grants from the General Court. In 1658 Willard successfully petitioned the Court for five hundred acres on the spurious grounds that he deserved recompense for a loan default by a Pawtucket Indian. At his death in 1676, Willard owned 1,521 acres of land and an overall estate estimated at £8,000. In the words of the foremost authority on the early New England fur trade, "The figure of the fur trader Simon Willard towers above all others in the early annals of [the Merrimack Valley]. Deputy from Concord to the General Court for fifteen years, Assistant of Massachusetts Bay 1654–1676, Captain, Major, and Sergeant Major of Middlesex County, Willard was the leading man in the successive towns in which he resided. Town builder, Indian agent, explorer, his services were most valuable to the people of Massachusetts Bay, and prepared the way for those who came to till the soil."[5]

Also strikingly similar to the career of John Pynchon was that of John Winthrop, Jr. Richard S. Dunn writes that Winthrop was

---

[5] Moloney, *Fur Trade in New England*, pp. 75–77; see also Bailyn, *New England Merchants*, p. 56.

"Founder of three towns, industrialist, scientist, doctor, governor, diplomat, farmer, [and] land speculator." As with Pynchon and Willard, Winthrop received land grants, monopolies, and special privileges and immunities for acting as a developer and mediator. In September 1650, soon after his arrival in the town of Pequot (New London), Connecticut, Winthrop and his heirs were granted the "priviledge and Right of ordering and disposing all publick Building and affairs of this towne, now and for the future." Dunn points out that Winthrop "was given a stone quarry, the town ferry, the right to build dams or watermills in any of the local streams, the right to hunt, fish, and cut wood anywhere within the town limits, and all of his land was made tax free. He was encouraged to manufacture glass, for which purpose the town gave him the 'great white sandy beach over against Bachelors Cove' and let him dig freely for clay. To manufacture saltpeter he was given Gull Island outside Pequot harbor. He built and operated the town gristmill as well as a sawmill outside the town, getting various timber rights for the latter."[6]

A third example of the successful merchant-entrepreneur is John Otis II (1621–1684) in Barnstable. According to John J. Waters, Jr., Otis "refused to be content with producing for a market controlled by others. Rather, John II took his father's land, capital lent by his in-laws, and money entrusted by neighbors and entered into trade, industrial activity, and long-term land speculation." Waters writes that "During his life the second Otis had been consumed by two objectives: the accumulation of property and the settlement of his family." After moving from Scituate to Barnstable, Otis became "the richest man in that small community of 145 householders" and left a patrimony of £1,500 for the next generation.[7]

Evidence is abundant that communities appreciated the importance of having a merchant-entrepreneur in their midst. Fearing, rightly, that John Winthrop, Jr. was contemplating leaving their town for Boston in 1637, fifty-seven inhabitants of Ipswich petitioned the General Court not to deprive "our Church and Towne of one whose presence is so gratefull and usefull to us." And, as Dunn observes, the townsmen also "bribed him with an additional grant of land on Castle Hill . . . if he would stay."[8] Moreover, Boston and Ipswich were not the only communities that vied for Winthrop's presence. In 1654 John Pynchon wrote his friend that "New

---

[6] Dunn, Puritans and Yankees, pp. 59, 75.
[7] Waters, The Otis Family, pp. 29, 36, 38–39.
[8] Dunn, Puritans and Yankees, p. 70.

Haven I heare have sent againe to you this weeke."[9] Likewise, in August 1675, Pynchon wrote to John Allyn at Hartford "Hast, Post Hast" that "They much desire the presence of some principall man at Hadley to direct, as need requires, and to expedite affairs."[10] When in 1706 the town of Enfield needed a spokesman at the General Court, as Edward M. Cook, Jr. notes, "the voters ignored their own leaders and attempted to persuade Joseph Parsons, Esq., of Springfield and Northampton to settle in their town and become their representative."[11]

The motives behind these desires for politically well-connected merchant-entrepreneurs are not difficult to fathom. Towns needed the political capital that flowed from the presence of a mediator, but, even more, they needed the financial capital of the entrepreneur. Pynchon, Willard, Winthrop, and Otis were all risk-takers, men who supplied the credit, technology, and leadership needed to turn a wilderness into a settlement. Through their trading activities, the merchant-entrepreneurs acted as corporate patrons for their regions, absorbing price variations and carrying charges in inventories of foodstuffs and soft goods to provide an economic cocoon for the townsfolk. John Pynchon, in Springfield, absorbed the costs and secured the benefits of price fluctuations, which he could do because of his wealth and profits from fur. He, like the other merchant-entrepreneurs, was an economic buffer to the outside world. And the benefits of this patrimonial world applied to (selected) workers as well as customers. For the skilled artisan, Pynchon could offer higher income, or higher security, or off-season employment (itself a form of security). Pynchon was also the employer of last (as well as first) resort—witness his taking as domestics the girls of particularly poor families. It is also likely that William and John's resources actually made it easier on the working people of Springfield in the early years when the general store was a place to turn to for work or provisions when hard times (or even starvation) threatened. The store, in times of financial distress, could function as a safety net.

It was not a zero-sum game. John Pynchon's presence meant that everyone was *potentially* better off. He supplied credit, employment, investment opportunities, and capital improvements such as mills that in his absence would not be available. Indeed, if one were so

---

[9] John Pynchon to John Winthrop, Jr., October 20, 1654, Winthrop Mss.

[10] John Pynchon to John Allyn, August 22, 1675, *Public Records of the Colony of Connecticut*, ed. J. Hammond Trumbull and Charles Hoadley, Hartford, 1850–1890, 2, p. 353.

[11] Cook, *Fathers of the Towns*, p. 180.

disposed, it would be possible to cast Pynchon's developmental activities in a near-heroic light. It was his assets, courage, and vision that released, amplified, and reinforced the energies of the hard-working, often skilled but propertyless New World settlers. We have encountered many men in these pages—Anthony Dorchester (the miller), Joseph Leonard (the carpenter), Rowland Thomas (the stonemason), and John Stewart (the blacksmith)—who profited handsomely from their association with the Pynchons. These were enterprising and determined individuals, men who recognized the possibilities offered by Pynchon and made the most of their chance.[12]

That their efforts—and his own ventures—enriched Pynchon even more, there can be no doubt. His £8,000 estate at death alone attests to that. But, like entrepreneurs in any age, Pynchon had the most to lose as well as the most to gain. In a time before the protection of investments offered by insurance, Pynchon's capital holdings were exceedingly vulnerable, particularly after the mid-1670s when the threat of Indian attack loomed continuously. It was *his* gristmill and sawmills, not the town's, that the Indians destroyed during the October 1675 attack. He was sorely tempted to retreat to the comfort and safety of Boston in that troublesome winter, perhaps for good. But, as he told the governor in a letter, such an action would have meant that "ale will fale here." Even during peaceful times, the entrepreneur stood to suffer financially if he didn't directly oversee his enterprises in order to ensure that all was being run efficiently. Rejecting a plea that he travel to Albany in the summer of 1666 to negotiate with the Indians, Pynchon told Connecticut Governor John Winthrop, Jr. that "myself having work men about a Mill [I] cannot well be absent without great loss at this tyme."[13]

Pynchon was a resource who could be used or abused. He offered his clients credit, access to outside markets, work, and leases for land, housing, livestock, and equipment. Those who availed themselves of his services thereby put themselves at risk. With luck—and pluck—they could translate these opportunities into genuine financial gains. But more failed than succeeded. These were the men who took the risk and ended up losing their gamble—and often their house and land as well. For them, a continuously mounting indebtedness ledger at the general store meant a life of no little anxiety and travail. For these individuals, the corporatist security offered by the less commercially oriented communities might have

---

[12] I am indebted to Fred V. Carstensen for helping to clarify these points.

[13] Mass. Archives, 68, p. 6; John Pynchon to John Winthrop, Jr., July 17, 1666, Winthrop Mss.

been appealing indeed. Fewer opportunities meant fewer risks, and a correspondingly higher level of psychic ease.[14]

It is reasonable to conclude, therefore, that a person's attitude toward John Pynchon was colored by his financial condition, and views probably ranged from willing fealty to grudging obeisance. Those men who enjoyed a modicum of success—or more—were presumably grateful for the opportunities offered by their affili-ation with Pynchon. To these men, he was a benefactor. To the others, however, men done in by their circumstances or their character, Pynchon's influence must have seemed blighting and oppressive. One can readily imagine the corrosive effects on personal happiness, family harmony, and neighborly relationships posed by economic dependency. We can envision, although not document, the anxious (sometimes desperate) conversations between husband and wife once the children were safely bedded down for the evening. Likewise, we can imaginatively recreate the sense of despair over impending foreclosures that would negate the toil of a decade or more. The potential damage to neighborhood reciprocity and obligations towards coreligionists in the church seems equally obvious.[15]

To some men, accordingly, Pynchon doubtless appeared grasping and possibly tyrannical. His monopoly of just about everything of major value in the community must have been a source of periodic frustration for many, perhaps most, of the town's inhabitants. Entrepreneurs are not always popular and American history is littered with business tycoons fiercely traduced in their day.[16] But, judged by the tenor of his time, Pynchon does not come off badly. While not a particularly warm man, and occasionally given to rigidity, and bouts of extreme self-pity ("all peckt at the Captain of our Salvation," and the like), he overall emerges as a decent, determined, and forthright individual. His account books show no evidence of duplicity or double-dealing, and he surely had ample opportunity for both. Likewise, in his treatment of debtors and tenants he appears to have been no worse than even-handed. For non-clients he could be draconian in enforcing contractual obli-

14 Robert Redfield, *The Little Community* and *Peasant Society and Culture*, Chicago, 1967, pp. 66–80.

15 For a recent study of the relationship between economic change and religious sensibilities, see Patricia J. Tracy, *Jonathan Edwards, Pastor: Religion and Society in Eighteenth-Century Northampton*, New York, 1980, pp. 147–170; see also Richard L. Bushman, *From Puritan to Yankee: Character and the Social Order in Connecticut, 1690–1765*, New York, 1970, pp. 3–195.

16 Richard Hofstadter, *Social Darwinism in American Thought*, New York, 1959, pp. 105–122.

gations, but he did not go *beyond* the law for his own advantage. And for clients, he modified contracts on their, not his, behalf. On several occasions he seized the encumbered estates of impoverished widows, but he followed this up by employing the family's children in his household. Compared to the landlords of East Anglia or the merchants on Fleet Street, Pynchon can be accused neither of rack-renting nor rapacity. The same is true for comparisons from later periods. While nineteenth-century rents usually amounted to from one-third to one-half of annual yield, his leases rarely exceeded ten percent of yield. Tenancy *was* dysfunctional in a frontier society because of the lost labor investment, but that responsibility cannot be laid exclusively at Pynchon's door. He did not force anyone to rent. By the same token, he was often exceedingly indulgent with client debtors, foregoing collection for extended periods or forgiving them entirely, and increasing the prices he paid to settle when he took the land. This solicitude, as we have seen, was partly motivated by his needs for skilled artisans and sufficient numbers of reapers. But, as Pynchon's frequent allusions to the hand of the Lord attest, he believed himself to be among the godly, and there is no reason to doubt that Christian restraint and charity ameliorated his economic dealings. That his commercial and speculative activities brought hardships (and even ruin) to some, there can be no question. We have seen too many sobering examples in these pages to believe otherwise. The texture of Pynchon's negotiations with his clients, however, suggests that, but for his restraint, things would have been a good deal worse.

Both Christian charity and economic self-interest argued for such restraint. The general store, like any paternalistic enterprise, functioned as a safety valve as well as a safety net. By deferring foreclosures, forgiving debts, ignoring unpaid rents, or hiring workers in the off-season, Pynchon blunted the force of any potential class discontent. There were, after all, no tenant rebellions in Springfield, in contrast to the Hudson Valley, which was riven with agrarian unrest throughout the eighteenth century.[17] Moreover, Springfield did not experience an atypically high level of out-migration during the seventeenth century. If the opportunities and conditions were discernibly better elsewhere, more would have left.

That more did not do so is a phenomenon worthy of note. Springfielders, even those experiencing genuine destitution, did not live lives of unrelieved desperation. They apparently believed that the future would bring better things. That for many this hope was

[17] Mark, *Agrarian Conflicts*, pp. 13–163; Lynd, *Dutchess County*, pp. 1–54.

chimerical we know, but they would not be the last Americans to
see the hardships of the present as but the necessary prologue to
eventual success.[18] The hope that the wheel of fortune will ultimately turn in one's favor is the most powerful damper on class
discontent. It is only the abridgment of hope that brings the rum-
blings of rebellion.[19]

But, to turn to the second implication of this study, this meant
that Springfield's inhabitants sacrificed political autonomy—as well
as corporate solidarity—on the altar of economic opportunity. Pynchon's dominion over the economic activities of his dependents
diminished their political independence at every turn. Whether
they were filing into the meetinghouse for an important debate,
choosing the church deacons for the coming year, or gathering on
the green to elect new militia officers, these men were never wholly
autonomous. The practice of voice voting at town meetings, of
course, made anonymity impossible. With John Pynchon always
wielding the moderator's gavel in the meeting, it would have taken
unusual bravery for dependent men to defy his wishes. Outright
intimidation, arm-twisting, or even veiled threats were all unnec-
essary in these situations. And, as the records reveal, these were
not tactics likely to be favored by Pynchon. The most invidious
dimension of economic dependency was that it was self-inhibiting.
Pynchon needed to do nothing, save gaze impassively down from
the dais. For men lacking the self-confidence offered by self-em-
ployment and a debt-free estate, acquiescence in the decisions of
their social superiors was the better part of valor.[20]

Third, there is the question of personal ambition and its effect
on the meaning of community in early Springfield. At first blush,
it seems less than surprising that migrants to the New World were
personally ambitious. The men and women who settled Springfield
left home and hearth to brave the terrors of the trans-Atlantic
voyage with only the foggiest idea what lay ahead. Once in America
they endured famine, Indian attack, and bankruptcy in forging a
town out of a wilderness. Their motives in taking on this formidable
task were myriad. Some came voluntarily, others as war captives.
Some were devoutly religious, others not, and given the complexity
of human nature, it is probably fruitless to seek a precise spectrum
of motivation. But, as Richard Hofstadter (among others) has pointed
out, the migration apparently acted as a kind of sieve, drawing

[18] Stephan Thernstrom, *Poverty and Progress: Social Mobility in a Nineteenth Century City*, New York, 1975, pp. 138–165.
[19] Crane Brinton, *The Anatomy of Revolution*, New York, 1965, p. 30.
[20] Gilmore, *People of the Plain*, pp. 51–127.

from the Old World its most ambitious, daring, unillusioned, and tough-minded people.[21] These were not passive "peasants" given to accepting the concept of a "limited good."[22] If Europe was largely populated by such people in the seventeenth century, they were not the ones who left for America. The men and women who came to Springfield—as their patterns of work, land acquisition, and social behavior reveal—came to the New World to get ahead. That they were acquisitive is not to deny that they were religious. Springfielders would have had little trouble accepting Samuel Johnson's aphorism that "There are few ways in which a man can be more innocently employed than in making money." As Max Weber and many others have pointed out, godly people often expect to be successful. Working hard and long to gain a patrimony for their children was not sinful for Springfield's early settlers. It was only when material goals became all-consuming that they became destructive.[23]

This acquisitiveness helps explain the weakness of communalism in highly commercialized towns like Springfield. Because theirs was an acquisitive—not merely materialistic—society, it tolerated diversity and heterogeneity. Rather than warning out a skilled artisan who was also a lecher and a drunk, the villagers profited by his skills and tried to minimize his excesses. Hence the high level of social conflict. Holistic, homogeneous communities are intolerant because they judge a person by his totality. Status, birth, wealth, education, or kinship, as well as diligence, self-discipline, temperance, honesty, and the like are assessed in determining one's acceptability.[24] Behavior in one sphere of activity affects all others. The fact that a cooper was a philanderer made him ineligible to pack one's furs. But Springfield was not a holistic community, only an economic community, based on skill and willingness to work. The key here, of course, is that Springfield's was a wage labor, not a manorial, economy. As Robert L. Heilbroner puts it, the "wage labor system in which workers are hired for a given length of time

---

[21] *America at 1750*, pp. 64–65.

[22] Two valuable, and contrasting, evaluations of the putative "peasant mentality" are Samuel L. Popkin, *The Rational Peasant: The Political Economy of Rural Society in Vietnam*, Berkeley, 1981; and James C. Scott, *The Moral Economy of the Peasant: Rebellion and Subsistence in Southeast Asia*, New Haven, 1981.

[23] Even the migratory servants to the Chesapeake studied by James Horn, although apparently defeated at every turn in their travels from city to city in search of work, had the forbearance to push on rather than remain in England to become public charges; see Horn, "Servant Emigration to the Chesapeake," Tate and Ammerman, eds., *The Chesapeake*, pp. 94–95.

[24] Carstensen, personal communication.

and then released from their 'servant' status effectively creates an 'economy' distinct from a 'society.' "[25] Separate spheres of activity were judged independently of one another. The hiring criterion was degree of skill, not personal probity. John Pynchon was impersonal in hiring in that he based evaluations of people on utilitarian, not holistic criteria. Unlike Old World patronage, this was one-dimensional. It was an economic-political axis, not a social, cultural, and spiritual one. Pynchon hired and fired on the basis of skillfulness and diligence, and a man's behavior out of the workplace was his concern, not Pynchon's. Social conflict in Springfield, therefore, was the reverse side of Pynchon's one-dimensional patronage.

The Springfield experience, in the larger frame, shows that migration to the New World brought a critical step toward the separation of spheres of authority that Weber characterizes as the legal/rational society. It is a world of individuals, not a community. The town's development corresponds with what J. M. Cameron has described as "the moment of transition from the old view of man as finding his fulfillment in his social role to the new view of man 'as an individual prior to and apart from all roles'—the transition, as Sir Henry Maine put it, 'from status to contract.' " And this transition came first in the New, not the Old World, as "it is only with the late eighteenth and early nineteenth centuries in Europe that we arrive at the notion of man as having moral substance apart from and prior to *all* social roles, as, for example, in the work of James Mill."[26] Such individualistic relationships, as Springfield vividly reveals, invite a society that was both litigious and market-oriented.

This brings us back to the question, posed at the outset, of how patron-client ties formed the bridge from the world of the manor to the world of the market, from master-servant bonds to those of employer-employee. The answer is that merchant-entrepreneurs like John Pynchon were not patriarchs responsible for *all* members of the community, but patrons answerable only to those selected individuals who had something to offer to—and gain from—an association with him. Because these were face-to-face relationships, they harkened back to manorial practices, but because at heart they were contractual and impersonal they prefigured—if they did not announce—the triumph of the market economy.

[25] "The Demand for the Supply Side," *The New York Review of Books* (June 11, 1981), p. 38.
[26] J. M. Cameron, "Can We Live the Good Life?", *The New York Review of Books* (November 5, 1981), pp. 45–46.

When viewed in the larger historical setting, it was not Springfield's commercialism but rather Dedham's corporatism that appears anomalous. Springfield's settlement and development fits naturally within the overall expansion of capitalism and empire in sixteenth- and seventeenth-century England. John Pynchon's construction of elaborate patron-client relations and his use of political privilege to gain enormous economic power within a new society are part of the story of late Elizabethan and Stuart mercantile expansion. Similar patterns developed in both Virginia and Ireland. The parallels with Ireland seem particularly inviting. There, too, a few people gained disproportionate control over land and rented it out to tenants, whose labor was extorted through the exaction of rent. Historians of Ireland stress that landlord-tenant relationships were a major barrier to agricultural improvement, because the tenant's efforts redounded only to the benefit of the exploiting landlord. This parallel suggests that the cast of Springfield is a cautionary tale of how New England might not have become so "exceptional" after all, how it could have gone the way of Ireland or old England if the fur supply had not run out or if a staple crop had been found. The Pynchons clearly were responsive to the mercantilist currents of their time. William Pynchon's condemnation of fur monopolies suggests that he favored a world of freer trade. Such ideas were taking root in the seventeenth century, yet could also be conjoined with patron-client exploitation under the notion that "free" contract was the basis of economic relationships. The merchant-entrepreneurs of the New World were laying the economic foundations of a liberal tradition at the same time that they were looking back to a manorial past.[27]

Finally, there is the question of the Glorious Revolution and its impact on the subsequent direction of social change. The overthrow of the Dominion, it seems, both prevented the possibility for a genuine gentry class in eighteenth-century New England and served as a dress rehearsal for 1776.[28] The eclipse of the old elites and their replacement by royal appointees brought in its train demands by the "common sort" for self-government and self-determination. Militiamen like James King publicly demanded leaders of "their own choosing." To use Locke's phrasing, after 1689 men such as King had "Confidence to turn [their] wishes into *demands*." But as things became more democratic at the local level, they became less

[27] I am indebted to Robert A. Gross for his contribution to these observations.

[28] David S. Lovejoy reached the same conclusion in "Two American Revolutions, 1689 and 1776," in J.G.A. Pocock, ed., *Three British Revolutions: 1641, 1688, 1776,* Princeton, N. J., 1980, pp. 244–262.

so at the colony level with the radical centralization of the flow of authority under the second charter. The "new men" who attempted to replace the Pynchons as leaders found themselves having to serve two contradictory masters: the Crown and their constituents. All was fine so long as public policy at both the local and provincial levels was in accord. But when the royal officials tried to implement unpalatable legislation—as they did between 1765 and 1776—the fragility of the system would be starkly revealed. Those local leaders who remained loyal to the Crown saw their community support evaporate with astonishing rapidity. The midcentury counterpart to John Pynchon in Springfield, Colonel John Worthington, learned this to his dismay during the Revolutionary crisis. Although he had long held a number of important civil, judicial, and military positions in the community, Worthington's continued fealty to the King brought expulsion from all town affairs and a hooting mob to the door. Among those who supplanted Worthington in the town's new leadership elite were two of the fifth generation of Pynchons, Charles and William. Ending the eclipse in local affairs their family had experienced since the turn of the century, they reemerged as leaders on the committee of correspondence and the committee of safety. Once again Pynchons were at the helm of local government in Springfield—but now under the mantle of republicanism.

The process of social, as well as political, change from the seventeenth to the eighteenth century is, therefore, in need of recasting. The communal, egalitarian, and quietistic models of the seventeenth century *do* make the later period seem considerably more factious and stratified. But if two of the three settlement zones in early New England—the coastal ports and the highly commercialized towns like Springfield—behaved in an acquisitive, market-oriented, and contentious manner in the seventeenth century, we cannot explain the Revolution by the sudden appearance of such behavior after 1740. Central to most of the existing arguments is an emphasis on an apparently dramatic rise in both wealth and poverty in the generation after the Great Awakening. While this study does not include an assessment of the distribution of wealth during the pre-Revolutionary generation, we do know that no one after 1703 remotely compared to John Pynchon in either wealth or influence. When the Pynchons lost their preeminence after the turn of the century, eager claimants—the Parsons, Hitchcocks, Dwights, and Worthingtons—arose to bid for the fealty of the general populace.[29] Accordingly, it seems reasonable to argue that

[29] Christine Leigh Heyrman, in her forthcoming study of Gloucester and Mar-

access to both land and political power came easier for ordinary inhabitants in the eighteenth century than before. By the same token, while religious and political disputes and community fragmentation continued into the 1740s and beyond, dissenters could now channel their energies into new churches or new precincts, rather than fighting it out in the old meetinghouse. Indeed, it seems possible to believe that it was the strength and unity of the New Englanders, not their privation and factionalism, that allowed them to stand successfully against the British in 1776.

---

blehead during the eighteenth century, likewise finds these communities becoming more, not less, harmonious as the Revolution approached. *Commerce and Culture: The Maritime Communities of Colonial Massachusetts, 1690–1750*, New York, 1983. See also, Gregory H. Nobles, *'Divisions Throughout the Whole': Politics and Society in Hampshire County, Massachusetts, 1740–1775*, New York, 1982, Chapter 1; and William Pencak, *War, Politics, and Revolution in Provincial Massachusetts*, Boston, 1981.

Index

account books (of John and William
Pynchon), 9, 27, 30, 39–40, 41, 51,
53–55, 58, 64, 66, 67, 68, 69, 74, 75,
76, 77, 83, 85, 88, 89, 92, 93, 94, 98,
101–102, 106–107, 111, 117–118,
119, 120, 122, 131–132, 177; as
source of socioeconomic data, xx–
xxi, 172
Addington, Isaac, Secretary of Massachusetts, 162, 164, 165, 168
Agawam. *See* Springfield
Agawam River (Westfield River, Woronoco River), viii, 6, 7, 27, 46, 59,
62, 70, 71, 114
Agawams, 6. *See also* Indians
agriculture: commercial nature of, xvi–
xviii, xx, 6–9, 10, 20, 33–34, 44–71,
72–73, 81–82, 106–122, 171, 176,
180–181; income from, 81; in England, 3; seasonal cycles of, 72–73,
105, 107n, 108, 113–117; subsistence, xvi, xvii, 44–45, 63, 82, 124.
See also field work; work
Aires, John, 35
Albany (Fort Orange), 21, 24, 25, 31–
32, 155, 176
Allen, David Grayson, 171
Allyn, John, 19, 23, 156, 162, 175
American Revolution, xv–xvi, xvii–xxi,
106, 182–184
Andover, xv, xvi, xvii, 44, 128, 148
Andros, Sir Edmund, 24, 88, 157, 158;
as Governor of Dominion of New
England, 154–156
Anglican church, 156
anthropologists, 20, 40n, 52n
Antigua, 29, 33–34. *See also* West In-
dies
Appleby, Joyce, 76–77, 172
apprenticeship, 9–10, 89, 92, 94, 100.
See also servants

Arrow, Kenneth J., 28n
artisans, 72, 73–74, 79–81, 82–104;
and social order, xvii–xviii, 129–133,
143; importance of for Pynchons, 3,
9–10, 80, 175–176; income of, 80–
81, 175–176; rent tools from John
Pynchon, 52; skills of, xvii–xviii, 48,
80, 83–84, 86–87, 88–89, 90, 94, 96–
97, 98, 100–101, 109, 129, 130, 133,
149, 175–176, 180–181; work day
of, 112. *See also* blacksmiths; brickmakers; carpenters; cobblers; coopers; millers; millwrights; sackmakers; shinglers; shoemakers;
stonemasons; tailors; weavers
Artsell, John, 74
Ashley, Joseph, 63
Ashley, Robert, 109n–110n, 145–146
assault, xviii, 129–132, 133–134, 141–
143. *See also* deviance; social conflict
Avery, William, 29

Bagg, John, 144
Bailyn, Bernard, 11
Baker, John, 69
Ball, Francis, 127
Ball, Jonathan, 55–56
Ball, Samuel, 143
Barbados, 33. *See also* West Indies
Barber, John, 84n
Barber, Thomas, 73
barley, 7, 8, 33, 56, 81, 114, 115, 116.
See also grains
Barnard, Richard, 22, 135
barns, 73, 109n, 115–116, 130
Barnstable, 151, 157, 173, 174
Bascomb, Thomas, 99
Beamon, Daniel, 133
Beamon, Symon, 139–140
Beamont, Alice, 118
beaver, 4–5, 16, 30–31, 33, 101, 155.

haymaking, 108, 114, 120. *See also* field work
Heilbroner, Robert L., 42–43, 180–181
Henryson, John, 69, 78–79, 109n, 143–144
Henryson, Martha, 144
historians, 172; on New England town, xv–xvii, xxi, 44–45; on rule of waste, 49–50; on wages, 74–75; on work patterns in England and America, 74–77
Hitchcock family, 183
Hofstadter, Richard, xv, 39, 179
Holeman, Hannah, 118
Holland, J. G., 29n
Holyoke, Elizur, 9, 10, 14, 47, 58, 79, 83, 119
Holyoke, John, 28
Hooker, Thomas, minister of Hartford church, 11–12
Horn, James, 75n–76n, 180n
horses, 8, 52, 54, 60, 73, 88, 109, 113, 127, 162, 163, 164. *See also* livestock
Horton, Thomas, 146
Housatonic River, 31
house of correction, 36, 109n–110n, 124
House of Deputies, 157. *See also* General Court
House of Representatives, 157, 158, 168–169. *See also* General Court
Hubbard, Margaret, 34
Hudson Valley, 6, 31–32, 51, 178
Hull, Richard, 146
Hunter, John, 110
Hunter, Katherine, 109n–110n
Hunter, Lewis C., 82
Hunter, Priscilla, 110, 141
Hunter, Sarah, 110
Hunter, William, 109–110, 141, 143
husbandmen, 51, 77, 149. *See also* agriculture

income, 11, 34, 48, 56, 57, 58, 72, 80–81, 87, 88, 89, 100, 119, 120, 121, 172, 175. *See also* wages; work
Indians, 7, 31, 65, 125, 173; corn dispute with, 11–12; economy of, 6; fur trade with, 10, 11, 29–32, 92–93; land transactions with, 6, 26–27; negotiations with, 22, 24–25, 155; trails of, 6; wars with, 19, 24, 25, 28, 30,

34, 57, 60, 67, 104, 111, 148, 156, 160, 162, 163–164, 165, 166, 176, 179. *See also* Agawams; Mohawks; Narragansetts; Nonotucks; Pequots; Wampanoags; King Philip's War
individualism, xvi, xvii, 3, 15, 38, 76, 78, 136–137, 139, 171, 181. *See also* capitalism; patron-client relationships
Ipswich, 34, 174
Ireland, 182
ironworks, 37

Jamaica, 33. *See also* West Indies
James II, 20, 46, 152, 153
Jedrey, Christopher, 48n
Jefferys, Goodman, 118
Jefferys, Goodwife, 117–118
Jefferys, Hannah, 117–118
Jefferys, Sarah, 118
Johnson, Edward, author of *Wonder-Working Providence*, 100
Johnson, Richard, R., 152n, 157n
Johnson, Samuel, 180
joiners, 66, 79, 80, 95, 131. *See also* artisans; carpenters
Jones, Griffith, xx, 89–90, 98, 106n
jurisprudence. *See* courts; magistrates
justices of the peace, 3, 152, 153, 155, 158

Kagan, Richard L., 129n
kilns. *See* brickmakers; naval stores
Kilum, John, 59
King, Gregory, 76
King, James (militia sargeant), 159–161, 165, 182. *See also* militia
King, William, 131
King Philip's War (Metacom's War), 19, 24, 25, 30, 32, 54, 57, 76, 82, 110, 111, 129, 130, 148, 176. *See also* Indians
Kirby, Francis, 5
Knowlton, Benjamin, 62, 135
Konig, David T., 128, 152n, 171

laborers. *See* day-laborers; field work; work
Lamb, John, 79, 142
Lancaster, 173
land distribution, xix, 14, 22, 28, 29,